People with a Passion
BUILDING CELL CHURCH TODAY

by
Colin Dye

This book is dedicated to the leaders and members of the cells in Kensington Temple, London City Church. You are truly people with a passion. May the Lord continue to bless your hard work and diligence in the cell vision.

Contents

Introduction

I

In the year 2000, I began to lead our church in London, Kensington Temple, into the cell vision according to the Model of 12. We had spent several years looking at other models and became interested in the G12 system, pioneered by Cesar Castellanos, the apostolic leader of the fast growing church, International Charismatic Mission in Bogota, Colombia. The flavour of the vision of 12, together with its structure of leaders working together in permanently established teams, suited us well.

One of our satellite churches saw astonishing growth through the G12 strategy. This Spanish-speaking group grew from a small congregation to almost 3,000 people within 3 years. We wondered if this was due to similarities in the culture of expatriate Hispanics in London and the people of Colombia. But, as we got to know the G12 model, we could see that it was applicable to all cultures.

We spent five years, learning and implementing the cell strategy with the help of Cesar and Claudia Castellanos, together with members from their Primary 12 Groups. During this period Cesar and Claudia Fajardo were leading the 100,000 strong Youth Net in Bogota. Their experience was particularly helpful to us, and they have remained close colleagues in the ministry.

After five years, we had fully transitioned into the cell model in Kensington Temple. Meanwhile, the G12 strategy, which had originally stood for 'Groups of 12' was being developed into 'the Government of 12' organised globally under the spiritual direction of the church in Bogota. The G12, as it was being developed, was no longer applicable to us. We were already under the spiritual covering of our own denomination, the Elim Pentecostal Churches of the UK. Nevertheless, we kept working with the principles we had learned and continued to develop the Model of 12 to suit our context.

Now 10 years from our launch, we can look back at what we have learned and how we have developed the principle of 12 in our own ministry. We have built on the apostolic foundations of the vision and have proved that it is wider in appeal and application than its original setting in Latin America. Our international work, both in Europe and further afield, proves that the Model of 12 is a strategy for the nations and not just for one ministry. The principle of 12 was Jesus' method for discipling the nations. It is not fixated on the number of 12, but focuses on the principle of training and releasing workers into the harvest fields of humanity. This, I believe is the Holy Spirit's true purpose for cell church.

We learned the vision, values and structure of the model in Bogota. However, the principles themselves come from the New Testament. The model is built on this foundation and is broadly-speaking applicable anywhere in the world, although the style and the details of its implementation will vary from place to place. In London, we have taken what we learnt and adapted it to our cultural environment without compromising a single element of the model we learned from Castellanos and his team of passionate and committed workers.

Every apostolic and prophetic vision the Holy Spirit gives one part of the church is a vital word for the entire church. We should take seriously the command repeatedly given in the letters to the seven churches in Asia Minor which is found in the second and third chapters of the book of Revelation, "Hear what the Spirit is saying to the churches." What God has been doing in Bogota for the past 20 years is of value to the whole body of Christ.

God has been highlighting cell church since the explosive growth of Yoido Full Gospel Church in Seoul, South Korea during the second half of the 20th Century. Now in the 21st Century, there is an increasing global interest in new ways of doing church.

The traditional 'local church' structure of single congregations meeting in church buildings, is no longer working. It cannot fulfil some of the basic New Testament requirements for church, such as every member ministry and expressing the body of Christ in the market place. The Mega church model, which came to the fore in the West in the 1980s, was an eloquent testimony to God's love of bigness, but it has proved inadequate when it comes to equipping the saints and raising disciples of Christ.

The Meta church model is the way of the future. The Greek word *meta*, here meaning 'beyond' or 'between', points to the relationships between small groups and the larger gatherings in this networking model of church. Meta church sees the full expression of church consisting of a network of three New Testament units of *ekklesia* (church) – small cell groups, medium-sized congregations and large celebration gatherings. These cells, congregations and celebrations of believers work together as a single church to see the Mandate of Christ fulfilled. Meta church adopts a 'honeycomb' approach, linking each unit together to form the greater whole.

The Model of 12 is not just about cells. It grasps their importance as the *basic unit* of church ministry but it sees beyond them to the larger context of church. It understands the role of the congregation in reaching communities as well as the big gatherings of the church to impact society and to reach the multitudes for Christ. It differs from the Mega church model as it is organised into small groups where every Christian is trained to be a disciple and a disciple-maker of others. That way, it keeps the call of Jesus in Matthew 28:18-20 as its central focus.

In a generation when secularists and false religionists are rampant and are using political power and social pressure to try and silence the church, we must surely rise up and fulfil our reason for being – to make, mature and mobilise disciples for Christ. Now is not the time to fight to retain our vested ecclesiastical interests or to keep on building our own 'empires'. Our success will depend on our ability to disciple every member of the body of Christ.

All this presupposes one indispensible thing – passion for Christ. Only people with a passion for his kingdom and his work in the world will be interested in the cell vision. It is too demanding for complacent 'Sunday Christians' who sit passively in the church. Jesus calls for passionate labourers to go to the harvest fields of our day. That is why I devote the first section of this book to stirring up spiritual passion in church leaders and members. Only a love inspired by the Father's love for us and poured into our hearts by his Holy Spirit will rouse us from sleep and drive us to our knees to cry out to God for the lost. Only his passion burning in our hearts will cause us to rise up and win our world for Christ.

Over the last few years, I have written a number of resource booklets in the *Discipleship Cell Explosion* Series. These cover many aspects of the Model of 12, but *People with a Passion* is my first attempt to bring teaching on the cell vision together in one publication. I draw from some of my previous writings but have resisted the temptation to 'cut and paste' too often. In the main, I have written fresh material and refer to the booklets for further information where that is relevant. The content of this book arises out of our practical experience both in Britain and overseas and it is good to know that it is not mere theory. It works!

I have written this comprehensive training manual primarily for our own church members and those who are interested in the cell model we are following. I have been deliberately non-technical in my approach in order to make cell church accessible to a broad spectrum of readers. I begin by showing the spirituality which must exist if cell church is to succeed. Then I look at understanding the cell structure before moving on to the basics of the Model of 12. Finally, I examine some principles for implementing the vision.

I pray that *People with a Passion* will inspire you in your love for the Master and help equip you to play your part in his Great Commission to make disciples of all nations.

Colin Dye

London, January 2011

Part 1

Stirring up your Spiritual Passion

Spiritual Passion

1

Mel Gibson's *The Passion of the Christ* shook the world in 2004 with its depiction of the sufferings and crucifixion of Christ. Accused by the press of anti-Semitism and of portraying "relentless gore" in the movie, Gibson defended himself. He affirmed the theological truth that neither the Jews nor the Romans crucified Jesus – we all did! The agonising scene portraying the Roman crucifixion included a close-up of Mel Gibson's hands hammering the nails through Jesus' hands and feet. This was Gibson's testimony to the fact that it was his sins along with those of all humanity that crucified Christ.

There is no doubt that the film is explicit, but students of the cruel practice of crucifixion and the public scourging that preceeded it, know that Gibson actually played down the gruesome reality of Christ's passion. But still people were shocked by the film, especially in its more adult version.

One man, who I was seeking to lead to Christ at the time, complained. "There's too much blood in the film", he said, "What's with you Christians? You are so fixated on blood!" He was clearly repulsed by the visual images of the suffering Christ.

The irony was my friend had just been speaking enthusiastically about Tarantino's *Kill Bill 2*. As in *Kill Bill 1*, the sequel revelled in blood and gore. I pointed out the inconsistency in my friend's different reactions to *Kill Bill 2* and *The Passion*. Aware that there was something going on beneath the conscious surface of his life, he became silent. It was an important moment of self-awareness for him.

Revulsion at the cross is not unusual. Isaiah the prophet spoke about it 700 years before the Messiah was born. What would he be like when he finally came? Isaiah answers,

> *He is despised and rejected by men, a man of sorrows and acquainted with grief. And we hid, as it were, our faces from him; he was despised, and we did not esteem him.*
>
> Isaiah 53:3

The image of Christ would be shaped by his Passion – his sufferings and death. How could the cross with its sickening shame and repulsive cruelty have become the defining moment for all humanity, according to Christian teaching? The worship of a crucified Christ is scandalous and contradictory. Surely we should exalt success and victory, not the inglorious blood-soaked Christ of the cross. And yet, Christians place the Passion of Christ at the centre of their faith. For us, it is the summit of God's redemptive purposes and the highest source of inspiration for every disciple who is nothing less than a cross-bearing follower of the Christ.

LIMITLESS OUTPOURING OF GRACE

The pieces of this puzzle begin to come together when, by the revelation of the Spirit, we perceive that Christ's death was neither a violent accident of history nor a cosmic blunder. It was the very plan and express purpose of God for the salvation and restoration of our lives. Turning to Isaiah, once again, we begin to understand.

> *Surely he has borne our griefs, and carried our sorrows; yet we esteemed him stricken, smitten by God, and afflicted. But he was wounded for our transgressions, he was bruised for our iniquities; the chastisement for our peace was upon him, and by his stripes we are healed.*
>
> Isaiah 53:4-5

The gospel hinges on this fact which is so clearly revealed in the New Testament. Jesus became the substitute sacrifice for the sins of the world. On the cross he paid the price for the total forgiveness of God who is so absolutely holy that he could never have otherwise accepted us into his kingdom. The cross reveals God's unrelenting love for lost humanity. It points to the limitless outpouring of his grace upon us and draws us out of our implacable rebellion into the love relationship with him which is true Christianity.

I longed for my friend to discover these things. Once we have bowed at the foot of the cross in gratitude and amazement at the perfect plan of God, we can never be the same again. We have experienced his grace and tasted his goodness. We are so captivated by his amazing love that we want the whole world to know it about it.

A pastor friend of mine who leads a growing cell church in Australia is one of the most passionate disciples of Christ I know. He is sold out for God and the good news of Jesus. He lives and breathes mission. During one of the very first commercial screenings of *The Passion*, he sat with members of his church mingled with regular cinema goers from Australia's non-religious general public.

When the film ended, a deep silence descended on the audience. No one moved. The pastor, profoundly affected by the reality of the movie's content and the beauty of Gibson's screen play, jumped to his feet and shouted, "Jesus! I will follow you anywhere!" The pastor's passion was palpable and it impacted the entire audience. They were catapulted into transcendent reality like the star ship Enterprise, suddenly boosted to 'warp speed'.

Such is the effect of the cross. It changes everything. It removes the tawdry irrelevancies of our self-centredness and banishes them to the sidelines of our existence. The Christ who died and who rose again is the Christ to be followed. No one who comes close to the cross could ever fail to hear the heartbeat of God. The Father's breast throbs with passion for his lost sons and daughters and calls out from heaven, "These are my beloved children!"

The cross has shaped countless generations of disciples who wholeheartedly agree with the apostle Paul when he declared, "For me to live is Christ and to die is gain." They share his God-inspired passion for Christ which also led him to say, "I want to know him, the power of his resurrection, and the fellowship of his sufferings, being conformed to his death."

SHAPED BY LOVE

The passion flowing from the cross breeds a like-for-like passion in our hearts. We love him because he first loved us. The gracious gift of his life surrendered for us, provokes a response – we give him our lives as "living sacrifices". The attraction of his sacrificial love compels us to follow him, and we never regret it. He is worth more than the entire world to us.

Disciples are passionate people. Gone is the colourless living that belongs to this monochromatic world where the best of earthly achievement and success is empty when compared to the glory being revealed in us. Gone is the preoccupation with self, both secular and religious. Christ is our inspiration and our motivation. We leave behind worldly ambitions. We also reject the religious preoccupation with guilt and condemnation. Clothed with the righteousness of Christ and emboldened by the flame of spiritual passion burning within, we follow him – no matter what the cost. An internet site I recently came across describes passion in the following way:

> *We all have a basic need to feel passion. We long to experience intense feeling, strong excitement, strong affection, love, intense desire and enthusiasm. Passion is the fire in our eyes, in our bellies and in our lives that drives us forward to achieve the object of our passion.*

When people lose passion or have no fire in their soul you can tell it right away. They go through their lives as if they are on auto-pilot and the joy seems to have leaked out of them. When people have a passion in life you can see it and feel it. Having passion is a way of living every moment of your life to its fullest. When it comes to having and feeling passion, you know when you have it and you know when you don't. We all need to decide what we are passionate about having or doing in our life and then be open to doing what we need to do to keep it that way.

We all crave purpose, destiny, beauty, skill and impact, and the Father wants us to find these things in him. Passion will lift you out of the ordinary and the mundane into the realm of the best possibilities of your existence. Irish playwright George Bernard Shaw spoke about passion and its capacity to break us out of boring conformity and release us into the excitement of changing the world. He wrote, "The reasonable man adapts himself to the world; the unreasonable one persists in trying to adapt the world to himself. Therefore all progress depends on the unreasonable man."

DISCERNING YOUR PASSION

When do you feel most alive, most excited in your life? What do you long for more than anything else? The things you find yourself constantly dreaming about or imagining, will give you some clues as to what your passion is. What you believe would give you the most pleasure or the greatest joy if you attained it, is your passion. How you would complete the following sentences reveals where your passion really lies: Wouldn't it be wonderful if…? If only I could…? What if I found…?

Your passion is that one thing you are most willing to spend your time, your talents, your energy and your efforts to pursue, even if you attain it only rarely and incompletely. Your passion energises you, invigorates you and galvanises you into action, even when you are tired, discouraged, criticised or opposed. You continue to long for, pursue, and keep on attempting to attain what you are passionate about, despite constant setbacks and disappointments.

Read the last paragraph again and ask yourself honestly, "What's my passion?" The cell vision calls for people to be passionate about Jesus and his mission. It expects them to centre their lives around Christ and his call on their lives. It champions wholehearted commitment to cell church as the best way of making, maturing and mobilising disciples.

Much of the later sections of this book will be about that last statement. I truly believe that without the cell vision (or something very similar to it) we will continue to fall short of Jesus' Mandate for the Church recorded in Matthew 28:18-20. However, even the greatest models of ministry or the best structures for church growth will fail without spiritual passion. That is why the first part of this book is about stirring up your spiritual passion. The driving force, the energy and power of the cell vision is spiritual passion.

Many Western pastors and church leaders see cell church in action while visiting Latin America or Korea. In typically Western fashion, they analyse the mechanics of the cell models being demonstrated. Envious of the growth and success of these non-Western churches, they often hastily adopt the cell church structure back in their home nations without paying enough attention to the spirituality that must be present before the cell model can flourish. When they do not experience immediate and dramatic results, they wrongly conclude that cell church is not applicable to the West. However cell models are ineffective anywhere in the world without the values that empower and sustain them. Passion for Christ is one of the most important of these values.

The spiritual fervour and passion I witness in many so-called developing nations in Africa, Asia, South America and the Far East never ceases to amaze me. It creates a longing to see such passion in Britain and other European nations I work in. We salve our consciences by saying these nations are in 'revival' – that's why the cell vision works there. By doing this, we mask our own coldness of heart and lack of courage to rise to the challenge of cell church.

It is true that evangelical revivals swept the African, South American and Asian continents during the 20th Century. These are the church growth success stories of recent decades. In the same time frame, European and (to some extent) North American churches have declined as our Western societies have turned to secularism, liberalism, atheism and false religion.

At the turn of the Century, social commentators and politicians were announcing the death of religion itself in the West. We were told that the 21st Century was going to witness the coming of age of pure secularism. It does not look like that now. An aggressive religious force is filling the spiritual vacuum created by a sleeping church. I speak of Islam which is now setting the public religious agenda in virtually every Western nation. Religion is back. While the doom and gloom 'prophets' were writing the epitaph of the church and bewailing the lack of religious interest in the West, others were executing long-held and carefully crafted plans, fulfilling centuries-old aspirations to 'take over' the world in the name of their faith.

PURSUING CHRIST WITH PASSION

It is time we stood up and took account of what is happening. People do have a desire for religion and they do want to think about God. He has still yet more grace for our nations. He will not rest or withdraw while the age of his mercy lasts. Jesus shed his blood for all humanity, and he will see the reward of his sufferings in every nation on earth. Our job is to recover our spiritual passion. We can rise up and change our spiritual environment with the message of the gospel and the power of the Holy Spirit. We can transform our churches filling them with vibrant, passionate people committed to the Great Commission. The cell vision will be of strategic importance but spiritual passion is indispensible.

True spirituality comes through the activity of the Holy Spirit. It is he who reveals to us the true identity of Jesus as the Christ, the Son of the living God and the true significance of the cross. Without the Holy Spirit we could never discern the loveliness of Jesus or feel the compelling attraction of the cross. The Spirit inspires, energises and sustains our spiritual desire. The Spirit-filled life is a life of passion. The Holy Spirit wants to re-energise Christians, drawing us away from the scandal of mere 'Sunday Christianity'. He wants to transform cold, inactive Christians who lack conviction into radical fire-brands of confidence and boldness, sold out for the kingdom of God.

Evangelical Christianity was birthed in passion and always flourishes when Christ is upheld as the one, true source of salvation and spiritual satisfaction. Martin Luther re-discovered the biblical gospel of salvation by faith alone and set Germany on fire for God, giving birth to the 16th Century Protestant Reformation. The Puritan Revival and evangelical awakenings of the 17th, 18th and 19th Centuries in Britain and North America upheld this passionate focus on Christ. The Pentecostal Revivals of the 20th Century in Africa, South America, Indonesia and China all focussed on passionate and personal relationship with Christ, transforming whole nations and sub-continents. We must find the same passion for Christ if we are to experience the significant moves of God we so desperately need in the 21st Century.

One of the reasons evangelicalism has been historically successful in reaching the multitudes is our bold presentation of Christ. We call people to make a decision – to put their faith and trust in Christ for salvation. We preach forgiveness of sins and assurance of heaven for every true believer in Christ. However, eternal life is not just for the hereafter – it begins now. The gospel is not merely an insurance policy against hell or a guarantee for entry into heaven. It is about having and enjoying eternal life now.

When Jesus spoke to the Samaritan woman who had come to draw water from the well of Sychar he obviously wanted her to find in him the way to heaven. But he also spoke into the depth of her being so that she could discover passionate and life-affirming purpose on earth. Her fruitless and disappointing relationships with men revealed a deep craving for true satisfaction. Her five previous husbands and her present live-in partner could never give her the quality of this eternal life Jesus was offering her.

> *Jesus answered and said to her, "Whoever drinks of this water will thirst again, but whoever drinks of the water that I shall give him will never thirst. But the water that I shall give him will become in him a fountain of water springing up into everlasting life."*
>
> John 4:13-14

CHRIST BECOMES YOUR PASSION

The experience of the abundant, eternal life Christ offers comes by pursuing him passionately. This is not just about finding Christ as a personal Saviour, or being assured of a place in his heaven. It means experiencing deep satisfaction, joy and fulfilment in him. It is about discovering in Christ the source, inspiration and driving passion of life. Physical things or human relationships can never bring lasting satisfaction. When you have drunk all you can take, you are still thirsty! But once you truly encounter the living Christ, you discover that there is nothing else that could ever bring such perfect peace and lasting fulfilment.

It changes you forever! You reject the cheap and superficial pleasures this world offers. Christ fills your vision and determines your direction. He becomes your very life. After the

Samaritan woman met with Jesus, she left her water pot by the well and rushed into the city to tell others what she had just experienced. Her focus had radically altered. No longer preoccupied with the mundane, she was now alive to spiritual realities. Set free from the reproach of her past, she was no longer ashamed to be seen in public and became a vocal and visible witness to the whole city:

> *"Come, see a Man who told me all things that I ever did. Could this be the Christ?" Then they went out of the city and came to him.*

> John 4:29-30

The cell vision presupposes this level of spiritual passion. No programme or system of church life could ever be a substitute for it. I personally make it my aim to preach and model this in my church. I know that unless the people are truly passionate in their pursuit of Christ, the cell vision is just another programme, just another method – only far more demanding than most! This vision is for people with a passion for Jesus.

Transforming your Spiritual Environment

During the 1990s I was involved in a series of city-wide evangelistic meetings called Mission to London. It was hosted by an American ministry led by a healing evangelist. The meetings attracted much media attention and not a little controversy. The British media, openly sceptical about evangelical Christianity, had a field day. Mocking the claims we were making about divine healing and miracles, they criticised the evangelist's 'hyped-up' preaching and mannerisms. However, their true controversy was not with the evangelist, but the message of the gospel itself.

This came to light in a specially arranged television interview during which a well-known journalist and television presenter attempted to discredit the evangelist in any way possible. At one point in the interview, the evangelist turned the tables on the interviewer and asked him what he believed about the gospel. The answer he gave was typical of the school of thought propagated by this particular brand of professional journalism. Often, doubt and scepticism are prized as marks of intellectual credibility and religious certainty is abhorred as a sign of fanaticism and intellectual stupidity.

Then came a fascinating moment, which was for me the highlight of the interview. The evangelist asked the presenter what he believed about the Christian gospel. His answer was bland, woolly and badly thought through. The evangelist leaned forward in his seat, looked the journalist in the eye and said, "You are the product of your spiritual environment."

That was an interesting and challenging statement. Is it possible that people are so influenced by their intellectual and cultural setting that unless the Holy Spirit intervenes they struggle to see the truth as revealed in Jesus? If so, does that same spiritual environment affect Christians even after they have believed? These are deep questions. Perhaps this is a key to understanding how we should engage our society and challenge its view of spiritual matters.

HOW YOUR ENVIRONMENT AFFECTS YOU

The scientific debate concerning theories of 'nurture versus nature' will continue for a long time to come, but one thing is sure – we are affected by our *spiritual* environment. Our culture influences how we approach spiritual matters. The claims of the gospel do not conform to the prevailing opinions of our world, either intellectually or culturally. But that's just the point. Our faith is not the product of our society. It is revealed from heaven. We need to know what we are up against when we preach and live by the gospel of our Lord Jesus Christ. Our spiritual environment is not neutral but hostile to faith in Christ.

The issue is far deeper than cultural and intellectual preferences which vary from time to time and from place to place. The source of hostility to the truth of the gospel is spiritual. Humanity is blinded to the light of the gospel by the prince of darkness, the god of the realm of darkness:

> *But even if our gospel is veiled, it is veiled to those who are perishing, whose minds the god of this age has blinded, who do not believe, lest the light of the gospel of the glory of Christ, who is the image of God, should shine on them.*
> 2 Corinthians 4:3-4

Our fallen human nature is dark and it obscures the truth of Christ. Only a miracle of grace can penetrate it and enable us to see the light of Christ. Negative influences resistant to truth are embedded within our cultural environment.

Cell leaders often share with me what they are up against when they try to motivate and inspire their members to be whole-hearted in the cell vision. Recently, my Primary 12 listed the negative aspects of our spiritual and social environment in London. They find themselves fighting daily against busyness, consumerism, selfishness, independence, self-satisfaction, false sense of security, media negativity, political correctness, liberal ethics, breakdown in traditional family values, lack of community, wrong concepts of Christianity, traditional church models, nominal Christianity, false religions, lack of spiritual understanding, prayerlessness and love of wealth. Above all, they face the barriers erected by the flesh at work in the life of believers.

Some of these issues apply particularly to life in London, but most are part of the culture of modern unbelieving Europe and the West. Non-Western nations also have their struggles. Life is made difficult, often by poverty, oppressive governments, pagan religions, tribalism and lack of infrastructure – including the basic means of transport and communication.

In the post-modern West, truth is no longer an objective reality but a confusing cluster of individual viewpoints and perceptions. This form of relativism teaches there is no such thing as *the* truth – only *my* truth and *your* truth. The exclusive claims of the Christian gospel sound arrogant and bigoted. In our current philosophical environment, it is the height of intolerance to say that Jesus is the *only* way to God. Ironically, one of the last remaining acceptable intolerances of official Western culture is intolerance against Christianity itself. Everything goes, as long as it is *not* Christian. It takes courage to stand for Christ in that environment.

This descent into relativism leaves the door wide open to confusion and despair. There is no sure word for our world. We are coming from nowhere and drifting into nowhere. There is no hope, no meaning and no purpose – only what you can think, perceive or invent for yourself. But the revelation of the God of the Bible tells a different story. We are created by God for his glory and we find our true purpose in him and his kingdom established in Christ.

THE SPIRITUAL REALM IS REAL

The spiritual realities of God's kingdom are true, life-affirming and enduring. Spiritual truths, revealed in the Bible and made visible in the life of Christ, are sure and certain. The faith of the Christian is neither a figment of personal imagination nor the product of individual perceptions in the midst of an ocean of a million other conflicting, yet equally-valid individual perceptions.

Our faith is solidly anchored in history and provides a reliable source of truth. The spiritual realm and the truths it contains are *real*. The rock of revelation is there whether people perceive it or not. Truth is truth whether people accept it or reject it.

I touch on these philosophical issues deliberately because they are part of the thinking of our age. These ideas have practical consequences in the way we live and behave, even for Christians seeking to love God and serve him in the world. Society tells you that the only world you can be sure about is the physical world of matter and energy. It allows you privately to choose whatever you want to believe about Jesus and his call upon your life. Sometimes you will be respected and admired for it, and at other times you will be ridiculed. But few will deny you your right to have a personal faith.

The problem begins when your faith begins to challenge others – when you refuse to keep it private and want to go public with the gospel. As soon as you assert that your gospel is a 'matter of fact' and that your faith is relevant for everyone, you go against the trend. It takes courage to be open about our faith and to attempt to share it with others in our modern society. This contempt for the Christian gospel is set to grow and become even more intense in the future. Pressure will increase from both other religions and from secularism in our generation. How should we react to these things?

Many believers see Christian witness as an uphill struggle, a battle they cannot win in such a hostile environment. They settle for the quiet life, just about managing to keep their own faith intact as they tackle the daily responsibilities of life. In short, they withdraw and find comfort in their small circle of Christian friends and the joy they derive from Sunday church services.

I do not want to come across as harsh or judgemental here. I am only trying to reflect the reality that our spiritual environment is oppressive and we do not always respond as we should. One thing is sure – the cell vision gives us a way forward. It shows us that as believers in Christ, we are not alone. We can develop strong, affirming and encouraging relationships within the church and we can work together to present to the world a credible witness to Christ. The devil wins when we are isolated. Together, we are a strong and powerful force, but we must never underestimate the influence of our spiritual environment.

THERMOMETERS OR THERMOSTATS?

Most Christians act like thermometers, reflecting the ambient spiritual temperature. If it is cold, they are cold. If the spiritual atmosphere is open, they are open. If the prevailing spiritual climate is conducive to growth, they grow. But God has not called us to be thermometers, taking the spiritual temperature. Rather, he wants us to act like thermostats and set the temperature both in the church and in society. We should be determining the spiritual environment, not succumbing to it.

By prayer, fasting, and spiritual warfare, we can change the spiritual climate in our church, our city and even our nation. This is exactly what has happened in many nations in the non-

Western World. Not so long ago we could speak of Africa as the continent of darkness, but now much of it is blazing the light of the gospel. Latin America has been transformed over the last 40 years, and is now home to a fast growing evangelical movement that is affecting its respective nations at every level. South Korea, once totally dominated by Buddhism, now hosts the largest evangelical church in the world founded by David Yonggi Cho, and has a Christian population of over 26% of the nation.

We have begun to learn these lessons in Kensington Temple. Zealous Christianity, confidence in the gospel, enthusiastic evangelism and effective witness may be waning in some churches across Western nations, but we, along with many others, determined a long time ago that we would break the mould and buck the trend.

OVERCOMING YOUR SPIRITUAL ENVIRONMENT

At a time when many British churches are declining, we are growing. We may be living in a 'national Nazareth' of unbelief, but we guard our hearts and carry the anointing for the ministry God has given us. Like a greenhouse in the Arctic, we maintain an atmosphere conducive for growth and preserve our 'on-fire' spirituality. That is how we achieve what we achieve. People come into our environment and grow rapidly, learning how to maintain high levels of spiritual passion, despite the external prevailing culture. Likewise, all those who pursue the cell vision must work on changing their own spiritual environment into one conducive for discipleship and growth through cells.

We must draw the line in the sand and refuse to allow the spiritual atmosphere to affect us. We must also tear down the strongholds of the mind. I identify the following effects our spiritual environment has on us, which we must learn to overcome by the power of Christ:

- Lack of confidence in the gospel
- Doubt and unbelief
- Spiritual coldness
- Fear and intimidation
- Spiritual ignorance
- Prayerlessness
- Mistrust and division
- Civilian mentality (non-engagement in the spiritual battle)
- Hardness of heart
- Barrenness
- Lovelessness
- Minding the things of self
- Neglecting the things of God.

All these things are rooted in the flesh, but can be overcome by the Spirit of God:

> *I say then: Walk in the Spirit, and you shall not fulfill the lust of the flesh. For the flesh lusts against the Spirit, and the Spirit against the flesh; and these are contrary to one another, so that you do not do the things that you wish.*
>
> Galatians 5:16-17

Passion brings transformation

We begin by refusing to allow our spiritual environment to dictate the level of our spirituality. Isaac sowed in a time of famine and reaped a hundredfold in the same year (Genesis 26:12). He refused to accept that his environment had more influence over his fruitfulness than the promise of God for his life. He sowed expecting a harvest, not paying attention to the negative surrounding conditions. God rewarded his faith.

In Isaiah chapter 35, we read of the miracle of a transformed environment. The dessert blossoms as a rose and the place of barrenness becomes a place of fruitfulness, watered by streams and bubbling springs. No matter how apparently hostile and unfriendly our environment, our true source is the promise of God and the provision of all that we need in him.

The Bible is full of examples of people who refused to bow to the trends of their day and fought against the constraints others placed on them. They stood for God and found they could break the barriers to fruitful growth forced upon them by negative circumstances and wicked people.

The godly kings, Josiah and Hezekiah, used their influence to reform the nation of Judah morally and spiritually, and to draw the people of God back to himself. Elijah prayed down fire from heaven and backslidden Israel turned to the Lord. Daniel interceded for the exiles in Babylon and prepared the way for them to return to their homeland. Stephen, the first Christian martyr, laid down his life for the truth that God was calling the Gentile nations to hear the gospel and repent. The apostle Paul blazed a trail for Christ across the then-known world establishing two vibrant sending centres of Christianity either side of the Aegean Sea.

We can turn the tide in our day also. In the cell vision, we stoke the flames of the fire of God through persistent prayer and intercession. We move in discernment and revelation. We are determined, we mean business with God and we persevere in faith. We live the supernatural life.

We teach our people to spend time with God, walking with him in intimate fellowship and worship. We love practicing his presence, meditating on his goodness, listening to his leadings and, above all, worshipping his greatness and glory. The cells provide true fellowship and friendship. 'Iron sharpens iron' when cell members get together as like-minded people, stirring one another up and investing in one another's lives. We value spiritual gifts and the miraculous power of the Holy Spirit.

We establish our new believers in the truth of who they are in Christ and we teach them that "all things are possible to him who believes." We encourage them to adopt their true position "seated with Christ in heavenly places", to lay hold of Christ "who is our life", to "have the faith of God" and to "speak to the mountains" that obstruct us. We teach them to live the overcoming life and to "be strong in the Lord" as they "put on the full armour of God." Together, we "pull down strongholds" and witness Satan "fall like lightning".

MAKING IT PERSONAL

The cell vision aims for 100% mobilisation of the body of Christ. This is not merely a good idea or a sound preaching theme. It is God's vision for the church and the cell strategy can make it happen. Jesus calls his disciples to be fruitful and promises to help us in this process, but we must play our part – each one of us.

If every believer won one person for Christ each year and discipled them in the faith, we would have an annual growth rate of 100%. I know that growth never happens according to such neat formulae. We all bear fruit in different measures, as Jesus said – some 30 fold, some 60 fold and some 100 fold. However, this teaching from the Parable of the Sower proves we have both the individual and corporate capacity to produce exponential growth for the kingdom of God.

The cell vision builds a model of church in which every single member of the church can grow and be fruitful. We emphasise individual responsibility for the Great Commission and we also ensure that no one attempts to go it alone. The very essence of church is corporate relationship – we operate as a body, but to do so effectively, we must be individually strong, healthy, and be functioning to full capacity.

That's why I am about to get personal with you! I want you to read the next section in a deeply personal way. Look at the pointers below and ask yourself if you are ready to adopt the mindset and lifestyle that will change your own spiritual environment and, together with others, influence the spiritual climate in your family, your church, your community and eventually, your nation.

"I am a world-changer"

We have already seen examples of whole nations and sub-continents being changed by the gospel. Sub-Saharan Africa, China, South America have all experienced dramatic spiritual climate change in the past six decades. This is the successful outworking of Jesus' mandate to the whole church: "Go, make disciples of all nations". Bear in mind the word *ethne* translated, 'nations' in Matthew 28:19 refers to ethnic people groups and not political nations as we think of them today. This makes Jesus' command all the more wonderful. It speaks of gospel penetration at every level of every society, resulting in global influence.

I am not thinking about world domination or other non-Christian concepts such as establishing a religious, political or military empire. I am picturing the fulfilment of Jesus' vision of hundreds of thousands of Christian communities penetrating, influencing and transforming every nation by their loving service and effective testimony to Christ.

The Lord Jesus is calling you to be a part of this. As you give yourself to his vision, alongside others in your cell group and in coordination with your whole church, you can become an effective agent for world change. Let's dream big and take small steps. We can change the world, one person at a time.

"I am a team player"

Individualism is one of the major spiritual barriers we face in the West. We are masters of our own destiny, determining our own path and choosing our own level of participation in society. Rather than confronting this, churches pander to it with their comfortable services, self-help sermons and their own brand of consumer Christianity.

Western Christians criticise the authoritarian church structures they find outside their nations, where group identity rules over individuality and collective thinking wins over personal opinion. The cell model itself is associated with non-

Western cultures where corporate choice is more dominant than personal choice. However, we must accept that in Western churches, where the individual is king, we have bred generations of shallow and selfish Christians who put personal comfort above the call of Christ.

The cell model seeks to redress the balance. We do need to be personally on fire for Christ, but we burn brighter and longer together. The networking structure of cell church means that every person is part of a team of people who in turn link with other teams. Every part connects with the whole and personal effort serves the corporate vision. We uphold both the individual and the community elements of our faith. Sharing and serving together in teams that are connected in interdependent relationships with the whole body is the essence of biblical Christianity.

"Christ lives in me"

The secret of passionate and vital Christianity is Christ. He lives in us individually and corporately. He is the source of our life, our joy and our fruitfulness. The apostle Paul spoke of living by the faith of Christ at work in his life (Galatians 2:20). He taught that when we die to the old life, Christ actually becomes our life and the 'faith of Christ' begins to operate in us. Jesus credits us with the benefits of his sacrificial death and indwells us with his sanctifying life. We are united with him. This is the summit of individual and corporate spirituality. We are joined to each other in him and he becomes our habitation, our true spiritual environment.

In John chapter 15, Jesus stresses that without him we can do nothing. But that also means joined in vital union with him, we can do all things. When we live in the conscious experience of this truth, we are transformed spiritually. Our repentance, consecration, wholeness and spiritual desire flow from Christ in us. When we stop trying to produce the life of

Christ ourselves, we discover that very same life is being supernaturally reproduced in us. Sustained by our true spiritual habitat, our fellowship and witness become natural expressions of who we are.

"I am a friend of Jesus"

We talk and sing about being friends of Jesus, but I wonder if we are really aware of what that means. It does not apply to everyone. It cost Abraham everything to be called the friend of God. Jesus taught that friendship with God depends upon two factors – hearing his Word and doing it. Some hear and don't follow his teaching, while others don't even listen. The steady flow of conversation with the Holy Spirit is the source of the spiritual life of the church. This presupposes intimacy, quietness of heart and a readiness to listen. Jesus said,

> *Greater love has no one than this, than to lay down one's life for his friends. You are my friends if you do whatever I command you.*
>
> John 15:13-14

Jesus has already given his life for us demonstrating his love. Such passionate, self-sacrificial love is the starting point of divine friendship. Now, we must respond to this startling fact – God, in Christ laid down his life for us. What are we going to do about it? More personally, what are *you* going to do about it? Are you going to become a passionate lover of God, or descend into the prevalent contemporary mediocrity of your spiritual environment? The right response is full-on, radical discipleship. Listen again to these sombre yet thrilling words of Jesus:

> *You did not choose me, but I chose you and appointed you that you should go and bear fruit, and that your fruit should remain, that whatever you ask the Father in my name he may give you.*
>
> John 15:16

"I am not ashamed of the gospel"

I have already highlighted the fact that it takes courage to stand for Christ in today's world. It is the same virtually anywhere, and it has always been that way. Christians have always run the risk of rejection and persecution. However, spiritual passion pays no attention to the cost. It is too focussed on Christ and his kingdom to be hindered by the hostility of the passing world order. Love for God and humanity overcomes the fear of negative consequences every time.

Our present life on earth is the only opportunity we have to own Christ in an alien environment. In heaven it will be too late. Like Joseph of Arimathea, who pleaded for a decent burial for the body of Christ, we must have courage to identify ourselves with the rejected, man of sorrows. Unlike Joseph, we stand not with a dead Jesus, but with the living Christ who is Lord of all.

We proclaim Christ, not ourselves. Therefore, we *can* be bold. We stand with him when we speak for him and live publicly according to his truth. Boldness means we do not back down when challenged by hostile secularism or Christ-denying religions. In love we hold firm, and by actions and words proclaim that life is found in him, and only in him. The gospel is still the power of God for the salvation of everyone who believes.

"I am a spreader of good news!"

The gospel carries a clear call of surrender to Christ as the only hope for a lost humanity. We must do this intelligently and compassionately, but we must do it. The "foolishness" of preaching is the only way people can hear and respond to Christ. The success of the very early church was due to this. Every believer was an evangelist, a spreader of good news.

The preaching of the gospel, backed up by righteous living and the convicting power of the Holy Spirit is just what the world needs. If we don't do it, who will? No other activity of the church is as important and nothing can substitute for it. Evangelism is truly the "life blood" of the church.

Determine you will be a witnessing Christian – that you will make it your daily prayer and your daily focus. Become skilled in presenting the gospel in every legitimate way possible. It is your mission and not just the responsibility of the official preachers of the church.

The Holy Spirit is the Spirit of witness and he will confirm your testimony in his own special way. Healing, signs and wonders were not just for New Testament times or reserved for special seasons of spiritual intensity. They are the tools of our trade. Expect God to use you just as Jesus promised,

> *And these signs will follow those who believe: In my name they will cast out demons; they will speak with new tongues; they will take up serpents; and if they drink anything deadly, it will by no means hurt them; they will lay hands on the sick, and they will recover."*
>
> Mark 16:17-18

If you recoil at any of the above, realise that it is probably due to the influence of your spiritual environment. Live in the revelation of the New Testament and reject the intellectual and moral compromise of your culture. It's a snare from which you must be set free.

"I am making a difference"

God has a plan for you far beyond your imagination. You have been masterfully re-created in the image of Christ and shaped by God himself to fulfil his divine purpose for you. Ephesians 2:10 teaches that God has a specially-prepared and tailor-made purpose for you on planet earth. It so perfectly fits you, that you will be able to say, "*This* is what I was born for!" When we reach out with Christ's love we become the hand of God to those he is touching with his grace. The partnership is powerful and irresistible.

The Christian faith spreads from person to person, and this impact brings radical changes that begin to transform the spiritual environment of a community or a nation. We are all influencers. History turns on apparently insignificant person-to-person encounters. 'Chance' meetings and unpremeditated conversations can become links in the divine chain of events. Human connections are the power sockets of heavenly purpose. That is why your life has the capacity to impact thousands. We are told that people living in the cities of today encounter more individuals in a single day that our medieval ancestors did in their lifetime!

The "salt and light" image Jesus uses in the Sermon on the Mount brings hope to everyone who would otherwise think they are insignificant. Our good works shine before men and bring glory to our Father in heaven. Traditional church models say to the world, "Come and hear." Cell church turns this on its head by equipping its members to be salt and light in the world. We say to our people, "Go and show" Christ to the world.

Cell groups bring structured and organised intentionality into the church's mission to the world. We build microcosmic expressions of the good news in every corner of the 'market place' of our generation. We take Christ himself to the multitudes and show them he is alive. As the Anglican Bishop, David Pytches wrote, "The meeting place is the learning place for the market place." Serving Christ in the context of Christian gatherings is not enough to win the world.

A constant refrain in my preaching is, "Your occupation is the location for your true vocation." The cell groups meet and operate where the people are – their home, place of work, place of education or recreation. We train Christians to be active in every aspect of modern life and to influence their world for Christ. We make sure cell groups never become holy huddles of Christian self-interest, but dynamic expressions of Christ in every part of society. As we reach people where they are, and disciple them for Christ, we fulfil our role as salt and light in the world.

Everything I have included in this chapter has to do with the spiritual environment we create by allowing the Spirit free reign in our life. It is not mere Christian activism but consistent spirituality. The Holy Spirit, the author of authentic Christianity, dwells in Christ's body, the church, and makes his presence felt in us and through us. He acts as the "go between" resonating God's heartbeat in the church and linking us with his dynamic life.

Prayer and intercession, the crucible of spiritual passion permeates the community of believers who throw themselves upon God's mercy and grace. Spirit-empowered living reaches the lost, the lonely, the broken-hearted and the hurting. First individuals and then whole communities are transformed. Intentional discipleship mobilises the whole body of Christ to rise up and be counted. That is how we can transform our spiritual environment.

The Spirit of Grace

By now you might be wondering whether the cell vision is promising too much. I hope you are rightly suspicious of any method that claims to be the panacea of all the Christian ills of our generation. I make no such claim for the cell model, or any other strategy for that matter. Furthermore, many ideas are good in theory, but fail in practice. I have met church leaders who were at first excited about cell church, but soon became disillusioned when they tried to implement it.

Later, I will offer some guidelines on how to introduce the Model of 12 into your church, but first I want to spend some time on an essential New Testament revelation without which the cell model cannot function. I am referring to the experience of God's grace, which is so foundational in fact, that no aspect of the Christian life can flourish without it.

Let me put the question this way. How can we hope to see this generation of Christians truly passionate for Christ – so passionate that they will happily pay the price it takes for cell church to thrive? That is an important question to consider. In my context in London, cell church is not a soft option. It rejects traditional ways of doing church and it goes against the trend of cheap populism.

Any vision that structures the whole of church life around the invitation to take up the cross, die to self and serve Christ totally, is bound to meet with some resistance. I have found that it's OK to preach these truths, but to insist that people put them into practice is another matter entirely! I remember the sombre moment when our church members realised that we were really serious about the cell vision. We were not just preaching about it, but were actually going to do it. I was challenging them to accept a completely different model of church which would call for their total involvement in the service of Christ.

SERVING GOD BY GRACE

For any serious church leader the question must be, 'How can I raise up a generation of believers so passionate about Christ that they are prepared to lose everything in order to gain him?' The answer is of course that we cannot do this, but the Holy Spirit can. When people receive a deep revelation of Jesus they will follow him anywhere. Without such a vision, people will never rise to the challenge. Put another way, this means we must learn to serve God by grace and not by our own efforts.

I remember a young man who came to Christ in a rather traditional church. He wore Gothic-type clothes and sported spiky, black-dyed hair. He also had a background of drugs and alcohol abuse. Needless to say, he stood out from the other members of the church. They were certainly not ready for someone of his appearance to get saved.

The church set to work right away. The piercings were the first to go – objects of the devil! The weird clothes were exchanged for a good 'Christian' suit. And the hairstyle was converted into something a saved man should wear. Everyone was happy, so they paid no more attention to him. He was expected to sit in the rows alongside the other members and be a good boy, like everyone else.

What was happening in this real life example so typical of what is taking place in today's churches? We could call it culture shock or a generational gap, but I have another way of describing it – legalism. This blight on Christianity has many faces and is supported by many fine-sounding arguments. However, it is literally choking the life and joy of Christ out of so many of today's churches. It is also a killer when it comes to delightful Christian service.

Without the revelation of grace, cell church becomes a yoke too heavy to bear and leads to a bondage almost as great as the Law of Moses! But once people have tasted the grace of God and learned to live under the favour he has freely bestowed on us in Christ, the cell vision becomes a joy. We welcome it as a God-given strategy by which we enthusiastically fulfil his call on our lives.

Take time now and allow me to minister the revelation of God's grace to you. I begin by asserting three things that are true of you before you even think about your duties or your responsibilities towards God. As one prominent 'grace teacher' puts it, "You are greatly blessed, highly favoured and deeply loved in the beloved Son of God." Think what this means. Totally independent of anything you have ever done, or ever could do, you are fully, freely and eternally accepted by God. This has absolutely nothing to do with you, but everything to do with Jesus.

Never again do you have to worry whether God loves you or whether you qualify for his blessing. You could never do enough to merit one single good thing God has for you. It all comes by grace – his undeserved favour. Doubtless you have heard this good news before, but perhaps it has never sunk in. More to the point, perhaps you have heard these truths preached or celebrated in the worship of your church, but you have never been allowed to enjoy what they mean in practice.

Legalism creeps in through many subtle and deceptive ways. That's because it is the devil's master stroke against God's people. He uses God's holy law to keep God's people under the bondage of guilt and condemnation. Bible teachers fear the consequences of preaching unlimited grace. They believe that to go down this line leads people into sin. People must be kept from the truth because they will abuse it. However, to think like this is to misunderstand God's grace and its power to shape our lives.

GRACE MEANS WE HAVE NOTHING MORE TO PAY!

Some will teach grace to a limited extent. They agree that we are saved by grace, but they quickly re-introduce the law to 'balance' grace with discipline. But you cannot successfully mix grace with anything – it must be all grace or it is simply not grace at all. Unlimited grace means that the good we receive from God is totally unmerited and free. If we contribute to our salvation, even in the slightest detail, then grace is no longer grace.

Grace is not a good offer, a bargain deal or a cheap way of gaining something priceless in itself. For grace to be grace it means we pay *nothing*. Christ takes full responsibility for 100% of the payment. That is exactly what he achieved for us on the cross. His cry of triumph rings down through the ages, "It is finished!" No more debt to pay, nothing more to do to qualify for God's favour. We are now and forever a part of God's kingdom by faith in Christ.

We are forgiven by grace, accepted by grace, saved by grace, sanctified by grace and we serve by grace. It is grace from start to finish. Think what this means in practice. We love God because he first loved us. We live right because we have been accepted by him and not in order to be accepted by him. We forgive because we have been forgiven, we live free because we have been set free and we serve God because he has served us.

All we do for Christ is based on our response to his grace and not in order to gain his favour. Paul knew this and made one of the most profound grace statements in the entire New Testament when he wrote,

> *For I am the least of the apostles, who am not worthy to be called an apostle, because I persecuted the church of*

God. But by the grace of God I am what I am, and his grace toward me was not in vain; but I laboured more abundantly than they all, yet not I, but the grace of God which was with me.

1 Corinthians 15:9-11

Paul was the first to admit that in himself he was unworthy before God. No-one disagreed! They were suspicious of his conversion to Christ and outraged that he was now claiming apostleship on the same level as the 12 apostles of Christ. Perhaps you feel completely unworthy and inadequate when it comes to the challenge of the cell vision. Maybe you have to face both internal and external doubts about your suitability to serve Jesus. Look how Paul dealt with it.

He was as amazed as everybody else, absolutely blown away by the kindness of God in taking a self-righteous, bigoted and arrogant persecutor of Christ, and making him the primary New Testament apostle to the Gentiles. All he could say was "I am what I am by the grace of God." He owed it all to Christ. We must learn the same lesson. Only when we are equally overwhelmed by the mercy and grace God has shown to us will we be ready to serve him willingly and joyfully. Only then will we be willing to take on something as radical and demanding as the cell vision.

SATURATED BY THE SPIRIT OF GRACE

At the beginning of our venture into cell church, I looked at the shallow response so many people in our church were making to the challenge I presented. I realised we needed a generation of people who were saturated in the Spirit of grace. I began to preach grace in a much more emphatic way. Some cell leaders complained, "Since you began to preach so much about grace", they said, "Our cell members have become lazy!" Can you guess how I responded to this? I preached grace even stronger than before. I preached grace, grace and still more grace! Do you understand why? It was because I knew the second part of Paul's testimony.

Paul did not only give God glory because he had been saved and called to be an apostle, but he also gave God the credit for inspiring him and empowering him in his ministry. In effect he said, "I am what I am by the grace of God", and, "I can do what I can do by the grace of God!"

Rightly understood, grace never produces lazy, fleshly Christians but workers, sold out for Jesus! Paul was so grateful for what Christ had done for him. His deep experience of the grace of God inspired and motivated him to live a life 100% dedicated to Christ. The same grace that saved him was now working dynamically in him, empowering him to labour tirelessly for the kingdom.

Grace teaches us – it shapes our lives – to be like Christ. Grace sets us free from sin's power and directs us towards God's holy glory. This is the motivation leaders must inspire in their members. Good workers for the kingdom of God are workers permanently infatuated by Christ. That's why pressure tactics, guilt trips, blame games and naming and shaming people, never work in ministry. Manipulating people by these means cannot produce the kind of willing response that God requires of his people.

Serving God is an honour and a privilege that can only be enjoyed by true lovers of God. The rest is dull, legalistic and dead religion. My friend I spoke of earlier had been given entirely the wrong picture of God through the legalism in the traditional Pentecostal church he had joined. He was puzzled by the fact that in the gospel God says, "Come as you are" while the church said, "You are not acceptable until you change!" He did change, at least externally, and the people backed off. As long as he looked like everyone else around him, they left him in peace. But he was not at peace within himself. He had so much to deal with concerning his past, but he could not bring himself to share these things with the judgemental believers he found around him. If they had judged his external appearance so harshly, what would they make of what was really happening inside?

The grace message states that God is looking for heart transformation, not behaviour modification. As long as we judge people from the outside, whether believers or unbelievers, we not only deny the gospel but we repel the very people the Spirit of grace is seeking to reach. God is looking for outrageous lovers and passionate warriors – not religious lawyers and judges.

MINISTERS OF THE NEW COVENANT

One of my greatest desires is that I might become a truly competent minister of the New Covenant – someone who is so taken up with gazing at the surpassing and permanent glory of Christ, that the Holy Spirit is free to transform my heart to be like him. That way the people around me might just get a glimpse of his glory also. The letter of the law always kills, bringing condemnation and guilt, but the life-giving Spirit always directs our attention to the perfection and fullness we possess in Christ. This is the ultimate spiritual attraction. That's why Jesus offended the religious as he drew sinners around him. Grace is not a doctrine or a theological statement – it's a person, called Jesus Christ, the Son of God.

Once you see him and taste his goodness and kindness, your heart is his forever. There is nothing too big or too small he could ever ask you to do that will meet with reluctance on your part. Your greatest joy and pleasure is in pleasing him. These are the amazing effects of grace and the cell vision is nothing without them. Once deeply experienced, grace produces willing and passionate people who love the cell vision because it gives them the opportunity to be effective workers for Christ.

In the next chapter, we look at one of the most important effects grace has on our lives – passion for souls.

Passion for Souls

A key verse in the New Testament reveals one of the most fundamental aspects of Christian living. 2 Corinthians 2:18 says,

> *But we all, with unveiled face, beholding as in a mirror the glory of the Lord, are being transformed into the same image from glory to glory, just as by the Spirit of the Lord.*
>
> 2 Corinthians 3:18

This is the Spirit of grace at work in us. Through revelation, the Spirit spotlights Jesus, drawing our gaze away from ourselves to the splendour of his glorious person. Captivated by what we see, our hearts begin to soften. The Holy Spirit is released to work the inner transformation that will begin to reproduce Christ's character and likeness in our lives. As we grow in our intimate relationship with Christ, he bares his heart to us. We start to see things as he sees them.

Our first discovery is his passionate love for lost humanity. His heart throbs with the compassion of a shepherd longing for his sheep. The same love that drew him to come to seek and to save the lost and wayward compels us also to reach the lost. This is our calling. We are sent on the same mission. His passion becomes our passion.

Spreading the good news of Jesus is at the heart of the cell vision. We work hard to keep the cell groups focused on evangelism. It is all too easy for them to become little havens of fellowship or support groups for our Christian friends. Outreach must become the lifestyle of every single member. We are committed to winning people to Christ. The regular cell meetings must be places where those who have not yet found him receive a warm welcome and feel accepted.

The biblical basis is clear. Jesus commanded us to spread the good news.

> *And he said to them, "Go into all the world and preach the gospel to every creature.*
>
> Mark 16:15

He promised us his power to do this effectively. But we must become both committed and skilled in the art of soul winning. It is estimated that 95% of believers never lead anyone to Christ. There are many reasons why evangelism is pushed to the sidelines. But no one can deny that it should be brought back to the centre as the church's main task. Most of our time, energy and resources are spent on those who already know and believe in Jesus, while a fraction of our efforts go on those who don't.

On a global level, over 25% of the world is without the direct influence of genuine Christian testimony, but less than 2% of church resources go into reaching them. In local church life also, most of our budget is spent on ourselves, while a fraction of it goes on reaching the lost.

Evangelistic church services, mass meetings, literature distribution, TV and radio – all have a part to play. But the genius of the cell vision is that we communicate Christ person to person, and we do it together, so that those more gifted in this art can help the others. We teach people how to spread the good news by witness (Acts 1:8), by signs and wonders (Mark 16:20) and by our works (Matthew 5:13-16 & Matthew 25:31-46).

We ask believers to think constantly about how they can evangelise in their sphere of influence – home, work, college, school, and neighbourhood. We teach people to share Christ within their social circle and to use their talents and recreational activities as a point of contact for non-Christians. We also focus on community projects as a means of demonstrating our Christian faith and building relationships with local people.

Evangelism is the natural overflow of people who are passionate about their faith. In Acts chapter 4, Peter and John were forbidden from preaching the gospel in Jerusalem following the ruling of the Jewish authorities. They had been arrested after the healing of the lame man who sat at the gate to the Temple. Acts records their reply, "We cannot help speaking about the things we have seen and heard!" Real faith is like that. You cannot keep it to yourself. After all, the issues the gospel addresses are vitally important.

FOUNDATION OF THE GOSPEL

The gospel is rooted in something far more solid than our personal enthusiasm. Our motivation for preaching is that we have found in Christ the truth God revealed for all humanity. As we saw in Chapter 2, exclusive claims to truth are unpopular in the intellectual climate of our day. Evangelical believers are derided more for this than for anything else. However, it is important to remember that Christ is, not just *our* Saviour. He gave his life for the whole *world*. This is why we make it a priority to preach the good news.

Our faith rests on historical facts. God has appeared, spoken and acted in history. Recall Peter and John's words to the Jewish Council – they were eyewitnesses to the events of the gospel. The appeal to public events known to have taken place by the general population is a recurring theme in the New Testament. The gospel events did not take place privately, in a corner.

However, the gospel revelation goes beyond the external events witnessed in history. It includes Jesus' explanation of their significance. To history, we must add theology if we are going to be sure of our message. It is a matter of history that Jesus was crucified in the time of Pontius Pilate, but it is a theological reality that he died to save the world. We must be sure of this, otherwise our witness will not be effective. It will always be just a matter of personal opinion.

I was once interviewed for a television programme in which a liberal theologian was mocking the evangelical message of salvation through the cross. His arguments were not new – the same liberal thinking that has sought to undermine confidence in the gospel for the last 150 years or more. Basically, he was saying that we cannot trust the New Testament interpretation of the cross. The theology of the sacrifice of Christ does not come from Jesus' teaching but from a later generation of followers who imposed their own thinking on the simple moral message of Jesus.

I was asked to produce proof that Jesus said he was going to die for the sins of the world. First of all, I did not accept the premise of my liberal opponent. The apostles were Jesus' closest associates. They were in a far better position to understand the significance of the cross than any of us today. The theology of the New Testament rests on the understanding of these 1st Century followers of Christ. What's more, the very existence of the Early Church is proof that what they taught came from God's revelation in Christ. The church came into being through the words and actions of Jesus. To say that the church invented the very things that caused its birth is historical nonsense. It would be like you saying that you invented the existence of your parents in order to explain how you came into the world!

The liberal theologian was wrong about Jesus' teaching also. Jesus clearly taught that his death was about saving the world when he said,

> *For even the Son of Man did not come to be served, but to serve, and to give his life a ransom for many.*
>
> Mark 10:45

Taken in the context of the whole of Jesus' life and teaching, this can mean only one thing. Jesus gave his life to set us free from the bondage of sin and all its consequences. This is why we must preach the gospel – it is the way by which humanity must be saved.

Nor is there salvation in any other, for there is no other name under heaven given among men by which we must be saved."

Acts 4:12

This means we have an urgent necessity to preach the gospel. We do so in the light of eternity. Jesus warned his generation about hell (Matthew 10:28 & Luke 16:23). Love will urge us to do the same (2 Corinthians 5:11, 14 & 20). We can never be ashamed of the gospel as it is humanity's only hope (Mark 8:38; Romans 1:16 & 2 Timothy 1:8). But we must do so in the wisdom and power of the Holy Spirit (Acts 2:43, 46-47 & 1 Corinthians 2:13).

THE FATHER'S HEART

If you draw close to the Father's heart you will discover it is breaking with love for the lost. He is the God of grace and mercy (Ephesians 2:3-5 & Psalm 103:7-8). His love for all humanity led him to send Christ to be the Saviour of the world (John 3:16). Judgement is described as his "strange and alien" work (Isaiah 28:21-22). He takes no pleasure in the death of the wicked (2 Peter 3:9; Ezekiel 18:23 & 30-32). But, he is absolutely just and cannot go against his holy nature (Genesis 8:25). If we reject his grace and his way of salvation, we remain under his wrath, his righteous reaction to sin.

Jesus died for all humanity (Hebrews 2:9 & 1 John 2:2) and the preaching of the cross draws us to him (John 12:32-33; John 6:37 & John 6:44-45). That's why "the second death" (hell) breaks God's heart (2 Thessalonians 1:8-9; Revelation 20:6 & Revelation 20:12-15). If this does not move us with compassion for the lost, nothing will. If we cannot be passionate for the lost souls of the men, women and children around us, I wonder whether we can be passionate about anything. Nothing could ever be more important than this.

REACHING THE LOST

One of the authentic hallmarks of the cell vision is that it places the gospel at the top of the agenda. The cells prioritise evangelism in their ministry. Technically, they are for both the evangelising of the lost and the encouragement of the believers, but we have found that unless we keep evangelism as our primary purpose, the cell groups easily slip into the comfort of Christian fellowship meetings.

That is why we centre all cell group activity on what we call the Evangelism of 3. Prayer triplets are not new, but they are an effective way of involving every single cell member to win people to Christ. We begin by asking cell members to make a list of 10 people whom they know, meet regularly and can invite to the cell meetings. Then we focus on 3 people the Holy Spirit shows us on each of these lists. Joining with 2 or 3 other people we begin to pray daily for those on our shortlists. A regular cell meeting will include time for prayer and strategic planning, in order to win these precious people for Christ. The cells then organise their meetings and activities around the goal of reaching their friends with the gospel.

Prayer is the single greatest evidence we have of our dependence on the power of God. Our prayer life also reveals our passion. We pray for the things we most want to see happen. That's why the cell meetings always include time to intercede for the lost, personally by name and with understanding. As we pray, God acts. C.H. Spurgeon, the great Baptist preacher who ministered in London in the 19th Century, said, "Prayer is the slender nerve that moves the muscles of Omnipotence."

Frequently, the cell meets around some social activity such as a meal, a film, a sporting event or a party. Evangelism becomes a lifestyle. We call the regular cell groups 'open cells' because they focus on reaching out to those who do not yet know Christ and bringing them to the cell meeting. The deeper issues of discipleship are reserved for the 'closed cells' which are leadership focussed. In these cell groups, leaders and potential leaders are trained to build their own cells. However, without a genuine passion for the lost, the whole cell vision falls to the ground.

Evangelism is the first step. To fulfil the Great Commission, we must also be passionate about discipleship. We look at this in the next chapter.

People with a Passion

Passion for Discipleship

Both Matthew and Mark pass on the Great Commission of Jesus with clarity and conviction. Their faithful records of Jesus' words complement each other, giving us the full picture of the task he entrusted to us. Mark focuses on preaching the gospel to the whole creation with accompanying signs, wonders and miracles:

> And he said to them, "Go into all the world and preach the gospel to every creature. He who believes and is baptized will be saved; but he who does not believe will be condemned. And these signs will follow those who believe: In my name they will cast out demons; they will speak with new tongues; they will take up serpents; and if they drink anything deadly, it will by no means hurt them; they will lay hands on the sick, and they will recover."
>
> Mark 16:15-18

Matthew stresses the discipleship aspect:

> Go therefore and make disciples of all the nations, baptizing them in the name of the Father and of the Son and of the Holy Spirit, teaching them to observe all things that I have commanded you; and lo, I am with you always, even to the end of the age. Amen.
>
> Matthew 28:19-20

For too long the church has acted as if Jesus intended us to make converts, not disciples. The goal of evangelism is raising up followers of Jesus. Evangelical and Pentecostal preachers are adept at winning converts but not so focussed on retaining them and discipling them into the church. The vast majority of converts do not get rooted in the life of the church – let alone go on to become fruitful disciples themselves. In my view there are two main reasons for this. We often have a wrong understanding of church and we rarely make discipleship our focus.

I will say more about our poor understanding of church later on, but for now, let me highlight the weakness of much evangelism which separates 'evangelistic decision' from 'Christian discipleship'. The word used of preaching the gospel in the New Testament means 'to proclaim as a herald'. This is a concept borrowed from the City State in ancient Greece. The herald's job was to announce the start of the city council meeting, the gathering of all the free men who deliberated on the affairs of the city.

The result of the proclamation was the council gathering, or *ekklesia*, which is the same word the New Testament uses for 'church'. The parallel is clear. We have not finished the task of evangelism until those who respond to the message are gathered into church fellowship. Until we understand this, evangelism and discipleship will always be disconnected.

I know many evangelists who break their heart over the lack of consolidation of new believers. In Africa, I once witnessed a mass evangelism meeting during which many thousands responded to the clear call of the gospel. Unfortunately, the church was not ready to receive these new believers. Very few were integrated into the fellowship of the church, and even fewer went on to become real disciples of Christ. In fact, I later learned that the vast majority of those who responded to the gospel were the same people who accepted Christ the last time the evangelist came to town – just two years before!

Another evangelist friend of mine spoke of a mission he held in a small church in the UK where he saw around 100 people give their lives to Christ. He discovered one year later that the decision cards which recorded the names and addresses of respondents were still sitting under the pastor's desk! There had been absolutely no attempt to follow up these new believers. Clearly something is wrong.

We have a responsibility to bring new converts into full and open expression of their relationship to Christ and to each other. We must make sure they have 'a good beginning' in the Christian life and have every opportunity first, to be personally discipled and then, to be trained to become disciple makers of others.

FRUIT THAT LASTS

Passionate followers of Jesus will care about this. They will not allow precious fruit to be lost. The single greatest reason the leadership of every church should look seriously at the cell model is that it retains the fruit of evangelism by organising the whole church – its members and activities – around the Great Commission 'to make, mature and mobilise disciples of Christ'. Jesus set this principle in motion from the very beginning. He said to those he called into the kingdom of God, "Come follow me – and I will make you to become fishers of men."

We recently finished two years of nightly evangelistic meetings in Kensington Temple. Over 5,000 people committed their lives to Christ and there were many outstanding miracles of healing. Each respondent was carefully followed up through our consolidation programme. By the end of the mission, 90% were being successfully followed up and 60% were already being discipled in the cell groups. We are learning to bear 'fruit that remains' and know that this is only possible when the whole church is involved in the process.

THE SCANDAL OF AN UNDISCIPLED CHURCH

Jesus placed discipleship at the heart of mission, but it is strange how the simple basics of Christ's teaching are so easily set aside by our human ideas of church. Even 'successful' churches that attract large crowds, often do so by neglecting discipleship. This is evident in the superficial consumer-based form of Christianity skilfully promoted by leaders, eager to boost their church numbers. A few mega conferences with internationally renowned speakers and famous Christian musical artists can provoke a popular response and add thousands to your church provided you can keep up the hype.

I have seen with my own eyes thousands of eager believers come forward to receive the blessings of prosperity, healing, joy or generalised 'success' channelled through some superstar guest speaker, usually as part of an aggressive promotional campaign to build a church of thousands. It seems God's people today will put up with almost anything, place almost any amount of money in the offering and be the most enthusiastic crowd possible, if only cross-carrying discipleship is off the agenda.

Few would want to argue that this is authentic Christianity, but many are trapped in the cult of popularism. Don't misunderstand me. I believe Jesus wants us to reach the multitudes. But we cannot do so by ignoring his true attraction. Jesus disappointed crowds of people who had attached themselves superficially to his ministry by testing their understanding of his true mission.

He did not come to be a popular preacher, but to give life. John chapter 6 records Jesus saying,

> *I am the living bread which came down from heaven. If anyone eats of this bread, he will live forever; and the bread that I shall give is my flesh, which I shall give for the life of the world.*

John 6:51

The offense was immediate. How could Jesus expect his followers to feed on his flesh? But he was talking about spiritual food. He did not come, in the first instance, to promise the comforts and provisions that lead to what is popularly understood as 'the good life' here on earth. He is our provider, but that is not the sole focus of the gospel.

The crowds forsook him, disappointed by such a hard message, because they were focused on physical things not on the spiritual life Jesus came to bring. Peter got it right when Jesus later challenged his 12. "Are you also going to turn away from me?" he asked. Peter replied with the inspired statement, "Where would we go? You have the words of eternal life."

This is the essence of passionate discipleship. We are motivated to go where our desires lead us, and we desire most what we believe will meet our deepest needs. Jesus came to satisfy the deepest longings of our humanity, created by God for life in him. Once awakened, this knowledge will lead us to feed on the very life of Christ. We are passionate about the things we believe will give us what we crave for. Once you understand that life – rich, satisfying, abundant life – is found in Christ and only in him, you will have no problem with spiritual passion.

That's why Jesus prefaced his invitation to discipleship with a call to awaken our spiritual desire.

> *Then he said to them all, "If anyone desires to come after me, let him deny himself, and take up his cross daily, and follow me. For whoever desires to save his life will lose it, but whoever loses his life for my sake will save it.*
> Luke 9:23-24

Two times in this passage, Jesus uses the word 'desire' – first to describe the desire he wants us to have for his life and then to describe the desire we already have to live our own life. The word in the Greek is *thelo*, and it carries the meaning of 'craving' or 'intense desire'. *Strong's Concordance* contrasts this word with *boulomai*, which is associated with a weaker form of wishing or wanting.

To be willing for something may mean we passively acquiesce to it and reluctantly comply with it, or it may mean we have a strong, overriding desire for it. This kind of desire (*thelo*) pursues its object with deep, driving passion. The choice is clear – either passion for self, or passion for Christ. A cross-carrying disciple abandons passion for self in favour of passion for Christ.

THE LIFE THAT SPRINGS FROM GRACE

Once this kind of passion for Christ is awakened by the grace of God, it leads us to forsake all to follow him. When we taste the goodness of God and realise that Christ offers the life we truly crave for, we begin to pursue him passionately. We become highly motivated to go in the direction of our new-found hunger.

Clifford Williams says, "Discipleship is simply the life that springs from grace." Once God reveals to us the grace found in Christ, we follow him willingly. There was a time when we found "no beauty in Christ that we should desire him", but the moment the Holy Spirit opened our eyes and began to show us his glory, we discovered that abundant life is found only in him.

Without this revelation of grace, discipleship will always be unpopular. The cell vision highlights discipleship, but we cannot force it on people. If we do, they will respond out of a *boulomai* kind of desire. They will comply, weakly, maybe even begrudgingly. But when we lead people to encounter Christ and his mercy, their desire for the life he gives increases. They become willing to "die to self" in order to experience the life of Christ. They begin to experience a *thelo* kind of desire for the abundant life he offers. In order to forsake our love of self, we must discover that Christ is the "true and living bread" that satisfies. Only then will we cease striving for the "bread which perishes". Like the 5,000 whom Jesus fed in John's Gospel chapter 6, we seek him because we have tasted his bread and want more.

The cell vision is always pointing people to Christ. The Encounter ministry enables cell members to meet with him regularly during the weekend retreats. Following the Encounter, our teaching focuses on true discipleship springing from the experience of God's grace. There is no compulsion from the leaders and no forcing of the issues – we simply present Christ in all his glory and draw close to him in our cell meetings, our congregational gatherings and our celebrations services.

MENDING THE NETS OF DISCIPLESHIP

The phrase "make disciples" occurs twice in Matthew 28, using two different Greek words: *matheteuo* and *didasko*. The former means literally to make a 'little follower', or a 'young follower'. It corresponds to the modern term, 'apprentice'. The second word relates to 'enlarging understanding or knowledge', but it implies that it cannot be enlarged unless it first comes by experience, which is why discipleship must be demonstrated in real life, not just in the classroom or in church services.

Matthew chapter 28 reveals four steps in the disciple making process: *preaching* the gospel, *baptising* new believers into the body of Christ, *teaching* them to observe everything Jesus commanded and *reproducing* this same fruit in others. Jesus is our model and we know that disciple making was central to his ministry.

We first see Jesus calling his disciples in Mark 1:17, "Come, follow me", he said, "and I will make you to become – fishers of men." In Luke chapter 5, Jesus confirms and completes that call. It was a call to become his disciple and to disciple others. He was inviting these fishermen to allow him to impact them with the kingdom of God and to train them to impact the lives of others, in the same way they had been impacted. It is also a call for us to follow Christ and to win the lost, forming his character in them. There is a personal dimension (follow me) and a vocational dimension (I will make you to become fishers of men). It takes a disciple to make a disciple.

Following Christ means we are called to follow both the man and his mission. The two go together and cannot be separated. We are called both to follow Christ ourselves, and to lead others to follow him. We slow the process down and make our work harder, if we allow people to think about the Christian faith merely as obtaining 'a ticket to heaven'. We are good at asking people to pray a prayer of salvation, but we hardly ever stand up and say, "follow me, as I follow Jesus." But this is exactly what Jesus teaches us to do.

The cell vision encourages people to follow Christ and become 'fishers of men' at the very beginning of the discipleship process. We take the lead from Peter's encounter with Christ in Luke 15:1-11. Believing that salvation is by grace alone through faith alone, we don't load people with legalistic requirements they must fulfil before they can be accepted by God. However, we make it clear that a life of disciple-making service is the only appropriate response for those who have been saved by grace.

We explain to our new believers that the call begins right now, where they are. Jesus indicated this when he borrowed Peter's boat in order to preach to the crowds assembled by the shore of Lake Galilee (Luke 5:3). Discipleship means you are engaged in the work of Christ from the start. You use whatever resources you have for the kingdom. You let Christ into your daily life, your work and your family. Your day-to-day life is your place of consecration and service to the Master.

The story in Luke chapter 5 continues with the miraculous catch of fish. Jesus did this to get Peter's attention, but also to teach him an important lesson. The nets began to break, so big was the catch (Luke 5:6-7). Peter had to learn that the task was bigger than he thought. He needed to be prepared for it. In effect, Jesus was saying, "You're not ready for my kind of fishing yet! I've got something for you to do, but you are going to need some preparation first."

I call discipleship 'mending the nets'. I think the nets of discipleship are wholly inadequate in most churches. If God were to send us a miraculous catch, most of us couldn't contain it – our nets would break. We are woefully unprepared for the task Jesus has set us.

In Mark 1:19 and Matthew 4:21 the disciples are found mending their nets. The word used is *katartidzo* meaning, 'to make ready, to prepare, to equip'. It's the same word as in Galatians 6:1, where it speaks of restoring those who are trapped in sin, so that they can become useful once again in God's service. A similar word is used in Ephesians 4:12, where it refers to preparing God's people for service. We are familiar with these concepts in today's world. An apprentice car mechanic on his first day at work will not be asked to overhaul the boss's Mercedes! For three months he won't even get to wash the boss's car. He must first be trained. A student doctor will not get to do brain surgery at the beginning of the course. He will be told, "Go and practice on the cadaver!"

In the same way, Jesus was saying to his disciples, "I have a work for you to do, but you are not yet ready for it. I want to take your lives and, like your fishing nets, wash them, mend them, strengthen them and prepare them for the great catch."

Our churches' nets are breaking. We need people to be ready, prepared and equipped for the great moves of God to come. We need strong and mature Christians who have found their place in the work of God, standing side by side and linked together in partnership for the work of 'catching men' for Christ.

JESUS' METHOD IS DISCIPLESHIP

Peter's experience is an example of what we need to happen in us if we are going to be ready for God's work. First, Peter had to learn to do it Jesus' way. The Model of 12 is a sincere attempt to do just that. We take seriously Jesus' method of working with a group of 12, training them and pouring his life into them so that they would be equipped to go and do the same. Peter, an experienced fisherman, thought he knew better than the Master (Luke 5:5). But he was relying on his traditional knowledge and experience. How can we expect a miraculous catch of fish today, if we act like that? Traditional models of church are failing us. We must get back to the strategy of Jesus.

When the big catch came, it revealed the next lesson Peter had to learn. He fell at Jesus' knees and said, "Go away from me, Lord; I am a sinful man!" (Luke 5:8). We all must pass through this experience. Jesus knows us through and through, and we definitely need to be healed, changed and formed into the character of Christ if we are going to be effective in his mission.

The discipleship process works from the inside out. That is why I am devoting the first major section of this book to the need to grow in our relationship with Christ before we implement such an ambitious vision as the Model of 12. In Kensington Temple we spend most of our ministry time leading people into wholeness and restoration. God is looking for a people who are shaped by grace and transformed from the inside out. We are grateful that Jesus told Peter, "Don't worry, I am going to form you, and make you into what I want you to be – an effective disciple maker" (Luke 5:10).

After this call, the real work of discipleship began. They left everything and followed Jesus (Luke 5:11). This is the only way disciples are made. It begins with a willingness to go all the way with Jesus. It must be a total commitment to the mission of Christ. Frankly, without this response, the cell vision will never work. Without this level of dedication and devotion to Christ, the church will never rise to fulfil her role in the world. We keep coming back to this point over and again in our work in London. Everything depends on our response to the call of Christ.

The disciples then entered into a three year training programme of walking with Jesus, listening and learning, watching the Master at work and gradually beginning to do what he did. They were there when the crowds listened to him teaching, "Blessed are the poor in spirit, for theirs is the Kingdom." They observed the stilling of the storm and asked, "Who is this that even the winds and the waves obey him?" They witnessed the blind seeing, the deaf hearing, the cripples walking and the dead being raised. They heard him recounting parables in public, and sat with him afterwards as he privately explained their meaning.

Jesus sent them out on early missionary adventures and they returned saying, "Lord even the demons are subject to us in your name!" They were present at the feeding of the 5,000 when he said to them, "You give them something to eat." And they counted the 12 basketfuls of food left over from the 5 loaves and 2 fishes. They all heard Peter's inspired confession at Caesarea Philippi, "You are the Christ, the Son of the Living God." Peter, James and John witnessed his face shining like the sun, and his clothes becoming as white as light on the Mount of Transfiguration where they heard the words from heaven, "This is my Son, whom I love; and with him I am well pleased. Listen to him!" They were among the crowds announcing his triumphant entry into Jerusalem, "Hosanna to the Son of David! Blessed is he who comes in the name of the Lord!"

Finally, he was taken from them through the dark events of the cross. Confused and hurting they asked, "What is it all about?" Then, by the shores of Galilee we see them again, fishing. The newly-resurrected Jesus calls out to them and there is another miraculous catch of fish (John 21:11). But this time the nets do not break! After three years of being with Jesus, they are ready – prepared by the Master to continue his work.

Several weeks later, the sails are set and the wind of the Spirit, sent by the ascended Lord of the church, begins to blow. Now Peter gets to understand he is a fisher of men. The wind of God has blown him right to where the fish are found. His nets are mended. He casts them into the sea of people before him and 3,000 men are brought into the kingdom.

Are you ready to begin your own discipleship adventure? Commit to being a disciple of Jesus, get ready to have your nets mended and you too will have a miraculous catch of fish. As you walk with Jesus step by step through the cell vision you will learn, like Peter did, that the Master is making you a fisher of men.

The Art of Imitation

As we have already seen, the cell vision is a vision for discipleship. Our goal is for everyone in the church to become a real disciple of Christ and to learn how to disciple others. Cell church is structured to make this vision a reality. But we must be confident about our goal. We find it easier to tell those who come to hear the gospel, "Believe in Jesus", but it is harder to say to them "Follow me."

At one time, a popular form of witnessing to Christ was through bumper stickers. One day, in the middle of one of London's frequent traffic jams, I noticed a bumper sticker on the car in front of me which read, "Don't follow me, follow Jesus!" I found this quite ironic, as immobilised by the dense traffic, nobody was going anywhere – rather like some churches I know! It also set me thinking about the message on the bumper sticker. What exactly was the owner of the car wanting to communicate? "Follow Jesus, not me" is a strange message. If the driver with the bumper sticker was following Jesus, then anyone following him would also be following Jesus. And if the driver was not following Jesus why should anyone else?

Discipleship is like that. It is not enough to tell people to do as you say. You must also be able to tell them to do what you do. Paul was not afraid to call people to follow his example. It was the bedrock of his ministry. He said to the Corinthians, "Imitate me as I also imitate Christ" (1 Corinthians 11:1). The implications of this for the discipleship process are profound. In an earlier part of his letter Paul gives a fuller insight into discipleship as the art of imitation.

> *Therefore I urge you, imitate me. For this reason I have sent Timothy to you, who is my beloved and faithful son in the Lord, who will remind you of my ways in Christ, as I teach everywhere in every church.*
>
> 1 Corinthians 4:16-17

The expression 'caught not taught' applies to discipleship. I would say Christian living is only taught when it has also been caught. We learn by imitating Christ in those who disciple us. This has enormous implications for the teaching ministry in our churches today. We have inherited an educational model which focuses on the impartation of knowledge, but the New Testament emphasis is on lifestyle.

For Paul, his doctrine was his manner of life and his manner of life was his doctrine. His lifestyle was more than an example of his teaching, it *was* his teaching. Look again at the scripture quoted above. Paul sent Timothy, his assistant, to help the believers in Corinth. His job was to remind the Corinthians of Paul's teaching, which he describes as "my ways in Christ." This implies that Timothy had imitated Paul and now the Corinthians could imitate Timothy. The ways of Christ are being passed on from person to person by teaching and imitation. This is true discipleship.

The teaching ministry is pure discipleship. The command to "make disciples" is the command to teach, or "to raise learners" of Christ. The call to teach is the call to form people in the lifestyle of Christ. That's why discipleship (teaching) cannot happen only through public preaching. It must also include imitation of lifestyle and that requires proximity. Prolonged personal contact of disciplers with disciples is absolutely essential.

One pastor who has a strong 'teaching ministry' told me that he would not be adopting the cell strategy in his church because, as far as he was concerned, he discipled people from the pulpit. But how much of the life of Christ can you model from the pulpit? You can give the people something to imitate, but only in a limited way. You can model how to preach a good sermon. You can show the people aspects of the character and personality of Christ by the way you speak, your tone of voice, your gentleness, your compassion and so on. But does the pulpit presentation of yourself really reflect all that is important to be imitated by your congregation?

SHOW AND TELL

People need to see for themselves how their teacher behaves at work and in the home. How punctual he is for his appointments. How she responds to a dressing down from her boss. How he speaks to his wife and raises his children. You cannot show that from the pulpit. And face it, church services are not real life. Real life is out there in the rough and tumble of daily living.

These are obvious but important points. I think the disconnection between the format of traditional church and real life is one of the greatest causes of ineffective Christianity in the Western world. Church is not about what happens in the church building on Sunday. It is how we conduct ourselves in the real world between the Sundays. The cell vision teaches people to express church not only in the vitally important Sunday services but right where they are every day of the week – in the offices, the schools, the cafes and the sports fields.

That why the discipleship model begins with proximity. Jesus called his 12 disciples in order "that they might be with him" (Mark 3:14). That way they could get to know him, learn how he lived and be trained to be like him in life and ministry. Discipleship is practical, not theoretical. It is about formation, not information. A good word for this is training. A fully-trained disciple will be like the master who disciples him (Luke 6:40).

Once I was working with a group of pastors led by a prominent theologian and Bible teacher. The purpose of our group was to develop successful models of biblical counselling which could be introduced into the practical training programmes of local churches. My colleague objected to the word 'training'. "It sounds like what we do to horses!" he said. Steeped in the tradition of pulpit-only approach to teaching, he could not understand that the way we model what we preach is almost more important that what we preach.

I say 'almost' because public preaching sets the standard and shapes the thinking of the whole church. Ideas have consequences and right believing leads to right conduct. But these same ideas must be seen in us – that is, seen to be in us, otherwise the finest of sermons are just words. Is it any wonder that we have a problem with people being hearers of the Word, and not doers of the Word (James 1:22).

Good preaching will include real life illustrations of truth applied, and clear examples of how to put the teaching into practice. But even that can only go so far. People need to see for themselves the teaching working in real life situations. They will learn best how to act and react when they see others do it. The cell ministry provides the context for this to happen. Cell leaders are shepherds who live among the flock. Cell groups build relationships in which Christians share their lives in a far deeper way than is possible when they are seated in rows listening to the preacher on Sunday.

ACTIVE ENGAGEMENT

When we first adopted the cell vision I began to re-emphasise the importance of having strong contact with people who do not yet know Christ. Genuine friendship with unbelievers is the best context in which to share Christ, provided our lives live up to it. Many Christians have far too few friends outside the church. I felt awkward about this, as I myself had very little meaningful contact with people who did not yet know Christ. My ministry was almost exclusively to the church, even though I often participated in evangelistic missions at home and abroad.

I felt I had to do more to model what I was preaching, so I took up a hobby – SCUBA diving. Apart from giving me much-needed recreation, it also brought me into contact with people. Up to then, most of my witnessing was done on the street, on planes, in hotel lobbies, in restaurants – anywhere I came into contact with people willing to talk about Jesus. Now it was different. I was regularly with people sharing a common interest and found the experience both challenging and liberating. However, my usual one-sided pulpit-style communication was useless in this context. These people did not share my presuppositions, were not impressed by my 'status' as a minister and they talked back!

The SCUBA training was itself enlightening – a perfect example of discipleship. It began with passion. I had once dipped my head below the water when I was on holiday near the Red Sea. Suitably equipped with my mask and fins, I discovered the magnificent underwater world of exotic fish and beautiful corrals. It was like stumbling upon a hidden cathedral of God's glory, and SCUBA diving offered me an opportunity to explore it more fully.

Motivated by this new-found passion I soon mastered the theoretical knowledge necessary for a first level diver. The instructors took us into the pool to learn the basic skills and, later, into the more demanding environment of the open water. We learned in the classroom, practiced in the pool and then honed our technique in the ocean. We learned to dive by listening to the instructors, watching them demonstrate their skills and then doing the same things under their close supervision. Then, as certified divers in our own right, we were able to venture into the deep.

Discipling people to become followers of Christ happens in much the same way. There is passion to share, knowledge to grasp, attitudes to adopt and skills to learn. Disciplers are instructors and they teach by explaining, showing and passing on their skills. The classroom will never be enough. They need to get into the water with you.

Later on, as I continued to progress through the various levels of training, I qualified as a dive instructor and learned from the other side of training the importance of example. Students will follow what you do more than what you say, and as an instructor, every detail of diving discipline must be exhibited at all times. If your students pick up bad habits from you, it may cost them dear in the future. Diving accidents are rare, but they almost always come about through diver error. Good training is everything.

Discipling others is similar to a parent-child relationship. We use the expression 'like father, like son; like mother, like daughter', and it is true. It is rooted in the revelation of the Trinity. The Son showed us the Father, visibly modelling his character through the incarnation, and then sent his Holy Spirit to enable us to show that same character to the world. We know what God is like through the example of Jesus. Jesus modelled life in the kingdom to his disciples and they passed on that pattern to those they raised up in the power of the Spirit. This is how the Christian faith has been passed down from generation to generation. Now, it's our turn to model Christ to our generation.

THEY WILL DO WHAT YOU DO

The very nature of gospel communication has the principle of imitation built into it. Those you preach to, will follow your example whether you like it or not. The cell model introduces intentionality into this process. Read carefully the following quotation from Paul's first letter to the Thessalonians.

> *For our gospel did not come to you in word only, but also in power, and in the Holy Spirit and in much assurance, as you know what kind of men we were among you for your sake. And you became followers of us and of the Lord, having received the word in much affliction, with*

joy of the Holy Spirit, so that you became examples to all in Macedonia and Achaia who believe.

1 Thessalonians 1:5-7

Can you see the process of discipleship at work in this example from Thessalonica? It begins with the gospel preached in the power of the Holy Spirit. That is essential. But the gospel was also preached by people who were living examples of it and who became the model for the new believers to follow. The process did not end there. The new converts themselves became examples of gospel living to the surrounding regions of Macedonia and Achaia.

The cell vision takes this principle and builds it into the very way we do church. We make discipleship intentional. We teach people to practice what they know and train them how to pass it on to others. The cell structure enables everyone to become both a disciple and a disciple maker.

The church is truly a reflection of its discipleship. That's why Paul and other writers are always talking about it. Look at the following statements drawn from the New Testament.

But you have carefully followed my doctrine, manner of life, purpose, faith, longsuffering, love, perseverance...

2 Timothy 3:10

Brethren, join in following my example, and note those who so walk, as you have us for a pattern.

Philippians 3:17

...nor as being lords over those entrusted to you, but being examples to the flock...

1 Peter 5:3

...in all things showing yourself to be a pattern of good works; in doctrine showing integrity, reverence, incorruptibility...

Titus 2:7

As Christians, we cannot escape from our responsibility to live and model what we preach and to make this the basis of our ministry to others. Leaders have a particularly serious responsibility to lead by their actions. Samson thought that his gift was enough. He used his supernatural strength to deliver God's people from their Philistine oppressors. But he didn't think he had to be an example in his character, and so lost his ability to lead God's people. David thought he was an exception to the rule and not an example to follow when he slept with Bathsheba and arranged for her husband to be killed. He displeased the Lord and the consequences were with him for the rest of his life.

CAN YOU SAY "FOLLOW ME"?

Jesus, on the other hand, was an example in everything – his teaching, his dealings with people, his acts of service and the way he raised up disciples. Discipleship is about forming Christ in people and, as we have seen, he must first be formed in us so that we can say to others, "Follow me". Ask yourself the following questions: "If they follow me, where will they end up? If they do what I do in private as well as in public, what kind of people will they become? Am I sufficiently like Jesus for people to follow me and end up like him?"

The honest answer to these questions may disturb you, but that is not my objective. We must accept the principle of discipleship by imitation, but that does not mean we have to be perfect before we start. The best example we can give is that we are moving towards the likeness of Christ. We are all on the same journey. Personally, I know that I fall short of the pure example of Christ, but one thing is sure – I am on the journey. When we disciple others we ask them to imitate this. Jesus is the perfect example – not us!

That is why I do not believe that we can gain everything we need in our discipleship by any one person. I am the product of the influence of many people – both fellow leaders and church members. Exclusive, one-to-one discipleship models are dangerous. They lead to control and suffocation. We are all called to disciple *each other* and we do this in the group setting. We can all learn from each other – no matter how young or old, experienced or inexperienced we are. After all, the Holy Spirit working in his church is the Master Discipler. We are just his instruments.

As we think about the discipleship process, it is important to ask what model of church can sustain it and cause it to flourish. *Accidental* discipleship will always happen whatever structures are in place, but surely we should aim higher than that. We must become *intentional* disciple-making churches. Multiplying effective disciples is the most urgent need in the 21st Century church. It is not enough to preach or teach this. We must devise ways in which every believer can be trained to become a disciple maker where they are – where they spend most of their time. We must train them and release them through lifestyle discipleship and this is exactly why it is so important for us to consider the cell structure as a model for today's church.

Fruitfulness

If we are passionate for Christ, we will be eager to bear fruit for his glory. Multiplication is one of the hallmarks of genuine discipleship. If you are passionately involved with Christ, you will love what he loves and reproduce that same love in others. This is how the cell vision works. Our love for Christ and passion for his name, not only shapes our lives around his person, but also leads us to engage with his plan for our own lives – to reproduce disciples. Jesus expressed this truth in the form of an image – the vine and its branches.

> *I am the vine, you are the branches. He who abides in me, and I in him, bears much fruit; for without me you can do nothing.*
>
> John 15:5

This teaching shows us that we are in vital union with Christ. As we draw from his life (abide in him) he produces the fruits of his character in us, as described in Galatians 5:18-22. He also enables us to reproduce that same fruit in others. The grapes on this vine are of the seed-bearing variety. There are no seedless grapes in the kingdom of God! This means every disciple has the capacity to reproduce other disciples. Just as Jesus sowed his life through his death and produced much fruit (John 12:24), so we die to ourselves and produce a harvest – that's multiplication.

Wherever there is true discipleship, multiplication will follow. I remember teaching on the cell vision at a conference in London during the early stages of our own implementation of the Model of 12. There had been much talk about multiplication from the Bogota team who pointed to the staggering levels of church growth they were experiencing at home.

One pastor at the conference was disturbed. It seemed he had little faith that this was going to happen in "barren, fruitless Europe". He suggested that we should not emphasise multiplication and only speak of discipleship.

This is an example of how we must learn to overcome the effects of our spiritual environment. The pastor could not see beyond his experience of barrenness. It is true that Europe is largely a spiritual wasteland. However, we must not forget that Isaac sowed his grain in a time of famine and produced a hundredfold harvest in the same year. With God all things are possible!

DISCIPLESHIP BRINGS MULTIPLICATION

My friend was right, the emphasis must be on discipleship, but the result will be multiplication. Sowing and reaping is a principle found in the natural world and it is also a principle in the kingdom of God. A harvest is merely the result of many seeds dying and reproducing themselves many times over. I once counted more than 100 grains in a single head of wheat. Imagine all that fruit coming from a single seed.

Everything in the kingdom of God begins as single seed, a life given, an action 'sowed' into the soil of someone's life. Jesus began as a 'seed' in Mary's womb and became great just as the angel had promised.

> *He will be great, and will be called the Son of the Highest; and the Lord God will give him the throne of his father David. And he will reign over the house of Jacob forever, and of his kingdom there will be no end.*
> Luke 1:32-33

Days before he went to the cross, Jesus explained the significance of his death,

Most assuredly, I say to you, unless a grain of wheat falls into the ground and dies, it remains alone; but if it dies, it produces much grain.

John 12:24

He then applied this same principle to his disciples saying,

He who loves his life will lose it, and he who hates his life in this world will keep it for eternal life.

John 12:25

As we die to ourselves we reap the fruit of eternal life in our own lives and Jesus multiplies it to others. We become productive for the kingdom and, as in the case of Jesus, our single seed brings forth much fruit.

Fruitfulness is not just a command; it is a promise. It was first given in the Creation Mandate, then re-iterated in the Abrahamic Covenant and finally expressed in the Great Commission. We can trace the theme of multiplication through all these phases of God's revelation.

In the beginning, God blessed Adam and Eve and said, "Be fruitful and multiply; fill the earth and subdue it" (Genesis 1:28). To Abraham he said,

"And I will make my covenant between me and you, and will multiply you exceedingly." Then Abram fell on his face, and God talked with him, saying: "As for me, behold, my covenant is with you, and you shall be a father of many nations. No longer shall your name be called Abram, but your name shall be Abraham; for I have made you a father of many nations. I will make you exceedingly fruitful; and I will make nations of you, and kings shall come from you."

Genesis 17:2-6

New Testament believers are heirs both of God's covenant with Abraham and the original Creation Mandate. We are to fill the earth and 'subdue' it, set it in order under the rule of God through the gospel, and be a blessing to the nations. This is what the Great Commission is all about – global influence through multiplication and fruitfulness.

The cell vision facilitates this process for every believer. Through the cells, we can all bear fruit and see that fruit remain. This is the central theme of Jesus' teaching about the true vine. It shows that God expects us to be fruitful. We recall that the kingdom was taken away from Israel and given to others that would bear fruit for God (Matthew 21:34).

That is why Jesus refers to himself as "the true vine" in John 15:1. He is saying that all God's purposes for Israel as a nation were being fulfilled in his person – including God's desire for fruitfulness. The kingdom is all about God's plan for fruitfulness. The kingdom of God will produce an abundant harvest of gospel fruit from every nation. There is no room for the 'little flock' mentality in the kingdom of God. The little flock will become a great gathering of sheep – the multitudes will come!

I know this does not accord with those who predict that the church will decline to nothing but a "faithful few" by the end of the age. "Look at the proliferation of false religion, the increasing hardness towards the gospel in nation after nation", they insist on repeating, as if this is God's plan for the end time church.

A man was puzzled when he had finished listening to a teaching series by Derek Prince, perhaps the greatest Bible teacher of modern times. Dr Prince had been expounding the parable of the wheat and the tares, showing that false teaching and apostasy were going to increase as the end of age approaches. He had also been speaking of this as the church's finest hour.

The man questioned Dr Princes' teaching, "You sound as if things are going to get better and better, and worse and worse – at the same time!" Dr Prince replied, "That's right! Just make sure you are one the things that is going to get better!" He then went on to explain that the same conditions that caused the tares to flourish were the same conditions that ripened the grain for the end time harvest. Don't let the fact that the enemies of the gospel are flourishing stand in the way of God's promise. We *are* going to reap a great harvest.

GOD'S BIG PLAN

God has never abandoned his plan to have a very big family. The gospel is going to be preached in every nation and bear fruit all over the world, before the end comes. The witness of the gospel to all nations Jesus speaks of in Matthew 24:14, must mean an *effective* witness – how else will the Great Commission be fulfilled? God will help us get the job done. I believe that the cell vision is one important way he is doing that in our generation.

Jesus is the real vine, and he is going to make sure that its fruit is multiplied for the glory of the Father. God's purpose is to call innumerable quantities of people who will carry his likeness. This purpose appeared to be failing, because Israel as a nation turned away from God, but now, in Christ, God's purposes are being fulfilled. Jesus is God's answer. In him, there is hope, life, peace – and fruitfulness. The question is, are you going to stay close to him and allow God's purpose for fruitfulness to be fulfilled through you?

THE FATHER IS THE VINEDRESSER

God wants what every good gardener wants – fruit. He is taking charge of your life, to tend it, and keep and to make it fruitful for him. He is absolutely committed to bringing you to fruitfulness. But fruitfulness is not automatic. No garden grows by itself. It must be cultivated. God does the cultivating, but you must allow him to do it. It takes your willingness, responsiveness, co-operation and obedience.

It is easy to dream big dreams and long for easy, instant results – but that's wishful thinking. You must do something about it. If you want to bear fruit, you must become active in the fruit-bearing business. As Peter says, you must add actions to your faith, if you want to be fruitful.

> *But also for this very reason, giving all diligence, add to your faith virtue, to virtue knowledge, to knowledge self-control, to self-control perseverance, to perseverance godliness, to godliness brotherly kindness, and to brotherly kindness love. For if these things are yours and abound, you will be neither barren nor unfruitful in the knowledge of our Lord Jesus Christ.*
>
> 2 Peter 1:5-8

Imagine this: Christians who bear no fruit! It ought to be unthinkable, but it is not – this is exactly what Peter is warning us against. Surely you do not want to end up barren and unfruitful in your Christian life. I know I don't! Peter's exhortation is strong and clear. He says that we have obtained the precious gift of faith. This is saving faith and like your salvation, it's free. You don't have to work to get it and you don't even have to work to keep it! It's a free gift – forever!

However, if you want to be a fruitful believer, you cannot just sit back and do nothing. You must add to your faith the things Peter lists. Fruitfulness comes by responding to God's grace and living under his favour, so that he can begin to bless you and make you fruitful. Jesus wants to produce his fruit in you first, and then reproduce it through you in others.

Fruitfulness comes by co-operating with God. He provides us with the vine to abide in. He brings us into a living relationship with Jesus. He tends us and works the right circumstances into our life so that fruit can develop. Our part is to abide in the vine.

ABIDE IN ME

Abiding is linked with obedience. Without obedience, the obedience that comes from passionate abiding in Christ, there can be no fruit, as Jesus explained,

> *Jesus answered and said to him, "If anyone loves me, he will keep my word; and my Father will love him, and we will come to him and make our home with him. He who does not love me does not keep my words; and the word which you hear is not mine but the Father's who sent me."*
>
> John 14:23-24

However, the obedience that leads to fruitfulness is not self-effort. Jesus said, "Without me you can do nothing" (John 15:4), which also means "With me you can do all things!" This is the quality of Christian God wants you to aim for. This is true discipleship, abiding in the vine, staying close to Jesus and drawing from him the fruit-bearing capacity of the Holy Spirit.

In the chapters that follow, we shall see how the cell structure supports the branches, enabling them to bear fruit – fruit that lasts. As a disciple who wants to be fruitful, you will welcome a model that helps you and your fellow disciples work together to be productive in the kingdom of God.

Part 2
Understanding Cell Church

The Heart of Cell Church

There is a world of difference between a church with a small group ministry and a cell church. This is something I had to discover for myself. I had always believed in small groups. Everyone needs the more in-depth relationships with fellow believers than the Sunday worship services of the church can offer. In London, people often live in one part of the city, work in another area and worship God in a building located in yet another corner of town. This is just a fact of 21st Century urban living, but it makes it difficult to build community into church life.

There had been many attempts by previous pastors to develop home group fellowships before I became Kensington Temple's senior leader. We had area fellowship groups, international groups, special interest groups and even the church planting programme was birthed through small groups. I continued with the experiment, even encouraging groups to adopt cell models that were successful internationally. But nothing really worked for us. We were clearly missing the point.

Then the Spanish-speaking church, planted by Kensington Temple during the time of the former Senior Pastor, Wynne Lewis, began to implement the Bogota G12 Model of cell church. They saw explosive growth with the church leaping quickly from 40 to 3,000 members. Together with the apostolic leaders of our London City Church network, I quickly came to the conclusion that we had to re-examine the way we approached, not just the cells, but the entire way we were doing church and how we were seeking to fulfil our Mission: London and the World for Christ.

THE BASIC FUNCTIONING UNIT OF CHURCH

It was clear we did not have a cell model that worked for us, but more than that, we had failed to understand the strategic place of cells as *central* to church life. Cells are not just one programme of the church. Rather, they are the fundamental means by which 'church' happens. We had to learn that the cells were responsible for every aspect of the church's ministry – evangelising, nurturing, training and mobilising the members.

The beauty of the cell church model is that it reflects many New Testament principles of church. From Matthew 18:20, we can deduce that the most basic unit of church is the 2 or 3 gathered together in the name of Jesus.

> For where two or three are gathered together in my name,
> I am there in the midst of them.
>
> Matthew 18:20

We uphold this principle in what we call 'the friendship factor'. Each cell is made up of clusters of friendship groups – 'groups of 3'. It helps cement genuine relationship and offers a useful means of breaking down the function of cell life into small, manageable units of fellowship, pastoral care and evangelism. This is the true 'one anothering' so frequently referred to in the New Testament where we are called to love, care for, teach and admonish one another. It is enjoyable and deeply rewarding, and what's more, it easily functions on a daily basis. The cell is more than a small group of believers who meet together once a week. It consists of several groups of 2 or 3 friends, who are drawn together in spiritual relationship and who are in daily contact with each other. Everyone is able to sustain this level of daily contact within the groups of 3 which are linked together through the cells.

Jesus himself had his group of 3 – Peter, James and John. However, this 'friendship group' was part of a bigger group – his 12. The 12 was the basic group through which Jesus conducted the major part of his ministry. It was his 'cell group'.

We can apply Jesus' methodology to the church at large. The Model of 12 draws inspiration from Jesus' way of working. The cell becomes the church in miniature – clusters of tightly-knit friendship groups sharing together daily in the work of the church, building one another up and reaching out to those who are not yet believers.

Cell church emphasises the cells as the primary means through which the church functions. These cells are neither isolated nor function independently, but see themselves as expressing the life of the larger body of which they are a microcosmic part. The cells cluster together forming congregations and celebrations which are the larger, more traditionally acknowledged expressions of church.

In a cell church, the Sunday services are joyful gatherings of people who have been together throughout the week, being and doing church. They celebrate what God has been doing through them in their homes, families, places of work or at school. The cells are groups of 24/7 Christians – whole life disciples. This, it seems to me, captures the essence of New Testament Christianity.

A NEW TESTAMENT APPROACH TO CHURCH

The apostles of the New Testament could never have achieved what they did without something very similar to what we would call cell church. For example, in Jerusalem on the Day of Pentecost, 3,000 people were added to the church. They were all baptised in water and they all continued steadfast in the faith. They were all schooled in the behaviour and practice of the apostles' doctrine – the lifestyle of Christ. They were all faithful in prayer and witness and all became a committed part of the fellowship of God's people. This is a far cry from today's situation where the vast majority of people who make a commitment to Christ never progress to any form of meaningful church involvement or take up their call to serve Christ.

There are many reasons for the success of the early church but without a doubt one of the most significant of these in the Jerusalem church was their small group or 'cell' emphasis.

> *So continuing daily with one accord in the temple, and breaking bread from house to house, they ate their food with gladness and simplicity of heart…*
>
> Acts 2:46

As well as the large meetings in the Temple courts, they met regularly in one another's homes. These were not just 'house meetings' or 'home fellowship groups'. They were cells – that is, 'micro churches' doing everything that church should do. They witnessed, they evangelised, they fellowshipped, they prayed, they nurtured and they cared for the poor – all through the cells. Nothing else adequately explains their effectiveness in making disciples or their sustained growth.

This concept of the cell group has very little in common with the traditional approach to small groups in many churches today. Home fellowship groups, prayer groups and Bible Study groups may all have something to offer, but they are not *cell groups*. What, then, is a cell group? David Finnell, in his book *Life in His Body* defines cells as, "The organising of the body of believers in small groups for the purpose of worship, experiencing God, ministering to one another, and ministering to and evangelising the community." In short, cells do everything that 'church' does – only in miniature. Once again, we see the emphasis in cell church on the cell as the *primary expression* of church – where the real work of the church goes on.

CELL CHURCH OR TRADITIONAL CHURCH?

This leads to a number of significant differences between a cell church and a traditional church. A traditional church is programme centred, but a cell church is people centred. A traditional church is built on the strength of its magnificent programmes. If you have bigger and better programmes then you have a bigger and better church! But church is essentially about people, not programmes. This people centred approach can only be consistently sustained in a church where the central thrust of its ministry is the small group setting, not the main services.

A traditional church is building centred. Usually, this is where it all happens. The size, location and architecture of the church building determine the activity of the church. People assume that once the meeting is over and the building is vacated, that church is over for another week. But in a cell church, that cannot happen. The main work of the church is undertaken by the members in their cells. Therefore, the cell church is community centred, not building centred. The central services are a celebration of what God has done throughout the week in the cell groups and a preparation for more of the same in the coming week.

The traditional church sends the signal to one and all, "Come to us". But the cell church's message is, "Go to them." The traditional church's model of ministry calls for a passive response, "Listen", and the cell church's clarion call is, "Do." It has an active model of ministry. The people are empowered to do the work of Christ.

All this implies a radical change of thinking. Churches must learn the power of cell life in the body of Christ. This is the only way we can successfully mobilise the entire membership to do the ministry of Christ and truly function as part of his body. Cell church equips every member to express Christ in the community, bringing the witness of the gospel through words and actions where they spend most of their time – in their daily life. Rather than encroaching on the valuable spare time of the members, cell church brings *ekklesia* right into every aspect of daily life. Church becomes a lifestyle and not a spare time activity.

Cell church seeks to build *ekklesia* in the heart of *agora* – the market place. It is the outworking of Jesus' compassion for the multitudes, which were "weary and scattered, like sheep having no shepherd". A scattered crowd is an oxymoron – a contradiction in terms. For those with the heart of the Good Shepherd, this is a call to build church at the core of the hurting community who gather in the 'market place', but are not yet gathered under his loving care.

Over the last 10 years, we have begun to prove for ourselves that cell church works. We would never return to the traditional church model. In fact, it was quite difficult in the beginning to accept that we were a traditional church. We were radical in many ways, but our understanding of the role of small groups in the church was traditional.

RETHINKING TRADITIONAL CHURCH
In Chapter 2 of this book, we saw some of the challenges confronting the church of the 21st Century. It is difficult to escape the conclusion that church as we know it and are doing it today is not very effective. Much of this has to do with the traditional church model we have inherited. It may have been relevant in its day, but I am now convinced that it is one of the main reasons we are failing to reach our generation for Christ.

What do I mean by 'traditional church'? The model that comes to my mind would reflect the vast majority of evangelical churches today. There is a pastor in charge of a congregation that meets in a church building and feels a responsibility to the surrounding geographical area. It may have a fine programme of teaching, preaching, worship, outreach and social action. But the focus is on part time church, perhaps demanding 5 - 10% of their members' spare time for 'church activities'. There is usually no comprehensive structure for the intentional discipling, training and deployment of believers for where they spend the other 90-95% of their life. At best, 10% of its membership is truly active in the Great Commission. The emphasis is on church services and not whole life discipleship or 24/7 church.

There are some positive aspects to the traditional model. It fosters a certain kind of stability in doctrine and practice. It is usually led by those who have had formal theological training. These churches are often a visible and established part of a local community and are doing a lot of good work. However, there are other aspects which are counter-productive to the promotion and growth of dynamic, New Testament Christianity. Usually, traditional churches are building-bound. A dedicated church building can lead church members to assume that 'church' is limited to what takes place in that building. Evangelicals believe that the 'church' is not 'God's building' but 'God's people', yet counter-intuitively they still talk about 'going to church' every Sunday. In New Testament language, we do not 'go to church' – we *are* the church.

The traditional church model is actually quite cumbersome and is not easily reproducible. If we insist on uprooting prospective 'ministers' for 3 to 4 years of formal theological training, spending vast sums of money on church buildings unused for the major part of the week, and waiting until we can afford to pay the pastor a salary for leading a group of 50-100 people – is it any wonder that church planting doesn't happen as often as it should?

Traditional church models reproduce an institutionalised form of Christianity promoting (knowingly or unknowingly) church as part-time Christians led by full-time professional ministers. They tend to be spectator-based, and programme bound. The traditional church model has moved us away from the simple, dynamic and fully-functioning organism described in the New Testament. As we have pointed out, the traditional model perpetuates the false distinction between the clergy and the laity – between 'professional' Christians and 'ordinary'

Christians. This has far-reaching and often negative consequences for our mission. It sharpens the unbiblical divide between the sacred and the secular, making church more and more irrelevant to daily life and increasingly inaccessible to those outside it.

The church leadership expends much of its time and energy trying to involve the members in 'church work'. They make demands on the spare time of these believers so that they can assist the professionals in some programme of 'in-reach' or 'outreach', but fail to see that the system itself is failing us. We are all ministers for Christ, right where we are, not only in church services, but where we spend most of our time – at work, school, recreation and home.

Our real objective is not to get our people involved in 'church work' but to put the church to work in the world. No amount of conference rhetoric, pulpit exhortation or church programming will ever fix this problem. It demands a root and branch re-evaluation of how we understand and are doing church in the first place. Only a model of church that is built on the intentionality of 24/7 Christianity and church as a lifestyle, will put hands and feet onto Matthew 20:18-20. Cell church is a practical model that answers the need for the total mobilisation of the 'work force' – the 100% servanthood of the body of Christ.

The traditional church model releases only 2% of its workforce into 'the ministry' while neglecting to prepare the other 98% to exercise their ministry in their daily life setting – as husbands and wives, parents and children, workers and employers, students and teachers. When we think of this, it is amazing how much of God's work actually gets done through this broken model. The Holy Spirit is gracious. Sincere leaders, gifted preachers and enthusiastic members will find ways of serving God, despite deficiencies in the system. But this does not mean we should not be more proactive in developing more suitable models of church. We must have the courage to face the truth and act. We need a new model of church.

ADDRESSING THE BIG ISSUES

The cell church model courageously addresses the two big issues in contemporary ecclesiology bringing us back to the fundamentals of New Testament teaching on the church's purpose and function. Traditional church models are founded on the failure to understand and consistently apply two key concepts concerning the church. The first has to do with *ekklesia*, the New Testament word translated as 'church', and *diakonia*, referring to 'service' or 'ministry'.

By pure derivation, *ekklesia* means 'the called out ones', but this does not give us its true definition. The best translation is 'gathering'. The church is made up of believers who have responded to God's call to gather to Jesus. We are in a permanent 'gathered relationship' to Christ and his people. Taking this into account, we can easily see that the biblical understanding of the word 'church' does not refer to 'a place of public Christian worship', as the *Oxford English Dictionary* defines it. Neither does it primarily mean the Christian meetings that take place in church buildings, as most Evangelicals use the word. Rather, it is the permanent 24/7 gathering of God's people. Nothing that we do together *makes* us the church. We gather together, we worship, we serve and we share because we *are* the church. Gathering in formal church services is a natural expression of *ekklesia*, but so is gathering in every other way possible. The big mistake is to think that the congregational worship we enjoy on Sunday is the totality of church. No wonder people think they have done 'their bit' when they have 'gone to church' on Sunday.

The other great error of our time, is how we define *diakonia* or 'ministry'. Traditional church goers will immediately identify 'the minister' as the person who stands before them Sunday by

Sunday. He or she may not be alone – there may be a team of 'ministers' and even an extended team of 'lay leaders', but the definition of the ministry remains the same. The ministers are the 'paid professionals'.

Even a cursory glance at Ephesians 4:11-12 will show that this is an inadequate model. Jesus warned us that wherever our traditions supplant God's Word they rob us of its power. Ephesians chapter 4 verse 12 clearly states that it is the "saints" or "God's people" who are the ministers. The leadership roles of verse 11 are present in the church to equip the body to do the work of Christ. I cover this in more detail in Chapter 29, but at this point, it is important to introduce some principles of the fivefold ministry.

It is clear that Christ has gifted some leaders with special abilities. There are five leadership ministries available to the body of Christ, but the traditional structure is built around just one of them. The pastor-teacher role is the most often acknowledged ministry and the traditional system is set up to keep it that way. It is tradition not scripture that tells us the pastor is "in sole charge" of the church. Perpetuating this error is one of the most damaging things we do to the cause of Christ today.

All the ministry gifts of Christ listed in Ephesians 4:11, including the vitally important role of pastor-teachers, are given for a wholly different purpose from that which is fostered by the traditional model of church. These leaders are not *the* ministers but are called to minister *to* the ministers, that is, the body of Christ. They are there to "prepare God's people" for the ministry of Christ. The ministry of Christ is done through the body of Christ. In the same way we work through our own human bodies, living, moving and acting in the world, so Christ does his work through his body.

It is time we were liberated from the traditional model. It is too restricting. It obscures the real work of leadership and the real ministry of Christ. Even though this model is so much part of our church culture and environment, we must have the courage to go against it. The church has been through one major reformation. It's time for another one! The cell model may not be the *only* way of doing church, but it points us all in the right direction. It addresses our faulty understanding of the church and its ministry, and it offers an alternative way of thinking about and doing church today.

People with a Passion

Cell Ministry Foundations

We are now ready to see how the cell ministry draws together many of the elements I have presented so far in this book. It begins with passion – passion for Christ and his amazing grace, passion to follow his example of ministry and passion to see the church equipped and mobilised in today's world. The traditional model I critiqued in the previous chapter must give way to a new approach to church in the 21st Century. A dynamic approach to cell groups goes a long way to redress the weaknesses inherent in today's church structures.

The cell model is an intentional discipleship structure. Every member can be trained and released to do the work of Christ. The focus is on empowering people, not merely attracting them through slick programmes. Cells are the fundamental unit through which the work of Christ is done. Cells work as microcosms of the whole. They form the basic unit of congregational church life and the bigger celebration meetings, gathering cell members together in one body.

The modern cell church movement originated in South Korea, under the ministry of David Yonggi Cho, during the second half of the last Century. He was not the first leader to work with cells in modern times, but Cho brought the cell system to prominence as it resulted in the world's largest church with up to 800,000 members – each one benefitting from the personal and intimate cell group fellowship as well as the mass gatherings of local church celebrations.

Later on, cell church also had proponents from the Western world such as Bill Beckham and Ralph Neighbour. All these men used a system of cells known as the 5 by 5 (or 'Jethro') cell model. That is, they worked with leaders who supervised 5 cells and appointed supervisors over of these supervisors, building into a pyramid-type structure incorporating the whole church. Much of the inspiration of this model was taken from Jethro's advice to his son-in-law Moses in Exodus 18:13-26.

Towards the end of last century, an alternative cell church model was developed by Cesar Castellanos in Bogota, Colombia. It is based on the number 12. This was an attempt to develop a model founded on the example of Jesus' way of ministering. The basic principle is that a leader gathers a 'group of 12' and pours himself or herself into these 12, discipling them, training them and sending them to reproduce cells. Today many churches throughout the world that are experiencing explosive growth are cell churches, using either the 5 by 5 Model or the Model of 12.

The system I adopted was the Model of 12. I will share more about this later, but I want to make clear that I do not hold to a doctrinaire view of this model. I just found it suited our ethos as a church and seemed to produce more fruit in our situation. In the first instance, what is far more important than the particular model we adopt is to understand what cells are and how they can operate in the church.

UNDERSTANDING THE BIOLOGICAL CELL

Ask any student of biology, "What is a cell?" and they will explain that it is the basic building block of the human body. Our bodies consist of multiple billions of cells working in complex co-ordination. Without them, the body could not live and function. They are the basic 'building block' of life. Each cell carries our unique genetic code, the 'blueprint' of life itself. By nature, cells multiply themselves bringing life, health and growth.

Little over 100 years ago, not much was known about the human cell. However, as scientific knowledge developed so did our understanding of cells. We now know that our cells are highly-complex 'factories' or 'mini-cities' carrying amazing diversity, working in finely-tuned harmony and astounding biological precision.

There are many different types of cells in the human body, each with their own specialised characteristics to enable them to fulfil their specific function. For example, the cells in our muscles, nerves and skin are all different – adapted for their special purpose in the body. Some cells have the capacity to transition or 'differentiate', that is, to develop the specific characteristics needed in any particular part of the body.

We can draw many parallels between the current biological understanding of cells in the human body and how God calls us to function in the body of Christ. One textbook statement on the cells of the human body shows us how helpful a cell model can be in our vision for church life:

> *"The body is made up of billions of cells, each a single unit of life working interdependently as tissues, organs and systems to create a complex single unity greater than the sum of its parts."*

Cells in the body of Christ carry exactly the same characteristics as described in this statement. They are microcosmic units of the life of the church. They are interdependent. They are part of larger structures in the body of Christ. They form a complex single corporate unit (the church) which is greater than the sum of its parts.

I return to this topic in Chapter 29, where we look back at the cell model in the light of these biological insights. But it is helpful to anticipate some important principles concerning the cell church structure and how it mirrors the way cells function in the human body. The following is a summary of some of these parallels. It will help us understand the attractive and dynamic nature of cell church.

A cell-structured church

1. The life of the church is in the cells.
2. The church is energised by the cells.
3. The church operates through the cells.
4. The church maintains its unity and diversity through the cells.
5. The church remains healthy through the cells.
6. The church grows, develops and reproduces through the cells.
7. The church maintains its unique identity through the cells.

There are many different ways of doing church and numerous models are possible that could express these principles of corporate life in the body of Christ. However, a cell-structured church seems to be the simplest and most logical starting point. Every aspect of cell church that we look at in this book, is essentially an expression of these fundamental insights.

SPIRITUAL DNA

We have seen that the discipleship process began with Jesus calling his 12. His "master plan" was to create a small intimate fellowship of disciples around him, pouring his life and his 'DNA' into them. In this small 'cell' gathering, Jesus built a relationship with his disciples, he taught and trained them, he imparted his authority and power to them, and finally, he sent them out to minister and witness in his name.

> *He appointed twelve, that they might be with him and that he might send them out to preach and to have power to heal sicknesses and cast out demons.*
>
> Mark 3:14-15

Later on, the Holy Spirit reproduced Jesus' ministry in the lives of subsequent believers. After Pentecost, we see the life and vigour of the early church expressed in the large gatherings in the Temple, complemented by their much smaller fellowship meetings in believers' homes (Acts 2:41-47). These are "the two wings of the church" that Bill Beckham describes as the basic structure of cell church.

THE HISTORICAL IMPORTANCE OF THE SMALL GROUP

History shows that the 'cell' group has often played a strategic role in world affairs. Frequently, small groups have championed subversive ideologies and counter cultures which have finally overcome resistant institutions, influencing and ultimately transforming whole societies. In the days before Al Qaida and modern Islamist terrorist cells, the historian Herbert Butterfield captured the historical importance of the small group. In his book, *The Second Reformation*, Bill Beckham quotes Butterfield's view of the historical importance of the cell:

> *The strongest organizational unit in the world's history would appear to be that which we call a cell because it is a remorseless self-multiplier; is exceptionally difficult to destroy; can preserve its intensity of local life while vast organizations quickly wither when they are weakened at the center; can defy the power of governments; is the appropriate lever of prising open any status quo. Whether we take early Christianity or sixteenth century Calvinism or modern communism, this seems the appointed way by which a mere handful of people may open up a new chapter in the history of civilization.*

With this in mind, we now look at a brief survey of 'cells' in church history.

THE CELL VISION IN CHURCH HISTORY

The church in Jerusalem was endued with the supernatural power of the Holy Spirit (Acts 2:43). The 'DNA' of Jesus, successfully reproduced in his 12 disciples, was passed on to the members of this burgeoning new church (Acts 4:13). They knew how to construct their lives upon the Word of God. They understood how to create close fellowship with each other so that no one was in need. They experienced supernatural power to reach the lost and to restore damaged lives. They came under the favour both of God and man (Acts 2:47). In all this, the Holy Spirit was dynamically active among them through the 'cell' gatherings.

After the destruction of the Jerusalem Temple in AD 70, the church grew rapidly and spread throughout the entire known world of that time. For over two centuries they erected no church buildings of their own. How, then, did they achieve such explosive growth? They continued to meet in each other's homes in 'cell' groups.

After the 'conversion' of the Emperor Constantine, Christianity became the official religion of the Roman Empire. The official persecution of Christians ended, and church buildings were erected all over the Empire. Church structures became more hierarchical and the ministry was increasingly controlled by professional ordained clergy, and the small group as the 'engine room' of Christian faith was emphasised less and less.

However, this formalism had not been present in the beginning, and it produced an unexpected backlash. The Monastic movement, active from the 2nd Century, began to include 'lay leaders' who met in small groups in defiance of the institutionalism of the church of the Roman Empire. These developed into a vibrant force of evangelism which penetrated much of Europe with small groups of missionaries establishing thousands of new churches.

Throughout the history of the church, whenever the Holy Spirit moved in revival power, the 'cell', in one form or another, was usually an integral part of his restorative work. Martin Luther, the father of the Protestant Reformation believed that a small group structure was necessary to give full expression to the principles of the Reformation. New wine needs new wineskins.

However, Luther did not take the project forward. In part, this was because he was under political pressure to establish a state church system for the Reformed Church of Germany. In the end, Luther opted to uphold an institutional church structure that accepted all members of society and not just those who were born again believers. Luther considered the idea of the gathered church which was being pioneered by the Anabaptists of the day, to be too extreme.

Martin Bucer, the great Reformer based in Strasburg, attempted to develop a small group structure, firmly believing that this was the secret of vital Christianity. This venture was vehemently opposed by proponents of the newly established Reformed church. They were opposed to the concept of the gathered church because they thought it would compromise the stability of the state church and threaten its place in society.

Philip Jacob Spener, who followed Luther in post-Reformation Germany, spoke of believers exercising their "universal priesthood" in small groups. He saw this as a natural outworking of reformation principles as well as a pastoral necessity. Another example of historical awareness of 'cell' during this period is Count Zinzendorf. He welcomed the persecuted Moravians who settled in the grounds of his vast estate in Germany. He supported the idea of the church being organised in small groups. *Koinonia* was regarded by the Moravians as the third sacrament, and this was expressed in the *banden* – small groups of people meeting for prayer, worship and world mission.

John Wesley in England was influenced by the Moravians and organised his emerging Methodist movement into *classes* of believers. These small groups were the cornerstone of his revolutionary structure and they spawned many thousands of disciples across Britain. George Whitefield, the great evangelist who lived at the same time as Wesley, also encouraged his converts to meet together in small groups to encourage each other through testimony and prayer.

I am not suggesting that these movements produced highly-developed cell church structures such as have been more recently developed by Cho and Castellanos. It seems that their ideas were Spirit led and instinctive, but certain factors stood in their way. Traditional church leaders resisted the idea of popular people-led movements. It cut across their vested interests. Also, there seems to have been no clear rationale for cells, apart from their natural and practical appeal. The lack of effective leadership training and education was also an issue.

The church has come a long way since then. Today, we have all the elements in place, not only to resist pressure from the traditionalists, but also to build a solid cell church structure into the fabric of our church life and practice. Perhaps the 21st Century is just the right time for cell church to blossom.

THE HALLMARKS OF A CELL

At the core, cell church is about cells. It is important to understand what we are talking about. For instance, what are the hallmarks of a genuine cell? There are at least five: worship, nurture, fellowship, training and outreach. Believers will seek to be Christ-centred, coming under his authority. They will nurture each other from the Word of God, applying its teaching to their everyday lives. They will fulfil Christ's command to love one another and build up each other in fellowship. However, they will go beyond considering their own needs and make sure each member is equipped to fulfil Christ's call to win the lost and make disciples (Matthew 28:19).

Holding all these components together is what distinguishes a true cell from a traditional small group which may focus only on 1 or 2 of these elements. Without worship, the group would be dry. Without the Word, it would eventually become sub-Christian. Without fellowship, it would grow cold. Without training, the people would be ill prepared to do the work of Christ. And without outreach, a cell would become introspective and self-absorbed. William Temple, a former Archbishop of Canterbury, once said, "A church that lives for itself dies by itself." The Church is the only institution that exists for the benefit of its non-members.

The Model of 12 with its focus on outreach and discipleship, ensures that the cell stays true to its purpose. The cell is the primary place for winning new believers, discipling, training and releasing them to become disciple makers of others.

Like the biological cell, a cell group of believers will be the basic building block of the body of Christ. It will transmit the 'DNA' of Christ. It will multiply, reproducing other cells, and when necessary, it will transition into a leadership group to take care of these new cell leaders.

HOW CELLS MULTIPLY

The Model of 12 facilitates the discipleship of every member of the body of Christ, the training of new leaders and the multiplication of cell groups. The aim of the model is for everybody to be involved in reaching the lost through the cell ministry. Then the goal is for everyone to lead their own cell, as soon as they are able. Everyone is ministered to, and eventually, everyone becomes a minister.

The cell groups do not simply divide – they multiply. When a person becomes part of a cell they immediately begin to reach out to their friends. One by one, people come to Christ and join the cell. When the group has grown to an adequate size, multiplication takes place. Each person in the cell starts to build their own new cell, while continuing to receive help, mentoring, discipleship, training and encouragement from their original cell leader. When a sufficient number of members from the original cell have started their own new cell, the original cell becomes a Primary 12 group. A Primary 12 group is for leaders who have their own cells and meet for leadership training, to share about their progress, and for encouragement and support. This process is illustrated in Figure 1 on page 111.

WHY CELLS?

We are beginning to see why cell church is an effective model for the church. At this point let me review some of the major ways the cells help us do church.

Fulfilling the Great Commission

The Lord Jesus has given us his Great Commission. We are to go and make disciples, maturing them in the faith and mobilising them into the harvest of the world (Matthew 28:18-20). This can only be done effectively when every believer becomes a true disciple. The small group setting is an essential part of this process.

The church is more than a building. It is also more than going to services in a certain building on a Sunday. To fulfil the Great Commission, we must be the church in the world – the church without walls. We have to live as the body of Christ every day and not just on Sundays. This means we will be active witnesses and representatives for Christ in our daily walk. The cells help us do that. They are established where people are – in homes, offices, schools, cafes and other places of recreation.

Reaching the lost

Evangelism is the responsibility of every believer. We are all called to make Christ known and to share his gospel with our non-Christian friends, neighbours and relatives. The vast majority of those who commit to Christ in any context do so through the witness of a believer whom they know and respect.

Cells can penetrate every part of the city we are seeking to evangelise – the schools, the businesses, universities, offices, and homes. A cell church is not bound by its building and so the

Open Cell to Leadership Cell

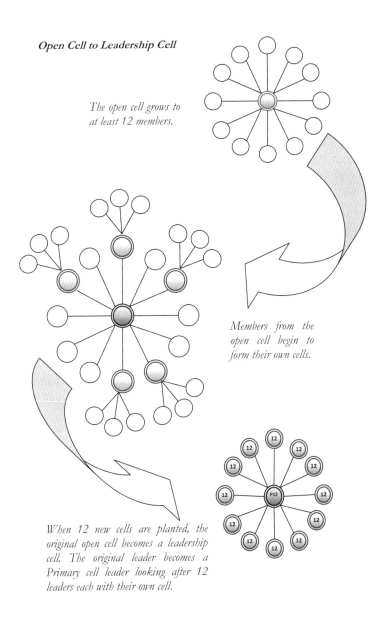

The open cell grows to at least 12 members.

Members from the open cell begin to form their own cells.

When 12 new cells are planted, the original open cell becomes a leadership cell. The original leader becomes a Primary cell leader looking after 12 leaders each with their own cell.

Figure 1

whole of the city can come under the influence of the gospel. I speak more about this aspect of conquering 'the giants' of our society in Chapter 29.

Nurturing new believers

New believers need to be firmly established in their faith so that they become strong and go on to be effective, fruit-bearing disciples of Christ. The cells help consolidate new believers. That is where they can receive the level of care and nurture they need. Face to face interaction is the only way. The cells provide support for new believers from a group of people who are committed to praying for them, teaching them and helping them practically. The cells make sure that the fruit of evangelism is not lost.

Discipleship

Every believer is called to be a disciple of Jesus Christ. This means we need someone to instruct us personally and to lead us in the ways of Christ. The cells provide the setting for these discipling relationships to develop. The cell leaders are accountable to the training and discipline of the church as well as benefitting from the resources, wisdom and counsel of their leaders. This helps prevent people being drawn into false teaching or being 'poached' by unaccountable people on the fringe of church life.

The cell is also where a new believer can begin to take up the call to be a disciple maker. Through the support and example of the group, cell members get involved in the discipling process from the beginning. They learn how to reach out to others and begin to disciple them.

Fulfilling the "one another" commands

There are many things we must do as an expression of our mutual relationship in Christ. There are over 45 different passages in the New Testament which specifically speak of the responsibility we have towards one another. We are called to love one another, care for, teach and encourage one another, and to exhort admonish and restore one another. The cells are the practical context for these things to be done consistently and comprehensively.

Cell ministry makes sure that every member is cared for in a personal way. Large Sunday gatherings can be impersonal and the individual can be lost in the crowd. But, in a cell church everyone counts, everyone is important.

Finding and fulfilling our ministry

Every believer is called to life in the Spirit. One of the things this means is that the Holy Spirit has called us and gifted us with his abilities. He anoints us with these abilities to serve Christ and to help build and strengthen one another. Most people never get to discover and fulfil their ministry.

The cells allow every member to respond to the call of God. The cell group is the ideal place to discover, develop and use the different ministries the Holy Spirit gives us. People can be trained in the exercise of the gifts of the Spirit and learn how to be released in their ministry.

Focusing our efforts

Cell groups help us coordinate our efforts as a church and become effective in reaching our goals. We work together and do not 'go it alone'. That is what it means to be part of the body of Christ. We benefit from the strength, wisdom, encouragement and support of the group. Also, when goals are openly shared, we become corporately accountable for them. That is a positive and productive experience for the church.

Cells enable us to work together strategically, as we break down a major task (like winning our city) into smaller, manageable and achievable units. For example, we have a godly goal to have a cell group in every street in London. That's between 50-60 thousand cells! But, it becomes possible, as each cell takes is share of the work.

Bearing fruit

As we saw in Chapter 7, disciples of Christ are called to become fruitful. The Creation Mandate: "Be fruitful and multiply; fill the earth and subdue it", the Abrahamic call: "Become the father of a multitude", and the Great Commission of Christ: "Make disciples of all nations" – all have to do with reaching the multitudes.

The cells are the place of blessing and fruitfulness. They are where multiplication takes place. As we fulfil God's call, walking in agreement with him, he blesses and prospers our work. In the next chapter, we begin to examine what takes place in the cell groups to bring about these desired results.

The Cell Group

A cell group is a small group of believers committed to a lifestyle of building each other up and reaching out to others. It is not just a small midweek meeting that takes place weekly, outside the main church building. When people say, "See you at cell tomorrow" or "I missed you at cell last week", I know they have not understood what the cell is all about. It seems traditions die hard. People easily slip back into thinking that 'church' is all about meetings!

Cells do gather their members in a weekly meeting, but it is far more than that. Cell members are a group of friends who are in daily contact, sharing life and ministry together. Cell life reflects what was happening in the Jerusalem church of Acts.

> *So continuing daily with one accord in the temple, and breaking bread from house to house, they ate their food with gladness and simplicity of heart, praising God and having favour with all the people. And the Lord added to the church daily those who were being saved.*
>
> Acts 2:46-47

The Jerusalem believers met together daily. Apart from the formal hours of prayer at the Temple, they fellowshipped with each other in their homes and in their other daily activities. Cell members are first and foremost friends who enjoy one another's company and share their life and experience together through the ordinary course of daily contact.

THE FRIENDSHIP FACTOR

In Chapter 8, I touched on an important aspect of cell life – the groups of 3, which we also call 'companionship groups'.

Jesus had his 12 close disciples but he had an even closer relationship with Peter, James and John. A group of 12 is an ideal number for a primary group – that is, a group of people who can know each other well and can sustain a high level of friendship. However, it is too large for everyone to be on the same level of intimacy. Jesus shared with his 'group of 3' things that he was not able to speak about in the wider group.

I notice the same tendency in our cell groups. Most cell members have 2 or 3 other friends in the cell with whom they relate at a deeper level. We understand this principle of human relationships to be an expression of our essential make-up as human beings. Everyone needs to have a group of 2 or 3 friends with whom they can share at a level of depth. We all should experience this level of companionship in our church fellowship.

Friendship groups of 3 facilitate the life of the cell. For example, it is not easy for every member of the cell to be in daily contact with every other member. The groups of 3 can do so easily and naturally – not because they have to, but because they want to!

The group of 3 includes your closest friends in the cell and you can meet each other often during the week and maintain daily contact through telephone, SMS or other forms of social media. You can pray for each other daily and be available for each other virtually 24 hours a day. The groups of 3 also spontaneously reach out to their closest friends who have not yet come know Jesus. That way, evangelism flows naturally on friendship lines and the cell group grows.

The groups of 3 facilitate the cell leader who cannot be everything to everyone all the time – no matter how small the cell group is. The leader's own group of 3 function as his or her assistants. This helps with communication as the cell leader seeks to disseminate information, delegate consolidation and generally look out for the well being of the cell group. I speak more about this in my booklet, *The Friendship Factor*, in the *Discipleship Cell Explosion* Series.

CELL MEETINGS

As we have just seen, the actual cell meetings are just one part of cell life, but they are important. That's why we say cell leaders should draw all the cell members together once a week. Usually, those who hold cell meetings only once or twice a month, find their cells lose their focus and stop growing.

The cell meetings need not be long – I recommend they do not last for more than one hour, as there are many things we must do alongside these meetings and we simply cannot afford to spend an entire evening on every single aspect of the cell vision.

The cell leader, together with other key cell members, should meet for prayer before the cell meeting. There may be some consolidation to do with the new cell members before or after the cell meeting, and perhaps also some extra support offered to struggling cell members.

The cell meeting follows a carefully planned strategy for the growth and advancement of the cell. Usually, this strategy is developed in the leaders' meetings so that the cells work in line with the overall plan and do not become isolated or side-tracked from the main vision of the church. During my meetings with my Primary 12, I share with them where I believe the emphasis should be placed at any particular time. I get my cue from the feedback the cell leaders give me, my own sense of where the needs are and also from the annual plan we devise as we set our goals and strategies for the coming year.

We do not always follow a set plan of teaching in the cells. From time to time, have made available notes for cell leaders arising out of the Sunday preaching and whenever we have done this it has been appreciated by the cell leaders. However, we want the cell leaders to develop their own teaching capabilities and to minister to the specific needs of their cell members. Quality control begins with the solid foundational training and on-going doctrinal and practical input the cell leaders receive. Regular feedback and supervision through the leadership groups, ensures that the teaching stays on track and does not deviate into doctrinal error or faulty practices.

Continuity and consistency are also maintained through the Primary 12 groups, where the principal leaders introduce a particular teaching emphasis, theme or topic for them to pass on to the cell leaders they are caring for. If, for instance, I believe we should be focussing on stimulating prayer and intercession during a particular season, I will minister on prayer in my Primary 12 leadership meeting and they will pass this teaching on to their cell leaders.

Also, we have numerous booklets covering various aspects of cell life and ministry, and we teach our cell leaders how to use this material in the cells. For example, we have booklets on *The Friendship Factor*, *Why Cells?*, *A Willing Heart* and *Evangelism through the Cells* – all providing valuable teaching material for cell leaders.

We are strict about maintaining the two different kinds of cell meetings – leadership cells (also called 'closed cells') and open cells. The purpose for each of these meetings is different – the open cells are primarily for outreach and nurture, while the leadership cells focus on training leaders and building them for effective ministry. Whenever these two agendas get confused, the cell ministry begins to lose focus and the meetings become neither a comfortable environment for visitors nor an appropriate place to minister effectively to leaders.

The key to holding an effective open cell meeting is flexibility. The format is informal and the timing and location of the meeting must make it easy for the cell members to meet. There is no set pattern. However, I do advise that the open cell meetings take place during the week and not in the church building.

The leadership meetings are different, and it makes sense for these to be held around the Sunday service programme. It is usually more convenient for all concerned. But this does not apply to the open cell meetings. The open cells reach out to people *where they are*. We want to change the pattern of church which says to those who need Christ, "Come to us."

The point of the open cell meetings is to give our members the opportunity to meet midweek, away from the main church building, so that they can grow as disciples at home, at work, at college or at leisure. This is where they spend most of their lives and where they meet with most of their friends. That way, cell ministry shows the relevance of the Christian faith to the whole of life and we move away from 'Sunday-only Christianity'.

While the time, place and agenda of the cell meetings are flexible, we do teach our cell leaders to include a number of important elements. We follow the 'classical' approach to cell meetings which include:

- Worship
- Word
- Witness
- Welfare
- Warfare.

Worship

Everything begins with worship. It's the highest order activity and principal purpose of a believer's life. Without passionate worship we cannot connect with God. The Father, not only seeks worship, but requires it. This is not just for his benefit, although he is blessed by worship in spirit and truth. When we touch him in worship our lives line up with his reality and everything we do for him flows from this experience.

We cannot worship God in the cell meeting the way we do so on Sundays, with a big band and shouts of praise. We must respect our neighbours! And we must also take into account the small group setting. There are many ways of worshipping

God in a small group where we cannot make too much noise: silent appreciation of a verse of Scripture, listening to a praise CD, reading a poem of praise, sharing something about God's goodness and blessing with each other, or even singing a chorus or two, softly and meaningfully.

However we do it, we must worship God in every cell meeting. We have found that testimony is a powerful means of giving glory to God. Worship in cell meetings often flows out of thanksgiving, in response to the testimonies members give at the beginning of the meeting.

Word

The ministry of the Word in the cell group should be short, interactive and practical. There is a tendency to turn the cell group into a regular Bible study, where the leader gives a long monologue and leaves no time for questions or contributions from others in the group.

The cell meeting is not a preaching or a teaching service. The Word must be ministered according to the principles of the small group dynamic. It must be personal, meeting the particular needs of the cell members. It must also be conversational, allowing time for interaction, questions and contributions from everyone in the group. It is a time of sharing together in the Word which focuses on working out the teaching of the Bible in the specific situations the cell members find themselves in.

This is not easy. It is a skill that must be developed. Some people will think that they have to communicate the Word in the cell meeting in the same way they hear it preached on Sundays in the church building. But that is not the case. The cell leaders must be trained how to lead a conversational Bible study in a small group setting. This is taught during our Leadership School and modelled by the Primary cell leaders as they train their members in these skills.

Witness

I speak about evangelism through the cells in several other places in this book. Here, I want to emphasise that no cell meeting is complete without evangelism. At the very least, we pray for our absent non-Christian friends and plan the next evangelistic opportunity or event. If there are visitors present, we make sure our teaching is understandable to them, we give time for questions and we invite a response.

Many cell leaders hold a totally evangelistic cell meeting once a month where the activity centres on something that will interest their non-Christian friends – a party, a meal, an evening at the movies, a cup of coffee, a DVD, a concert, or a football match.

During a certain period, I encouraged the cell leaders to do this every week as I felt the emphasis of the cells had shifted from evangelism to fellowship. Those that responded to this idea found it a timely reminder to keep the cells open and outward looking. The new believers were still consolidated during the 'evening out' and the fellowship among the group deepened. We do not always have to be doing 'spiritual' activities in order to do the Lord's work. We can have fun too!

In Chapter 29, I show how our witness extends to world mission. This is always on the agenda in the cells.

Welfare

I am maintaining the standard alliteration here, and use another 'W'. Welfare represents the nurture, care and encouragement of believers through the cells. The cell leaders are the 'pastors' of the church. During their time of training, they are taught all the elements of pastoral care: prayer, counselling, visitation, practical support, correction and training. It is amazing how fast the church grows when pastoral care is shared out among the whole church.

Before we transitioned into the cell vision, we had a strong pastoral team, who were on duty during the week to take counselling and pastoral appointments. We still do this, as we do not want new people to the church who are not yet in cells to miss out. But our message is loud and strong – pastoral care happens through the cells. The more experienced cell leaders, many of whom are pastors in their own right, help the less experienced leaders who may struggle with some pastoral issues.

I am amazed at how effective the cell leaders are in caring for their members. When people miss a cell meeting, the cell leader calls them and if there is a problem, a visit is arranged. If this becomes too much for the leader to handle, other cell members get involved. The group of 3 principle means that no one is without a friend on hand to help out if things get tough.

During times of difficulty the whole cell is there for the cell member. Hospital visits, family visits and support at work – all this is made possible through the cells. There is no way that the traditional approach to pastoral care could match this level of support. In a large church, you may not be missed by anyone if you are absent from the meetings for a while. But, in a cell church, your fellow cell members are always in touch with you.

When we were quite new to the cell vision, I was highly-impressed by one of our cell leaders from the youth. One day, I saw him leaving the church building in a hurry. He told me he had a call from one of his cell members who had a problem. He explained that a young convert was expecting a baby by a man 40 years her senior, and that her family was not going to allow the couple to get married.

By any standard, this was not an easy pastoral situation to deal with. I asked the cell leader what he was going to do and if he had enough support from his cell leader who was more experienced than he was. He explained how the leader and he were going to approach the situation pastorally, and I let him go. He returned later to say all had gone well. The young woman had agreed to submit to the counsel of her parents. The older man had not really wanted the marriage and had broken off the relationship. The cell was there to support, not just the girl, but the whole family, who were now showing interest in the gospel. I realised then, that the cell vision works!

Warfare

Prayer and intercession is one of the principle weapons in our armoury. The whole cell vision must be soaked in it. We teach the cell members to become passionate people of prayer. The cell members pray every day for each other, for their leaders and for the lost. Simple petitions and prolonged periods of prayer and fasting are both modelled in the cells. No prayer request is too small to be ignored and no prayer request is too big to be tackled.

COVENANT-TYPE RELATIONSHIPS

The regular cell meetings help cement the bonds between the cell members and develop them into strong covenant-type relationships. The cell leader gets to spend individual time with cell members outside the cell meetings keeping watch over them like a shepherd. The cell members accept their responsibility to become their "brother's keeper" and to take their place in the ministry of the church. The whole cell functions as a unit but not independent. The 'friendship factor' takes effect as the cell members help one another find Christ and grow to be like him. These relationships are the spiritual bonds of the body of Christ and, like the ligament and sinews in the human body, hold the church together. The whole is built up as each part does its work. All the key activities of the cell work together to grow the church:

- Evangelism
- Consolidation
- Mutual discipleship

- On-the-job training
- Development of spiritual gifts
- Ministering to one another
- People development
- Relationships
- Helping one another grow
- Sharing life's joys and setbacks
- Encouragement
- Prayer
- Personal testimony
- Goal-setting
- Strategic planning

SAMPLE CELL MEETING

I will end this chapter with a sample list outlining a typical cell meeting to help us see how all this comes together.

- Assembling together – time for a quick catch up, ice-breaker and welcome.
- Short opening prayer followed by worship.
- Time of testimony – "What has God been doing in your life? Your family? Your Evangelism of 3?"
- Prayer time in groups of 2 or 3 – "What are you believing God for? What prayer needs do you have? How can we pray for those on your Evangelism of 3 list?"
- Opportunity for someone (a budding or established leader) to share a short inspirational word of experience or testimony.
- Vision word from the cell leader.
- Closing prayer.
- Time for social interaction – a snack, a simple meal or just a cup of coffee.

The Principle of 12

The cell model we work with is based on the principle of 12. It is not a dogma, and we are not fixated with the number 12, anymore than those who follow the 5 by 5 Model are addicted to the number 5. The number 12 does carry some scriptural significance. It is, however, the principle that counts more than anything else.

The key is to understand that Jesus spent most of his time with a small group of chosen disciples, and concentrated much of his ministry on discipling, training and ultimately releasing them to do the work of the kingdom of God. If this is what Jesus did, who are we to try and do it any other way? Surely the Lord's example is something we should follow.

If every church leader focussed on training a group of 12 and preparing them for leadership, we would have no shortage of workers and the expansion of the church would be rapid and solid. It seems we are not the only ones to come to this conclusion. Writing about Jesus' method of training leaders in *The Master Plan of Evangelism*, Robert Coleman records the opinion of Dr Billy Graham, perhaps the greatest evangelist of modern times. Dr Coleman writes,

> *In this connection, it is not without great significance that the leading evangelist in the world today, Billy Graham, recognises the tremendous potential of this plan when used properly in the church. In response to the question, "If you were a pastor of a large church in a principal city, what would be your plan of action?" Mr Graham replied: "I think one of the first things I would*

do would be to get a small group of eight or ten or twelve people around me that would meet a few hours a week and pay the price! It would cost them something in time and effort. I would share with them everything I have, over a period of years. Then I would actually have twelve ministers among the laypeople who in turn could take eight or twelve more and teach them. I think one or two churches that are doing that, and it is revolutionising the church. Christ, I think, set the pattern. He spent most of his time with twelve men. He didn't spend it with a great crowd. In fact, every time he had a great crowd it seems to me that there weren't too many results. The great results, it seems to me, came in his personal interviews and in the time he spent with his twelve."

This, in essence is the principle of 12. It means we spend quality time and expend the lion share of our efforts on those who are gifted and willing to take what they learn from us and pass it onto others. It is seen clearly in 2 Timothy 2:2, where Paul tells Timothy to pass on what he learned from him to other faithful leaders so that, in turn, they could pass it on to others.

If it is the principle that is important, not the number 12, why do we build a model around Groups of 12? Will not 4 or 8 have the same effect? Growing a group of 12 leaders as Jesus did is a godly goal and not a doctrine. As we shall see, there are some practical reasons for thinking in terms of the number 12, even though it is not a theological necessity.

MORE THAN A NUMBER

Numbers in the Bible do carry symbolic significance especially when they occur throughout the Scriptures, but biblical numerology is fraught with difficulty and can lead to speculative theories and subjective interpretations.

For example, I do not believe that when Elijah took 12 stones and rebuilt the altar of the Lord in Samaria, he was thinking about a church structure that we might find helpful in the 21st Century. However, the number 12 was significant for him and his actions symbolised the fact that God wanted to draw the whole nation (the kingdoms of Israel and Judah) back to himself.

In choosing 12 disciples, Jesus was thinking about the spiritual restoration of Israel. His disciples would govern the 12 tribes of Israel in the kingdom of God.

> *I bestow upon you a kingdom, just as my Father bestowed one upon me, that you may eat and drink at my table in my kingdom, and sit on thrones judging the twelve tribes of Israel.*
>
> Luke 22:29–30

It is obvious that this is a spiritually and historically unique use of the number 12. The 12 apostles were to become the foundation of the New Testament Church and of the City of God. But Jesus' method of working with a manageable number of leaders must surely tell us something about an effective model of doing what he calls us to do today.

There have been many uses of this principle of 12 in Church history. Britain was evangelised by monks who built cells around the small group principle. As we saw in Chapter 9, Luther, Spener, Wesley and Whitefield all accepted elements of this principle.

In our time, interest in the principle of 12 has also been intense. As we have just seen in the quote from *The Master Plan of Evangelism*, Robert Coleman wrote about it 40 years before the G12 model of Castellanos. Here is another useful comment on Jesus' method found in Coleman's book:

> *Here is the wisdom of his method, and in observing it, we return again to the fundamental principle of concentration on those he intended to use. One cannot transform a world except as individuals in the world are transformed, and individuals cannot be changed except as they are moulded*

in the hands of the Master. The necessity is apparent not only to select a few helpers, but also to keep the group small enough to be able to work with them... All of this certainly impresses one with the deliberate way that Jesus proportioned his life to those he wanted to train. It also graphically illustrates a fundamental principle of teaching: that other things being equal, the more concentrated the size of the group being taught, the greater the opportunity for effective instruction.

The principle of 12 is a well-established foundation for leadership training. The cell model of 12 simply builds on this, working intentionally with leadership groups of 12. Whatever other significance of the number may 12 hold, it is the optimum number for intense and personal discipleship. This is shown by the Lord's example as well as the work of others today who confirm this principle.

One of the greatest advantages of the Model of 12 is that everyone can be personally mentored and discipled into leadership. It is a relational, not a supervisory model, and that is characteristically how discipleship happens. People can make rapid and sure progress in their Christian life and ministry when they know they have the support and backup the Model of 12 gives them.

RETURNING TO JESUS' ORIGINAL PURPOSE

Since the year 2000, when Kensington Temple adopted the cell vision, developing groups of 12 has been one of the most significant aspects of our church life. Many hundreds of cell leaders and potential cell leaders have been formed and supported in the cell ministry through these groups. It has been thrilling to see the levels of fellowship, pastoral care and practical equipping that has emerged in what is without a doubt the most effective initiative in training and releasing leaders into God's work we have ever undertaken.

Jesus' choice of 12 establishes a principle for evangelism and discipleship. This was God's appointed method of reaching the multitudes and discipling them in the kingdom of God. It points to the practical way we can respond to his call to gather the multitudes – to bring the crowds of the market place (*agora*) into the gathered fellowship of disciples (*ekklesia*).

One account from the Gospels makes this point particularly forcefully. Jesus' compassion on the multitudes was clearly visible and always led to practical action. He healed the sick among them, he taught them the truths of the kingdom, he fed them and he called his 12 to reach them.

Matthew chapter 9 shows Jesus being moved with compassion at the sight of the crowds who were attracted to his ministry.

> *Then Jesus went about all the cities and villages, teaching in their synagogues, preaching the gospel of the kingdom, and healing every sickness and every disease among the people. But when he saw the multitudes, he was moved with compassion for them, because they were weary and scattered, like sheep having no shepherd. Then he said to his disciples, "The harvest truly is plentiful, but the labourers are few. Therefore pray the Lord of the harvest to send out labourers into his harvest."*
>
> Matthew 9:35–38

The reason why Jesus was moved with compassion for the multitudes is compelling. Matthew says that Jesus saw them as "sheep having no shepherd" and were therefore "weary and scattered" (the NIV says, "harassed and helpless"). As we saw in Chapter 8, this introduces us to a strange concept – that of a scattered crowd. The crowd was part of the general *agora* or public society of the day. Jesus wanted them to become his *ekklesia*, a community of disciples gathered to him. But they were sheep without a shepherd. The question was, how could the lost sheep be gathered under the pastoral care of the Good Shepherd?

Jesus' remarks to the disciples were poignant, "The harvest is plentiful, but the workers are few." Today, we make the mistake of wrongly focussing on the harvest fields, often wondering whether people really want our message or whether we can really be fruitful, as if there were no harvest waiting to be gathered. However, Jesus said that the problem is not with the harvest, but with the workers. The harvest is plentiful but the real question is how can we gather it in?

Jesus' analysis of the problem is as true today as it was then. The workers are few. Jesus solution was simple yet pointed: "Therefore, pray the Lord of the harvest to send out labourers into his harvest." We tend to think about the harvest, but Jesus taught us to concentrate on the harvesters. This is a clear indication of Jesus' call upon the church. We are to train, equip and release workers for the harvest field, praying to the Father to bless our efforts.

JESUS' STRATEGY FOR REACHING THE MULTITUDES

However, the passage does not stop at this point. Jesus goes much further. Unfortunately, the follow-on from his statements in Matthew 9:37-38 is obscured by the fact that those who were responsible for dividing up our Bible into chapters and verses, chose to end Matthew chapter 9 at verse 38. But Matthew 10:1 actually is part of the same passage. In it, Matthew goes on to show what Jesus did practically to reach the multitudes.

Jesus' strategy for reaching the multitudes was his 12. Look at how Matthew chapter 10 begins.

> *And when he had called his twelve disciples to him, he gave them power over unclean spirits, to cast them out, and to heal all kinds of sickness and all kinds of disease.*
> Matthew 10:1

Immediately, Jesus called his 12 and gave them power to heal the sick and to cast out demons. In other words, Jesus equipped his 12 to preach the gospel of the kingdom. Remember, Jesus never sent anyone out to preach without also giving them authority to heal and to deliver, and he never gave anyone power over sicknesses and demons without also commissioning them to preach the gospel.

This shows us what kind of workers Jesus wants to release into the harvest fields – workers like him. Matthew has shown us how Jesus reached the lost – by teaching, preaching and healing (Matthew 9:35). This now makes sense of his calling of the 12. He wanted to disciple them at close proximity and train them for their work of reaching the multitudes.

Notice that to reach the multitudes, Jesus actually turns from the crowds to his 12. But the very reason Jesus focussed on the 12 was to reach the multitudes. We now see clearly the practical reason why Jesus worked with his 12. He chose to equip others so that they could do the work of the kingdom, and this implies that he also taught them how to train and raise up others so that the process would continue uninterrupted until the work was completed.

This clearly and unambiguously establishes discipleship through the principle of 12 as the means of spreading the gospel, growing the church and expanding the kingdom of God. That is why the principle of 12 is at heart a discipleship vision. As we have seen, Paul draws on this principle when he writes to Timothy.

> *And the things that you have heard from me among many witnesses, commit these to faithful men who will be able to teach others also.*
>
> 2 Timothy 2:2

Here are four generations of spiritual communication, with no indication that it should stop there. Reaching out to others and training them also to reach out to others, is a process that should not end until the mission has been completed. That is how the multitudes are won for Christ. Beginning with one person who follows this principle, it takes just 10 generations, or cycles of discipleship, before there are over 1,000 followers of Jesus. Once multiplication according to the factor of 12 sets in, even more dramatic growth begins to occur. The 12 leaders grow to 144, and then to 1,728, to 20,736 and so on. In the model of 12, we focus on leaders, and so these numbers relate to cell groups. 20,000 cells would have at least 100,000 people.

A PRINCIPLE NOT A FORMULA

Of course, the cell vision never works according to this neat mathematical formula – people grow and reproduce at their own pace and some bear more fruit than others. However, the underlying principle still stands – we multiply through the cells.

After his ascension, Jesus sent the Spirit to empower his disciples to continue his work. Without a doubt, the 12 began to work with others just as Jesus had worked with them. They gathered disciples and developed them into effective disciple-makers. Christianity, from the beginning until now, has always been essentially a discipleship movement. Discipleship groups similar to those we know as cell groups today, are the only conceivable way the early church could have grown so rapidly and was so successfully able to consolidate new converts to the faith.

The book of Acts shows that all the 3,000 people who were converted on the Day of Pentecost were integrated into the church. This level of consolidation is almost without precedent in modern Christianity.

> *And they continued steadfastly in the apostles' doctrine and fellowship, in the breaking of bread, and in prayers.*
> Acts 2:42

The secret lay in the discipleship methods of Jesus in which the small groups played a crucial role.

> *So continuing daily with one accord in the temple, and breaking bread from house to house, they ate their food with gladness and simplicity of heart.*
>
> Acts 2:46

The daily 'house to house' contact was more than just the opportunity for friendship and table fellowship. It was also the ideal context for discipleship development following the model of Jesus and his disciples.

Jesus' method of raising up teams of people, focussing on their discipleship training and releasing them to do the same, is clearly established and indisputable. But what about the number 12? Why should we follow Jesus' practice of raising up 12?

First, let me again make it clear that there is no New Testament injunction that states every leader must grow and develop his or her group of 12 leaders, in the numerically literal way that Jesus did this. However, we can learn spiritual lessons from the Bible's use of the number 12. It is a symbolic number pointing to the principles of nationhood, apostleship, discipleship and government in the church.

This is not to say that there is a dogmatic necessity that binds us to build everything we do on the literal number 12. However, Jesus' choice of 12, gives us sound and practical reasons why we can develop a Model of 12 and work with it today. This is not a doctrine, but a strategy.

Sociologists tell us that 12 is the optimum number for people to relate to each other and be involved with each other on a regular and personal basis. Every person can get to know everyone else in the group at a level of depth and can have personal and intimate knowledge of each other's character and life experiences. This means that the number 12 is an effective building block for discipleship. A primary leader can grow his or her 12 and release them to do the same, optimising the small group principle for the purpose of propagating the Christian faith.

Therefore, we can say that the Model of 12 is a practical way of implementing the example of Jesus. It is an accessible model for those who want to be effective soul winners and disciplers. It is a significant strategy for churches to adopt in order to train and equip workers into the harvest. Today, as in Jesus' day, the principle of 12 is an effective principle to build on.

Homogeneous Groups

The model of 12 we use in London uses the homogeneous principle in the cells. This means the cells are organised into several different categories, or 'Nets' – one each for men, women, youth, and children. As we shall see, there are a number of ways of applying the principle of homogeneity, but we must first understand why it is an important component of effective discipleship.

THE HOMOGENEOUS PRINCIPLE

In practice, homogeneous cells simply mean that we run the men's, women's and youth ministries through the cells. Three main facts help us grasp the importance of these homogeneous groups:

1. The church is a family
2. Each member has special interests, needs and concerns
3. Each group is best equipped to reach and disciple others who share the same interests, needs and concerns.

This means that men are best equipped to reach and disciple other men, women best reach women, and so on. When we first adopted the cell vision in Kensington Temple, we were already familiar with the principle of homogeneity. We knew that the gospel spreads fastest along pre-existing kinship lines and had used this in our church planting programme. Many groups were already organised along homogeneous lines – for example, the ethnic and language based churches in our network. But we have also always stressed the need for the corporate expression of the body, where all the parts join together. The individual parts enrich the expression of the whole, as this snap-shot of the future life reveals:

> *After these things I looked, and behold, a great multitude which no one could number, of all nations, tribes, peoples, and tongues, standing before the throne and before the Lamb, clothed with white robes, with palm branches in their hands.*
>
> Revelation 7:9

We will see aspects of culture redeemed and glorified in heaven! These distinctions are not barriers between people. Rather, they form the diversity that enhances our unity. Our unity is enriched when we receive one another and celebrate our diversity within the body of Christ. We love one another for our differences and not in spite of them!

Another point to understand is that our unity in Christ does not mean we must always be doing the same thing, at the same time, in the same way or in the same place. We are one body, one family and one church, and this means there will be regular times when the whole family gathers. However, there will also be times when the children are doing one thing, the teens are doing something else and the mother is engaged in something else, and so on.

We must always remember that our first cell is our family. The cell vision is about building families up not splitting them up! The first port of discipleship is our own family, and the second is our homogeneous cells. We also make sure that the whole church comes together in congregational meetings and in the celebrations.

THE ADVANTAGES OF HOMOGENEOUS GROUPS

Homogeneous groups allow people to learn and grow in the company of like-minded people who have the same needs, face the same challenges, share the same interests and identity with the same cultural group. Most churches accept this principle in their youth groups, women's groups and men's ministry. Young people have special interests that enable them to identify with one another. Their music, their style and their mind set all relate to their time of life. We can best address their questions, pressures, and temptations in the context of youth ministry.

The same applies to women. Many women's ministries are being raised up today. These recognise the special dynamic that operates when women come together to minister to each other. The same is true of men's ministry. Men find it easier to talk about certain issues in their lives in the company of other men. They need to be ministered to by men who share the same needs, desires and pressures.

Discipleship involves role modelling and teaching by example, and the homogenous principle facilitates this process. Only so much can be achieved by opposite gender role models. How can a man model to a woman how to be a godly wife? And how can a woman demonstrate to a man how to be a Bible pattern husband?

A general principle is 'like disciples like'. When you disciple others, you reproduce yourself. Jesus' 12 disciples where male, although he also had many women followers. In fact, they were often his most faithful, loyal and supportive disciples. Women backed his ministry in practical provision. He elevated them and gave them a very high place in his ministry, teaching and mission. But his close disciples (his 12) were men. Even when you take the culture of the day into account (theirs was a patriarchal society in which men and women were separated in most public gatherings), you can still see how this homogeneity could apply today.

Paul seems to be acknowledging this principle when he gave the older women a clear directive to teach the younger women and to disciple them.

> *The older women likewise, that they be reverent in behaviour, not slanderers, not given to much wine, teachers of good things that they admonish the young women to love their husbands, to love their children, to be discreet, chaste, homemakers, good, obedient to their own husbands, that the word of God may not be blasphemed.*
>
> Titus 2:3-5

The homogeneous principle does not suggest that the sexes or the age groups should be segregated. Rather, it means that they are discipled as men, women, youth and children. They become better husbands, wives, fathers, mothers or children, as they take their place in their families and in the wider body of Christ. As I have explained, the congregational gatherings and celebration services include everybody. The church is a family and the family must come together.

The homogenous principle works. We have seen our Christian families benefit through the men's ministry, the women's ministry and the youth ministry as each member of the family finds their special place in the work of God. We are discipling the whole family, one member at a time.

During the time of transition into cells, it is important to start where you are. Churches should introduce whatever homogeneous cell structure it is feasible at that moment and gradually implement the full homogeneous structure over time, ending up with cells for men, women and youth. Some churches transitioning into the Model of 12, may already have mixed cells in the church. These should continue until leaders are raised up who can lead the men, the women, the youth, and so on.

I strongly recommend the homogeneous structure, but please understand that not all Model of 12 cell churches work in the same way. Some have mixed cells and find other ways of ministering individually to the men, the women and the youth.

There is power in corporate strategy. Whatever method is agreed should be adopted by the whole church, for the sake of clarity and unity. Homogeneous cells should never be a point of contention. However, we should not reject something just because it challenges some of our pre-conceived ideas. For our part, we have certainly found the benefit of introducing an element of homogeneity into our discipleship process.

GATHERING THE NETS

An important part of the cell strategy is the gathering of the cells from the various Nets in the Net meetings. We regularly gather the men, the women, the youth and the children in their respective corporate meetings. These can take place weekly, monthly or quarterly. The main purpose of these Net meetings is evangelism, spiritual warfare, prayer, celebration and vision. Spiritual forces are routed and God's victory is stamped on the spiritual atmosphere. And because our Net meetings are homogeneous, the focus remains steady. When the cells get together it is like the troops assembling. All the little companies gather in their battalions and begin to think, feel and act corporately. They are part of the greater army of God and must fill their function.

This level of gathering is essential. Those who make commitments to Christ in the cells need to confirm their decision publicly and discover the wider family of God. During the Net meetings the vision is held up once again and people are renewed in their determination to fulfil it. There is an opportunity for fine tuning and repairing the breaches. Issues are addressed corporately and everyone hears the same thing at the same time building stronger and stronger unity.

But one of the greatest purposes of the Nets is to bring everyone together to praise and celebrate the name of the Lord Jesus Christ. There is nothing like going to a big meeting where

Jesus is being glorified by those who are fighting shoulder to shoulder in the trenches. When we come together we encourage each other in the fight and learn to stand strong in the battle. During these meetings, the net is cast for the lost to be saved. The Spirit of salvation is poured out and hundreds make commitments. And they do so in the presence of people ready to receive them. The consolidation process begins right away and disciples are made. The Net meetings are a powerful and effective means of winning people to Christ.

When these Nets start to operate across the city, salvation will not be far away. The Nets can grow very large. The process begins with a single cell, but before too long their numbers can multiply into the thousands.

Some ask us if we intentionally plant cells according to other aspects of homogeneity, such as ethnicity, language, or special interests, such as professions or hobbies. We find that all this falls naturally into place as people reach out to those with whom they are in regular contact and share a special affinity. We have people, for example, who have planted cells in the music industry and the legal profession, but that is not because we have deliberately planned it that way. People just reach out to others like them – it happens naturally.

MACRO CELLS
However, there are two other ways of gathering the cells that we do deliberately plan for. One is what we call 'macro cells' or 'Subnets' and the other has to do with congregational gatherings.

A macro cell is a gathering of a particular generation of cells under the leadership of their primary cell leader – whether male, female, or from the youth. We have found this a helpful way of building and envisioning the cell leaders and the cell members. The primary leader is able to speak directly to the entire generation of cell members. It gives a sense of identity to this group of cells and can help ensure that the message is not getting diluted as each leader communicates it to their cell members.

As we shall see in Chapter 22, where we deal with planting new cells, the macro cells are ideal for launching new cell groups. These macro cell gatherings are called 'launching groups' in the men's ministry and 'birthing groups' in the women's Net.

Macro cells can also take the form of congregational gatherings. Groups of leaders from the different Nets gather their cells together for worship, Communion and witness. They operate according to the principles found in 1 Corinthians 14:26. Each member comes to the gathering ready to share and participate in the service. The participants grow in their corporate identity and exercise the kind of 'body ministry' suited to these gatherings. The Communion services build the sense of fellowship and identity and keep people focussed on the New Covenant in Christ.

The congregational gatherings are larger than the cell groups and have a strong family feel with men, women, youth and children worshipping together. They are smaller than the celebration services which do not allow for 'every member participation'.

NETS FOR FISHING!

Cell church is a networking vision. All the ways of linking and gathering together I have just described, work together like a giant net. And we always remember nets are for fishing. The networking strategy of cells is bound at some point or other to be attractive to the fish!

Jesus first met some of his disciples mending their nets. They were fishermen, and Jesus said, "Come, follow me and I will make you fishers of men." As they obeyed that command, Jesus spent the next three years equipping them for the work of catching, gathering and cleaning a different kind of 'fish'. The picture of the net is an abiding one. The process Jesus established has continued down through the ages. Using it, we catch the fish of today – men, women and children in need of the life he offers.

The cell vision acknowledges that there is much more to church life than the cells. The basic work is done in the cells, but the cells must come together in the Net meetings, in macro cell gatherings, in congregational assemblies and in the celebration services. All these occasions introduce the new believers to the wider church body of which they have just become a part.

KIDS IN THE VISION

Many people understand how the cell vision works for the men's, women's and youth Nets. We simply build the cells through the Ladder of Success. But how do we minister to kids through the cells?

This work was pioneered in Kensington Temple by our children's pastor during our time of transition into the Model of 12. The Sunday services give us the opportunity to gather the children of our members and minister to them through cells.

Children's cells

Under the supervision of the adult leaders of the Children's Net, the regular 'Sunday school' ministry of the church was organised into kid's cells, with the older children helping lead the younger children.

The *Womb Ministry*, which offers pre-natal support for pregnant women and their husbands, instils the need to think of children in the womb as 'belonging to the Lord'. According to 1 Corinthians 7:13, the children of Christian parents are 'targets' of God's grace and covenant blessings. Through this ministry, expectant parents receive prayer, counselling and advice and, from the very beginning, the vision for ministry to children is explained.

The children are never considered too young to be involved in the vision. They are part of the church of today, not just of tomorrow. The crèche is named *Baby Praise*, and we minister to the babies with music and play activities that build the values of the cell ministry.

When the children are old enough to start their own cells outside the church building, they already understand the cell vision and are skilled in all its disciplines – prayer, witness, consolidation and discipleship.

The children's workers gather the children in the regular Kids Net, lead mini Encounters (within the church building) and take the children on missions. The children pray for the Lord to give them messages from Jesus to those they will meet in the shopping centre or another 'safe area', under the close supervision of parents and adult children's workers. Healings, words of knowledge and conversions to Christ are a regular feature of these outings.

Some of the older children (9 years and above) start cells with their friends in their homes and the schools. Parents are always involved and the children's team helps direct and supervise the children's activities. Some children are proving to be effective cell leaders winning many of their school colleagues to the Lord. By the time they are 14 or 15 they are accomplished 'ministers' of the gospel!

The transition into the Youth Net begins with the 'boys to men' and 'girls to women' programme. This is an important season in their lives and each child is given an older mentor to look up to and to prepare them to join the youth ministry. These teenagers move into the younger youth group that meets every Sunday near the church and soon become an active part of the Youth Net.

Age groups

More information on how we work with the children is detailed in our booklet *Kids in the Vision*. Here, I will draw from this material and explain the various stages we implement for the age groups within the children's ministry.

I have mentioned the *Womb Ministry* for the unborn and the *Baby Praise* for children from 0–4. The 5–9 year olds are grouped together as *Capital Kids* children. This is a time when they can begin to make progress on the Ladder of Success. At the age of 5, they can be consolidated, and at the age of 7, they can enrol in the School of Leadership (assuming that they have completed the other two steps, love Jesus and want to become a leader). These children are growing into their leadership. Our vision is to see them grow up in a church where the biblical pattern of Christianity is the norm, where all share the gospel without fear and where signs and wonders are experienced by every age range.

Carrying the Fire Worldwide, is the name for the 10-14s group. This is a key age range that covers an important transition from childhood to adulthood and marks another important transition from the Children's Net into the Youth Net.

We choose to start this step at the age of ten, so that the leader for this group can begin to build a strong relationship with the cell before they transition into secondary or high school, where peer pressure to conform to non-Christian ideas is stronger. This relationship with the cell leader helps to keep them strong in their faith. Indeed they can start their new school with the attitude that they are going to impact it for Jesus.

From children to youth

Many children's ministries transition children to the youth ministry at the age of 12. However, this is often a key time of searching and working out personal identity. It is a time when a familiar leader can have a great influence in a young person's life, reminding them of the promises of God and holding them within the church. By the age of 14, the young people are more established as to who they are in themselves. They are more ready to be able to have a transition that does not rock their whole lives.

The young people have also reached a stage of maturity where they are more able to interact as friends with those who are older than them. A 15 year old and a 20 year old can get on with each other, but between the ages of 13 and 15 there are vast developmental differences. The speciality of children's ministry is the ability to adapt the cell material to groups of children with a wide range of development and to communicate to all of them in an age appropriate way.

Of course, the terminology used for this age group is important. They do not want to be seen as children, and indeed they are not children from the age of 13. That is why we give them a special Subnet meeting of their own, rather than the regular Children's Net. This frees them to be themselves without the fear of being labelled 'children'.

These different age groups each have their own unique ways of being ministered to. They each have their own individual challenges and joys (each is made up of individual unique children). They each have different ways of relating to the adults over them. Many leaders will feel more comfortable working with one age group rather than another. Because of this, most children will remain with the same leader within one Subnet, enabling a good relationship to be built up and then they only change leaders when they move up an age group led by someone who is more comfortable relating to children within that age range.

We explain how we minister to the youth in the booklet, *Ministering to Youth*. Both this booklet and the brief description of Children's ministry I have given here show the kind of flexibility possible in all the different Nets. There is no blueprint, no 'one size fits all' approach. We need to bear this in mind as we approach the next section of this book where we begin to look at the detail of the Model of 12.

Part 3

The Model of 12

Why a Model?

So far in this book, I have been emphasising general principles of Christian life and ministry. I have been building a foundation, using the values that undergird the cell vision. From now on, we begin to look at the specifics of the Model of 12. We are going to see how this cell model enables us to fulfil the plan of God for his church by organising ourselves to obey the Great Commission. But we must be sure we understand the importance of having a clear and workable model that will enable us to act on our godly desires to be disciples and disciple makers of others.

If you show people the possibility of reaching their potential for God and equip them to do it, they will respond with enthusiasm and energy. God has placed in every believer the desire to reach out and attain to their high calling in Christ. The role of leadership is to recognise that desire and find ways of helping people fulfil it. That's where a model becomes necessary. It simply will not happen unless we organise ourselves practically around the vision and purpose God has for us.

The cell model is just such a structure. It is proven to be an effective way of fulfilling Christ's Mandate. The structure that supports the cell vision is like the scaffolding erected around a building. It is not part of the building, but enables the building development to go ahead. The cell model is also like the support structure that upholds the vine trees in a vineyard. Without such structures the vine would not yield fruit – or at least not as it could. This is the difference between wild vines and cultivated ones. In vineyards, vine trees are usually supported by posts, wires or some other physical framework, such as a trellis. The structure does not produce the fruit – the vine tree does that. But the structure supports the vine and maximises its fruitfulness.

The way we structure ourselves as churches, either helps or hinders the life of the 'vine'. But, no model can do the work of the 'vine' itself. In other words, the cell model is only a tool. We must use it with skill and, as we do, rely on the Holy Spirit to produce the fruit.

WILD OR CULTIVATED VINE?

You can have a brilliant cell model in place, but that does not guarantee results. But without a model to use, the chances are that the discipleship in your church will be haphazard and patchy. It will resemble the wild, uncultivated vine growing in the forest, which bears some fruit but falls short of its full potential. With an effective model you can involve the whole church in intentional discipleship. Cooperating with the Holy Spirit in this way, leads to an abundant harvest of quality fruit.

When leaders set in place inspiring structures for fruitfulness and work together with their people united in heart and purpose, it is amazing what can be achieved. The highest levels of ministry attainment come when passionate people rise to Christ's challenge, provided you resource them, support them and release them into his purpose for their lives.

Structure and planning are important in daily life. We plan our holidays, make arrangements with our friends, make shopping lists, and so on. We also set goals and organise ourselves to accomplish the things we really want to achieve. Even when embarking on a simple journey, we ask ourselves where we want to be in relation to where we are and work out the way to get there. If we do not order our lives, we will not achieve much. We must structure our lives effectively in order to fulfil the goals that are really important to us.

This is why it surprises me that some people think the cell structure makes the process of serving God mechanical. The cell-structured church releases people to fulfil the call of God, provided we remain flexible and open to the Holy Spirit, depending on him rather than on our structure. After all, the church is a living organism not a corporate organisation, with its goals, targets, sales techniques and management systems. Nevertheless, a church that is serious about serving God and being fruitful for him, will set goals, plan well, put structures in place and release resources to fulfil the vision it is passionate about.

STRUCTURES CARRY INTENT

For churches, structures are their statements of intent which, if taken seriously, lead to specific action which in turn brings about a desired result. They are statements of faith about what we want to achieve for God. Quite simply, they hold us accountable to our purpose.

Church leaders must recognise it is not enough to tell people what they ought to be doing. We must also show them by our example and give them a practical model to follow. Take the case of prayer. We do not help people by repeatedly giving them motivational sermons, telling them that they don't pray enough, or that they ought to pray more. They know that already! But if we pray with them, demonstrating a practical and effective model of prayer, they will soon become excited about prayer and begin to do it themselves.

This happened to the disciples of Jesus. They saw Jesus communing with the Father in prayer and they said, "Teach us to do that!" They saw an example of effective prayer and they wanted to know how they could pray like that. Jesus then gave them the model prayer, which we call the Lord's Prayer. It was a model to help them put their desire to pray into action. Jesus modelled prayer himself and gave them a practical model to follow.

Paul also devised practical means by which the Corinthians could put into action their godly desire to give financial help to those in need in Judea. He didn't just motivate them to do it, but he also showed them how it could be achieved. He gave them a structure, a method they could follow in their giving. This in itself motivated them to follow through on their desire to give. People will become highly motivated to do something if they see how they can do it. Look at how Paul achieved just that.

> *Now concerning the collection for the saints, as I have given orders to the churches of Galatia, so you must do also: On the first day of the week let each one of you lay something aside, storing up as he may prosper, that there be no collections when I come. And when I come, whomever you approve by your letters I will send to bear your gift to Jerusalem. But if it is fitting that I go also, they will go with me.*

1 Corinthians 16:1-4

Paul's instructions were a simple and practical way of fulfilling God's will for them to be generous to those in need. His suggestions were clear, practical and 'do-able'. Paul, in effect, provided them with a model which they could easily follow and would enable them to achieve the desired goal. I believe that this is an important part of motivational leadership. We must provide means or models by which the Word of God can be fulfilled in the life of the church.

PRACTICAL OUTWORKING OF VISION

The cell vision is just such a model. It is of course much more than a programme or a method, but it is a model that people can follow if they are serious about obeying the Great Commission. It goes much further than mere motivational preaching about making disciples.

Preaching without providing a context for the practical outworking of what is being preached, encourages mere lip service and leads people into a false sense of obedience. Many times I have met pastors who think that believing something and preaching about it is enough. They seem to think that the church is actually fulfilling the Great Commission because they preach about it. But obedience is more than preaching or listening to sermons. It means *doing what is being preached.*

Leaders should understand that preaching a sermon is the easy part. The question is what does the leader do when the sermon is finished? Unless you offer the people a practical way of doing the very thing you have just preached, then the sermon will probably be forgotten. This Sunday's sermon will be shelved until next Sunday when another topic will be on the agenda. Unless the leader gives the people a practical way of putting the message into practice, and helps them do it seeing the process through, obedience will either be partial or not happen at all.

The cell model avoids this error. It is a way of putting Jesus' Great Commission into action. Jesus' command in Matthew chapter 28 is broken down into four practical steps: win, consolidate, disciple (or train) and send. It covers the whole process of making, maturing and mobilising disciples. The cells provide the practical context for people to grow, be discipled themselves and make disciples of others. The cells offer people constant opportunities to apply the Sunday preaching practically to their own lives and to help their fellow cell members act on the Word in their daily lives.

In the next chapter, we look at the heart of the Model of 12, the Ladder of Success.

The Ladder of Success

Success is a positive word in today's world. Everyone is seeking it. But what does it really mean for a believer? What is success in the eyes of Jesus? As far as he is concerned, there is only one criterion by which we may judge success. All that he has told us to do can be summarised by his final instructions to the church.

> *Go and make disciples of all nations baptising them in the name of the Father, the Son and the Holy Spirit, and teaching them to do everything I have commanded you.*
> Matthew 28:18-20

Your life will be judged successful only in so far as you have personally fulfilled this commission of Jesus. It means making disciples and maturing them into his character and image. The Model of 12 is a practical means by which we can all obey the call of our Master and be successful in his eyes.

Another way of expressing this is to understand that Jesus is looking for us to bear fruit. As we saw in Chapter 7, one of the main ways we bear fruit is by winning others to Christ and helping form his character in them. As branches of the True Vine, the fruit we carry is seed bearing fruit. The Vine of the kingdom of God does not produce seedless grapes. We have the privilege of abiding in him and the responsibility for reproducing fruit according to his nature in us.

This aligns precisely with the Great Commission. As we grow in discipleship, we reproduce other disciples and bear fruit as branches of the Vine, and as Jesus said, bring glory to the Father.

By this my Father is glorified, that you bear much fruit;
so you will be my disciples.

John 15:8

The secret of fruitfulness is "abiding in the Vine", or staying "connected" to Jesus. It is a natural outworking of the life of Christ in us, but it does require our active participation. A church structured according to the Model of 12 is a church where everyone works together to bear fruit. Every member accepts his or her responsibility to grow the church.

FRUITFULNESS COMES WITH BLESSING

There is great blessing in this kind of fruitfulness. God said to Abraham, "I will bless you and make your name great; and you shall be a blessing… and in you all the families of the earth shall be blessed" (Genesis 12:2-3). When you obey the Great Commission of Jesus you spread the blessing of Abraham to the nations and you step deeper into the blessing of Abraham yourself. And remember, he was blessed in all things! This promise is confirmed in John chapter 15, where Jesus says, in the context of our fruit-bearing mission,

You did not choose me, but I chose you and appointed
you that you should go and bear fruit, and that your fruit
should remain, that whatever you ask the Father in my
name he may give you.

John 15:16

As we go about the Father's business, raising up disciples of Jesus, we can depend on him to supply us with everything we need, both personally and for the mission he entrusted to us. At every level of life and living, the secret of success is to allow the Holy Spirit to form Christ in you and to use you to lead others into the same blessing – fruit that lasts! This is our calling, whether we are pastors, bankers, dentists, car mechanics, factory workers, musical entertainers or students. That is why we are here.

THE WAY TO FRUITFULNESS
The backbone of the Model of 12 is the Ladder of Success. Some may prefer to call it the 'Way to Fruitfulness'. The expression 'ladder of success' came about in Bogota when Cesar Fajardo, who together with his wife Claudia, led the youth ministry, numbering many thousands – arguably one of the largest youth groups in the world! Fajardo was giving a seminar outlining the elements of the cell vision that brought fruit into the church, and listed the following: win, consolidate, disciple and send. He then said, "Those are the four steps on the ladder of success!" The term was adopted by the whole church as a useful summary of the discipleship process.

These four steps are not unique to the Model of 12, but are embedded deep within its structure. We will expand the model more fully in the following chapters, but we begin with a brief explanation of these four steps. The Ladder of Success is not a formula but a reminder of the important elements in the discipleship process.

THE LADDER OF SUCCESS

Win
The process begins with evangelism. New believers are added to the church through friendship evangelism, the celebration services and the regular church meetings where the gospel is always presented. At the end of each of the services, the leader takes the congregation through the sinners' prayer and invites those who want to commit their lives to Christ to make a public response. The counselling team, which is made up of cell group leaders and members, joins the new believers either in the service or in a separate room, and the process of consolidation begins.

Consolidate

At this point, contact details are exchanged and the gospel is shared once more to ensure that the person understands what has just happened to them. The person is then told that someone will call them within two days to encourage them. It is the responsibility of the consolidator to ensure that the new believer is called within 48 hours, receives a personal visit within a week and is introduced to a suitable cell group.

The consolidation process continues through a series of one-to-one Bible studies followed by a special Encounter Weekend. This Encounter retreat focuses on leading the new believer into a profound experience of Christ. The Weekend covers such areas as assurance of salvation, repentance, inner healing, deliverance, the fullness of the Spirit and the vision of Christ for his church. After the Encounter Weekend there is a 10-week Post-encounter course, either in a central venue or in the cell groups. This helps establish the new believers in Christ and shows them how to live the life of freedom they discovered during the Encounter. The Post-encounter programme ensures that everyone keeps on growing in the Lord and learns how to stand firm in the faith.

Disciple (Train)

The consolidation process gives way to leadership training. The aim of this stage on the Ladder of Success is to enable every new believer to become a leader of a new cell. We believe every person is called to be a leader – to lead others to Christ and to lead them deeper in the faith. According to Ephesians 4:12, every believer is called to be prepared and fully equipped to do the ministry of Jesus Christ, which is to make, mature and to mobilise disciples for Christ. The leadership training is there to bring out and develop this leadership potential in every believer so that they will be ready to lead their own cell.

Therefore, when each disciple has completed the consolidation process they are encouraged to enter the Leadership School. The School of Leadership involves training one night a week for about six months. During this time there is a Re-encounter Weekend which helps each person strengthen their lives as they prepare for the task of leadership.

The Leadership School provides every person with teaching on Christian doctrine, personal holiness and character development as well as the fundamental principles of Christian leadership. Every student is taken through basic cell leadership training, equipping them to open and lead a cell. The goal is that at the end of the leadership training, every person is ready to start their own cell.

Send

Ideally, each person graduating from the Leadership School launches an 'open cell'. As we have seen, these cells are designed to receive people who are not yet Christians. The leader of the new cell continues to receive support, help and instruction from their original cell. As the members of the original cell start their own cell groups the original group transforms into a 'leadership cell' also called a 'Primary 12 group'. This Primary 12 (P12) group continues to multiply other cells. The 12 grow their own 12, each of whom eventually has their own cell. This process is shown in Figure 1 (see page 111).

When each of the original 12 have grown their own Primary 12, the next step is for these to begin to form teams to lead Encounter Weekends and for them to develop their own Leadership School. As the multiplication takes place, more people are needed to teach in the Leadership School. Therefore the School of Teachers trains more teachers to teach the cell model. Then the leader is free to go on and plant many more cells.

The goal is for the cells to penetrate every level of society with active Christian witness and to bring transformation through the gospel. The cells equip people to be good news in their place of work and in their community. The presence of these tiny Christian communities influences the spiritual environment, right where they are.

Our Missions focus also means that people who have grown 144 leaders are given the opportunity go and plant cells and churches overseas. We are particularly concerned about the 10/40 window. That is the part of the world which has most of the world's population of unevangelised people. A cell strategy is definitely the most effective way of reaching them. Many of these people live in remote areas of the world and are found in countries which are hostile to Christian teaching.

From all this you can see this cell vision is not just another programme. It is an effective tool to reach thousands of people, disciple them and send them into the harvest fields of the world.

PRODUCTION LINE OR DISCOVERY ADVENTURE?

You may be thinking that all this appears to resemble a factory conveyor belt. That is not a good way of looking at it. Obviously, the Christian life does not function like an automated machine. People grow at their own pace, and cannot be treated as items on a production line.

I recently heard a sermon illustration that I want to apply to working with the Ladder of Success. Imagine a multi-storey department store. The entrance is warm and welcoming. As you go inside, you notice all the goods on the ground floor. You may wish to spend some time there, browsing through the items on offer. Then, you notice the escalator to the next floor and check out what departments it houses. When you are ready, you step onto the escalator and it lifts you effortlessly to the next level. You are then drawn to the next level, and the one after that. Eventually, your interest takes you to the top floor and you look at the goods on display there.

In many ways, the four steps of the Ladder of Success are exactly like those escalators in the department store. They are always available, but never intrusive or demanding. It is your interest that draws you to the higher levels. As you discover what interests you on the next floor, the escalator is always ready to take you there. That's how people progress on the Ladder of Success. They begin on the ground floor and are drawn to the higher levels as they go forward in their adventure of discovery. No one forces them, but the next step is always available. Here is a summary of that process.

LADDER OF SUCCESS SUMMARY

Win
New believers are won by personal evangelism, through the cells and through the celebration meetings.

Consolidate
The new believer is consolidated through the Pre-encounter Bible studies, the Encounter Weekend and the Post-encounter Bible course.

Disciple (Train)
The disciple is then trained in the Leadership School and in the cell group to which they belong. During this time there is a Re-encounter Weekend and each person is equipped to become a cell leader.

Send
The disciple launches a new cell group and becomes part of a P12 group. The original leader's 12 grow their 12, making a potential total of 144 cells. The leader then forms teams to run his or her own Encounters and starts a new Leadership School. The cycle continues and the cells multiply. Congregations are

formed and people are mobilised for mission, transforming society at home and reaching nations abroad.

In the following chapters, I will deal with each of these elements in turn, beginning with 'Win' and the work of friendship evangelism.

Friendship Evangelism

15

The greatest untapped resource for the work of the kingdom of God today is the body of Christ. Any evangelistic strategy that fails to train and successfully mobilise church members, simply will not be effective. That was the secret of the New Testament church. Every member was a propagator of the faith – or to put it another way, they 'gossiped the gospel' wherever they went.

In Chapter 4, we spoke about having a passion for souls. It begins with this, but we must also work on ways of channelling that passion into effective evangelism. After 2,000 years of church history, personal evangelism is still the best way of communicating the gospel. We believe in mass evangelistic events, communication through literature, television, radio, and of course, evangelism through church services. However, the vast majority of those who come to Christ speak of the personal contact they had with Christians who loved them enough to pray for them and share the gospel with them.

Evangelism begins in our 'Jerusalem'. That means we should all share the gospel with our friends, our family and our closest associates. Kensington Temple church members find street evangelism to be effective and we win many of our converts through this method. However, friendship evangelism is our primary method, and this happens through the cells. The Model of 12 uses 'prayer triplets' or the Evangelism of 3 as a basic tool for evangelism. This means we ask cell members to think of their personal circle of influence and list the 10 people they are most likely to reach with the gospel. We then encourage them to pray for at least 3 of these people the Holy

Spirit particularly impresses on their hearts. They pray daily in groups of 3 and in the weekly cell meetings. The cell members then begin to build genuine friendship relationships with these people. In time, this creates an opening to share the gospel.

FRIENDSHIP LINKS

Genuine friendship is a key factor in communicating the gospel successfully. People are more likely to accept the message if they accept the messenger. It is a principle of mission. We have a two-fold responsibility in following Christ's call to preach the gospel – first to 'earn the right' to preach it, and then to preach it in such a way as it is most readily understood and received.

Friendship is the first step. It begins by valuing people, appreciating both their dignity and their destiny. CS Lewis, the great literary scholar and Christian apologist of the 20th Century, said in his book *The Weight of Glory*, "There are no ordinary people. You have never met a mere mortal… but it is immortals that we joke with, work with, marry, snub, and exploit – immortal horrors or everlasting splendours."

The Bible places a high value on friendship. It says, "A friend loves at all times" (Proverbs 17:17), and, "There is a friend that sticks closer than a brother (Proverbs 18:24). Genuine friendship is honest. It speaks the truth and understands how to communicate it: "Faithful are the wounds of a friend" Proverbs 27:6. Friendship is a Christian quality that should be extended to all – irrespective of their interest in the gospel. Jesus befriended Judas, knowing how things would turn out. He loved him as a friend to the end (Matthew 26:50).

This example should be enough to counter the arguments of well-meaning Christians who say we should withdraw from society and have no contact with the world. Such isolationism, which exists today in certain forms of narrow evangelicalism, hands our world over to those who have their own vision for it.

We must learn to penetrate every part of our society, linking both with 'ordinary' people, and with the 'movers and the shakers' of our age – politicians, artists, educators, medical people, scientists and philosophers. That way, we can more easily influence our world with the gospel and build a generation of disciples who make a difference where they are. That's why the cells are so effective. They bring the gospel to where people are – workplaces, homes, schools and colleges.

In the world, not of it

In John 17:14-16, Jesus explains that we are *in* the world, but not *of* it. We must love the world but refuse to submit to its evil God-hating system (John 3:16). We are to love and accept the sinner but have nothing to do with their sin.

Friendship evangelism means loving people enough to be their friends and caring enough to tell them the truth about Christ. It breaks down barriers to witness, builds bridges for the gospel and establishes a good foundation for on-going discipleship through the cells.

This means we must make time to develop genuine friendships with those who do not yet know Christ. We meet them on common ground – shared interests, social links or professional calling. We 'show ourselves friendly' by caring genuinely about their concerns, enjoying being with them and generally being there for them.

However, we must be careful to avoid some common pitfalls. Compromise never wins souls. If we do not give a good testimony to Christ and the difference he makes in our lives, our witness will be weak. We should never 'use' friendship as a tool for religious headhunting. This kind of insincerity will be exposed in a moment. The world is very discerning on this issue! We should always avoid playacting – pretending to be what we are not. Our friends must see our struggles, doubts and weaknesses. One wise Christian once told me, "Just be real, and the Holy Spirit will do the rest!"

We must not be afraid of telling our friends the gospel in clear terms even if it puts a strain on the relationship. The good news is the most important thing we have to offer others. However, the gospel must be 'incarnated' in us if we are to be good witnesses. Jesus must be seen in us. He calls us to *be* good news, not just to *preach* good news. This is where the rubber really hits the road.

What would be good news for the homeless, the rejected and the marginalised? What would genuine friends do in such situations? The answer is obvious. Loving our neighbours surely means helping them practically. Our 'good works' demonstrate the practical relevance of our message.

We are not just called to preach the gospel but to transform our society by putting Christ's love into practice. The transforming *presence* of effective Christianity is, in itself, a form of evangelism, and this must accompany the more overt forms of *proclamation* or *power* evangelism. These three elements together ensure the gospel is communicated both with practical relevance and spiritual authority.

Transformation in the work place

The workplace is a fruitful harvest field. When people begin to look at their daily occupation as God's opportunity to win people to Christ, the cell vision suddenly begins to make sense. It equips people for where they spend much of their lives – their place of work or study. This is how we can engage with today's world and bring real transformation in our society.

A lawyer, working in a busy office in the City of London, once complained to me about the expectations of the cell vision. He lived a good distance from his workplace, leaving his home very early every morning and returning quite late each evening. He wondered how someone with his schedule and commitments could possibly have time to be involved in a cell group.

I explained that the cell vision is a lifestyle and not a church programme. He began to use his daily journey to work to listen to CD recordings of the meetings he could not attend, to spend a time of personal devotion and Bible meditation and to plan and strategise for his cell ministry.

On the way home he would telephone his friends who had not yet become Christians, his cell members as well as people he had recently won to Christ. His lunch times became opportunities to speak to his clients and colleagues about the Lord. Soon he became one of the most fruitful men in the cell vision, and his witness had begun to change the atmosphere of his workplace.

SUCCESSFUL EVANGELISM

Friendship evangelism in all its forms is crucially important. Fruit does not always come immediately. I have testimonies of people developing genuine friendships for several years before these eventually led to commitments to Christ. Other times, all it takes is an invitation to the cell meeting or an evangelistic event, and the person comes along and gets saved. The significant factors are faith, prayer and patient persistence.

One cell leader was frustrated to see that by October in one particular year, she had not won a single soul for Christ. She was determined to change that. She got together with the other members in the cell, focussing on prayer and fasting during the month of November for all those who were on the Evangelism of 3 list.

She visited each person during that same month and presented Christ to them. Two out of her three friends immediately accepted Christ, and one of these had been particularly hostile towards Christianity. Without being prompted to do so, she fell on her knees and confessed Christ wholeheartedly. The cell leader wrote to me later saying, "All I did was to fast and pray for a month, visit each person, present the gospel and ask if they wanted Christ. I was surprised how easy it was!"

Street evangelism is also a successful way of winning people to Christ. Contacts are made and friendships begin right there on the street. Sometimes this is through presentations of street drama, music and public preaching. The cell team witnesses to those in the crowd who are willing to talk.

One youth team went onto the streets with a video camera and invited people to take part in a simple interview. They asked people three questions: Would you consider yourself a good person? Who would you consider a good person is like? Do you have faith in anything? The team were amazed at the willingness of people to share their thoughts on camera. The interviews opened up the way for the gospel to be shared. By the end of the morning, 15 people had committed to Christ.

The team leader later testified, "We were amazed at God's faithfulness, but we were also overjoyed by the effect it had on our cell members who had dared to believe God and to step out to win souls. Their faith has been lifted to a new level."

These kinds of testimonies are frequent. People discover the joy of sharing the most important passion in their lives with others. Fear and timidity are soon exchanged for excitement and boldness. All the effort, inconvenience and rejection they have experienced along the way are soon forgotten when the Holy Spirit uses them to lead someone to Christ. Cell church can only be successful when evangelism becomes the passionate lifestyle of each member.

Once someone has been won for Christ, the next step is to consolidate them – we must learn 'to service what we sell'. The Ladder of Success takes the new believer through a series of important milestones in their new life in Christ. We now turn to look at these one by one.

Caring for New Believers

16

Being committed to Jesus' mission means that we do more than preach the gospel. We want to see people respond to the message, become genuinely born again and go on to follow Christ all the days of their life. The cell model organises the whole church around these objectives.

Through the cells, we form strong relationships with people who do not yet know Christ. Often these friendships lead to clear commitments to Christ in the cell meetings. Therefore, many new believers are 'born' into the cell ministry. That makes follow-up and on-going discipleship much easier. The cell group that introduced the new believer to Christ is the most natural environment for nurture and on-going discipleship.

However, we ask the cell members to make sure that new believers make a public commitment to Christ during one of the main church services. We call this making an 'affirmation'. We want new believers to understand right away that there is more to church life than the cell groups. In a climate of mistrust of 'organised religion', we find people more easily accept an invitation to attend a small meeting in a home or place of work than to come into the 'alien' environment of a church building. Also, as we have seen, the cells focus on evangelism where people are – that is why the open cells are not usually held in the regular church building on Sundays. The cell vision emphasises 'go, show and tell' rather than 'come, listen and see'.

But this can present another problem. New believers can love the cells but see no need for the other expressions of church. Some cell churches have more people in the cells than those who attend the regular church services. We avoid that pitfall by ensuring that every new believer makes a public commitment before 'the whole family' of believers. They begin to understand that church involves being a member of a group far larger and diverse than the cell group in which they found Christ. The consolidation process roots new believers in the life and ministry of the whole church.

But for this to happen we must be ready to receive the new lives he gives us. Preparing to receive a new baby in a family is always an important event. When Amanda was expecting our first child, Elizabeth, I had to move out of the little office in our home. We turned it into a nursery. I was thrilled to do so – we were expecting a new life! We prepared the room beautifully, with "happy people" wall paper, a deep pile rich green new carpet, a cosy cot, a soothing night light and a cupboard full of baby clothes.

This contrasts with the inconsiderate attitudes found in many churches. There is almost no thought given to the new members – what they need, how they feel, and so on. Often, they receive a handshake at the door, with the parting words, "God bless you. See you next Sunday!" Imagine if we acted like that to a newborn baby – just pushed it out the door and told it to come back next Sunday! It's unthinkable, but that's in effect what we do with many of our new believers. As with a physical life, a new born believer needs constant care, nurture, feeding and attention – it's hard work!

THE SCANDAL OF ABANDONED BABIES

God is the supreme nurturer of new life. The parable found in Ezekiel 16:1-14, shows how he took care of the baby nation of Israel. He found her abandoned in a field, newly-born, still covered in blood and exposed to the elements. God, in his love and compassion, washed her, fed her, clothed her and nurtured her to maturity. Consolidation calls us to have the same compassion on the new-born Christians he has entrusted to us.

Do you remember what it was like to be a new believer and to be in church services for the first time? There was joy and excitement of your new discovery of life in Christ, but there was also some fear and apprehension. Perhaps you came to Christ with many problems, looking for answers. You probably wondered if the people around you really cared about you and if they could help you. A thousand questions about God, the Bible and church life probably flooded your mind. But the central question you asked yourself was, "Do I really belong here?"

New believers in your church will probably all have the same thoughts. They will be looking to you for answers and will follow your example. Above all, they will be looking for people who will be there for them and help them feel that they belong. Consolidation is all about helping these new believers find their feet and make a good start in their Christian life.

THE GOALS OF CONSOLIDATION

Consolidation refers to establishing new believers as fruitful members of the church of Christ. It is the process of retaining the fruit of evangelism and gathering the harvest into the storehouse of the church. It also means releasing these new believers into their destiny as disciples and disciple-makers of others.

It can also be defined as the care and attention we should give to new believers in order to produce Christ's character in them. By doing this, we ensure that they will fulfil God's purpose for their lives and bear fruit that will last (John 15:16). We must care for people properly and value them in the same way that God values them.

Consolidation generates commitment and faithfulness because everyone has a role to play. It mobilises the church and employs every believer in the work of the ministry. Therefore, we must be diligent in consolidation. When we are motivated by love and a deep desire to fulfil God's purpose to love and care for souls, we experience great satisfaction and bring glory to his name.

HARD WORK

Bringing up children is hard work! After the birth of our first daughter, an experienced couple with several children in their family told us to say goodbye to a good night's sleep for the next 10 years! Nurturing spiritual babies is no different.

Consolidation is like a 'second labour'. This is what Paul seems to be describing when he writes to the troublesome Galatian believers.

> *My little children, for whom I labour in birth again until Christ is formed in you.*
>
> Galatians 4:19

The first labour could well have been Paul's agonising over the souls of the Galatian people as they came to Christ. We know what a labour that is. People passionate for souls, have to 'labour' in prayer and 'agonise' in the Spirit, just like a woman in the pains of giving birth. We wrestle with 'dark angels' over the souls of men and women as we testify, preach, persuade and plead with them to come to Christ.

Then, the second labour begins. Once again, we agonise in prayer and loving concern as we weep with new believers, listen to them as they share their problems and patiently teach them the Word of God. It is hard work, a spiritual battle that Satan wants to win. Zechariah 3:1-5 reveals Satan bringing condemnation and discouragement upon Joshua, the High Priest. We must help protect new believers from similar tactics the enemy employs against them. They too, are "brands plucked from the burning flames".

I recall that after my conversion to Christ my elder brother who had helped lead me to the Lord found out that, in the few days since he had last spoken to me, I had 'come across' several heretical publications, which had been planted in my hands by strangers who were working for the other side! How quickly the enemy tries to draw us back. He hates losing a single soul.

I tell my people that if we don't immediately consolidate the new believers, the devil will! Once we have come to Christ, Satan has lost us forever, but that does not stop him from deploying has his 'anti-consolidation' processes! He certainly does not want to see new believers grow and become fruitful in Christ. We cannot fail them. We must act promptly. I insist that everyone who has made a commitment to Christ must be personally followed up, within 24-48 hours. Any later than that is too late!

There are many obstacles and ups and downs in this ministry. We are often disappointed and feel like giving up. One young woman was assigned a new believer to consolidate. The address was quite far from her place of employment and that day she had been asked to work late. She was tired and hungry and the weather was cold and wet. She had to catch several buses to get to the new believer's home and she nearly turned back.

When she finally arrived, she found the whole family waiting for her with a meal on the table. They were so glad she had come, because the daughter had told them all about her visit to the church, how wonderful it was and how she had committed her life to Christ. As well as helping the new believer with some prayer and simple Bible study, the consolidator was also able to lead the whole family to Christ. She was now happy that she had not turned back!

With consolidation, as with everything in the cell vision, relationship is crucial. The keys are persistence, patience, faith and above all, love. Consolidation is a spiritual discipline, a labour of love. But the rewards are great. We get to retain the fruit of evangelism (John 15:16) and we receive the rewards of obedience (1 Peter 5:4). There is no greater joy than seeing growth, development and the unfolding potential of a new life in Christ. We get to reach out to others and build our cell, knowing that we are about the business of the kingdom.

CONSOLIDATION TEAMS

Consolidation takes place primarily in the cells. If someone commits to Christ in the cells, then naturally the cell group takes care of the new believer. However, many come to Christ in the services or during an evangelistic event. Through our School of Consolidation we prepare teams from the cell groups to begin consolidating those who come to Christ who have not yet had any contact with a cell group.

Teamwork is essential. Jesus' words in Matthew 4:19, "Come follow me and I will make you fishers of men", were spoken to a group of disciples. He trained them in his 'cell group', and they learned to work as a team. Many of them were professional fishermen and knew the importance of teamwork in the fishing industry. Normally, they fished from two boats side by side. It took cooperation and team effort to haul in the fish caught in their nets. Then the fish had to be cleaned and prepared for the market. They all had to work together.

In the same way, the work of keeping the fruit is not the responsibility of the pastor or a small group of people. Success does not depend on one person, but upon the entire church. We have large teams of trained consolidators on duty every meeting – and we have five services on Sunday and several more during the week.

Not all the members are expected to attend all these meetings, but different groups of cells support the different services and are ready to participate in the ministry and consolidation teams. It is a big effort, but the whole church is involved in the whole vision. We all reach the lost, consolidate them in the faith, lead them into discipleship and send them out to serve the Lord.

NEW TESTAMENT FOUNDATIONS

The consolidation process is founded on the example of the New Testament church. Acts chapter 2 shows us a number of elements that the Jerusalem church incorporated into their care of new believers.

Verifying salvation (Acts 2:41)

It was normal for the genuineness of salvation to be verified beginning with repentance from sin and confession of Jesus Christ as Lord and Saviour. Water baptism was also part of Christian initiation and all those who genuinely responded to Peter's preaching were baptised.

Teaching doctrine to the new believer (Acts 2:42)

The apostles persevered in teaching the new believers the doctrines of the faith. Every day, they were to be found in the Temple and in people's homes consistently teaching them the ways of life in Christ. Because of this, the new followers of Christ became an influence in the city of Jerusalem and later, all over the world. This shows that they lived out in their lives everything they had learnt.

The fellowship (Acts 2:46-47)

By nature people are social beings and we need one another to grow and develop. New believers must become integrated into 'the fellowship' or *koinonia* of the church. This is not just the informal expressions of fellowship in Christ, but also the formal commitment to a church – the fellowship of believers organised and structured together as a Christian community.

We see the new believers of Acts chapter 2 meeting daily in the 'celebration' gatherings that took place in the Temple courts and also in the 'cell' meetings in their homes. Fellowship was expressed in both these kinds of gatherings. That was one of the secrets of their success. The home meetings included table fellowship, which would have been an opportunity for celebrating the Lord's Supper. They met together in these groups for evangelism and edification.

The prayers (Acts 2:42)

The new believers participated in the regular set prayers of the Jewish Temple, but they also learned the value of Christian praying. We know that the Jerusalem believers were great prayers (Acts 4:23-31). This point cannot be over-emphasised. They learned the power of prayer and when they prayed, heaven came down and the whole city was impacted.

Fear of the Lord (Acts 2:43-46)

The fear of the Lord was the natural response to the awesome presence of God that filled the Jerusalem church. God manifested his power through signs and wonders as he attested to his Word. That way, the new believers were able to rejoice and grow in holiness of life.

Evangelistic testimony (Acts 2:47)

The new believers came to faith in the context of a witnessing community. They would have been taught the importance of sharing the gospel with their friends and their family. The Jerusalem church spread rapidly through evangelism and church planting. This would not have been possible if the new converts were not trained in the art of disciple-making.

THE CONSOLIDATION PROCESS

Building on these principles, we have established a seven-fold process of consolidation. Our consolidation training covers each one of these elements. We help cell members develop all the skills needed to participate effectively in this work. The seven elements are:

1. After service counselling (verification)
2. First week contact (phone call and home visit)
3. Introduction to a cell group
4. First steps of discipleship: *Walking with Jesus* (4 Bible studies)

5. Encounter preparation: *Preparing for Your Encounter with Jesus* (4 Bible studies)

6. Encounter Weekend (3 days away)

7. Post-encounter course (10-week course).

Beginning in the next chapter, we will look at each one of these elements and explain how the Model of 12 establishes the new believers in Christ and brings them into a life of discipleship.

Consolidation Begins

17

Consolidation begins the moment a person responds to the gospel. This response to the pure grace of God is simple faith in Christ – with no strings attached. Salvation is a free gift and we do not add any legalistic preconditions. Our appeal to follow Christ makes it clear that Jesus accepts us just as we are. However, we also stress that new believers are beginning a new life as disciples of Christ. Each respondent is invited to pray a prayer of salvation including the following elements:

- Their need of God: "I need you"
- Their condition: "I am a sinner"
- Their repentance: "Forgive me"
- Their acceptance: "I put my trust in you – I want to live for you".

We usually invite those who pray the prayer of salvation to the front of the church to emphasise that they are joining the family of God who publically welcome and celebrate their arrival. They are accompanied by their friends from the cell group and the consolidators who are on duty at that meeting. We explain the gospel again in simple terms and emphasise that if they have genuinely prayed the prayer of salvation then Jesus is now with them, just as he promised. Next, we pray for each person that Christ would make this experience real and help them as they begin new life in him.

Then we find a quiet place so that we can spend brief uninterrupted moments one-on-one with them after the service. We have a consolation room behind our church platform dedicated to this purpose. We suggest that a friend joins them and make sure that children are always accompanied by an adult responsible for them. Then the process of After Service Counselling begins.

AFTER SERVICE COUNSELLING

The After Service Counselling is done with great care but in a relaxed way, without 'clip-board' bureaucracy. Men counsel men and women counsel women.

Verification

The first objective is to verify the decision the respondent has just made and to be sure that they have understood what they have just done. We also assure them of Jesus' promise that whoever comes to him, he will not turn away.

After welcoming them and setting them at ease, we give the respondents a brief restatement of the gospel and lead them personally through the sinner's prayer once more. This is to help them be sure of the gospel and the life-changing significance of coming to Christ. According to Matthew 13:19, those who do not understand the good news of the kingdom of God are easy prey for the enemy who snatches the seed away from them.

> *The seed that fell on the hard path represents those who hear the Good News about the Kingdom and don't understand it. Then the evil one comes and snatches the seed away from their hearts.*
> Matthew 13:19 (New Living Translation)

The consolidators are taught to be clear about the five major themes of the gospel.

1. Teaching about love – God loves every individual (Jeremiah 31:3, John 16:27 & 1 Peter 2:8-9).

2. Teaching about sin – everyone without exception has sinned (Romans 3: 10-12 & 23).

3. Teaching about Christ – the only sufficient Saviour (John 14:6, Romans 5:8, Galatians 3:13, Ephesians 2:8-9, Isaiah 53:5 & 1 John 1:7).

4. Teaching about repentance – turning from sin to follow Christ Acts 3:19, 1 John 1:9, Isaiah 1:18 & Proverbs 28:13).

5. Teaching the Lordship of Jesus Christ (Matthew 7:13-14 & John 1:12).

Prayer for the new believer

We begin to encourage the new believer to understand that they are loved and accepted by God in Christ (Ephesians 1:6). We want them also to begin a life of trust and dependence on God to meet their needs, so we ask them if they have any particular prayer needs and immediately begin to pray for these. This prayer will be a good point of contact later when the new believer is contacted within 24 to 48 hours. We often find that God has already begun to answer their prayers and this becomes a powerful testimony that he is at work. The new believers learn the reality of God's presence from the very beginning.

We determine whether the person is making a 'first time' decision for the Lord or a public 'affirmation' of their commitment to Christ made beforehand, during one of the cell meetings. Those who have come to Christ through the direct ministry of a cell group will be consolidated in that cell. Those who have come to Christ without the support of a cell group eventually will be introduced to an appropriate one.

Verification pack

At this stage, we explain how the consolidation process will proceed. There will be a telephone call within the next day or so to see how they are getting on and, if possible, a personal home visit within a week. The new believer then receives a Verification Pack containing a copy of one of the Gospels, an information leaflet on the church, a letter from the Senior Minister, a gospel tract explaining salvation, a declaration card they sign and an invitation to a Welcome Party. The consolidator completes a Verification Form in a sensitive manner as it contains the contact details of the new believer.

Allocation

The next step is to allocate the new believer to a consolidator for the next stage in the follow up process. As we have said, if the person has come from a cell group, they are allocated to the leader of that cell. If not, then the person who counselled them after the service will personally take care of the next step in the consolidation process. This is because the consolidator on the night has already begun to build the relationship.

The consolidator may eventually introduce the new believer into his or her own cell group. However, the objective is to link the new believer to the most appropriate group. We take into account any existing relationships they may have with members of the church. Hopefully, the cell will be in a geographical area that is accessible to the new believer.

Naturally, if a person already has some friends in the church, we involve them in this process. Perhaps they are not yet in a cell themselves and this gives us the opportunity to encourage them to join the same cell as their friend who has just come to Christ.

THE FIRST WEEK

The first week of a new believer's life is critical to their on-going Christian experience. We aim to do two things within this time frame: to make personal contact by phone and to arrange a face-to-face meeting in the home or another appropriate place.

Phone call

We aim to contact each new believer by phone, or other means, within 24 hours of their commitment to Christ. It is crucial to the whole consolidation process. Much fruit will be 'lost' if this does not take place. Other influences are at work in a new believer's life and we must be there for them to help them overcome the obstacles the enemy puts in their way.

Often, doubts are quick to creep in, unbelieving friends discourage them and other pressures from the world bear down on the new believer. The phone call is a significant source of encouragement, showing that we care and are ready to stand by the new believer as he or she steps out in their new-found Christian faith.

The objective of the phone call is to continue to build a relationship with the new believer, to encourage them and to make ourselves available to serve them in any way possible. This also is an opportunity to make arrangements for the person-to-person visit either in the home or some other place which may be more suitable. The conversation is kept simple, warm and friendly. No pressure is exerted and the contact is strengthened. Each person is treated as an individual and with genuine interest and care.

The consolidator is able to follow up on the previous prayer request and gives assuring words concerning the promises of the gospel. The new believer needs food to help strengthen them and ammunition to use against their spiritual enemy, the devil. This phone call is an important part of meeting the initial needs of the new believer. The consolidator can also assess the spiritual condition of the person. They may be jubilant or doubtful, but the consolidator is there for them. In these days of technology the phone call may be substituted by SMS texts, Twitter messages or other forms of interactive communication. It's the personal element that's important.

At this point, the consolidator will confirm the appointment for the personal visit. We give the new believers the option of a few alternatives: their home, a cafe or another suitable place. We try to make sure the meeting takes place on territory that is familiar to the new convert and not in the church building. We want to avoid the impression that everything now revolves around the church meeting place. We finish by leaving them with a short verse of scripture and pray a brief and encouraging prayer.

The home visit

We have found that personal contact within the first week is pivotal to the new believer's progress. There is no substitute for a person-to-person meeting within this time frame. It shows we are genuinely interested in the new believer's life, but we make sure that we do not behave in a pushy or intrusive manner.

Many of Jesus' miracles and most significant encounters were with people in their homes. Peter's mother in law was healed in the home (Matthew 8:14-15). It was where Zacchaeus had a change of heart (Luke 19:1-10). We also see the importance of visiting the new believer in their home in Acts 9:10-19, which tells of the 'consolidation' Saul of Tarsus received from Ananias.

The purpose of the home visit is to find out what the new believer's impression was of the church service or Christian event they attended. It is to find out what their needs are and to minister to them under the guidance of the Holy Spirit. It is also to introduce them to a cell group. At this point, we also begin to talk about the Encounter Weekend and explain the benefits of this short time away. Obviously, the consolidator does not put any pressure on the new believer and is extremely sensitive to his or her feelings. Sometimes suspicion is an obstacle to be overcome, but with careful explanation the new believer becomes more responsive.

The home visit is an ideal opportunity to answer any questions the new believer has and to give some basic Bible teaching. A short time of prayer is also appropriate. The consolidator is usually accompanied by someone from the cell group that has been recommended to the new believer. It is a time for friendship to develop. Plans are made to accompany the new believer to the cell meeting just as soon as it is practical to do so. At this point, the consolidator is ready to begin to hand over the consolidation process to the cell leader if the new believer is not going to join the consolidator's cell. The handover is done with sensitivity and the consolidator will always be available if needed.

INTRODUCTION TO CELL GROUP

The new believer is always accompanied to his or her first cell meeting. We do not just give them an address and hope they will show up. Meeting up for a cup of coffee nearby, or a simple chat somewhere convenient is always advisable before the cell meeting. That way the new believer is not left to meet a group of strangers on their own. Friendship is always the key. Each person begins to feel that they belong and that they have a new circle of pleasant and caring friends. The cell group will have already being praying for the new believer and is ready to welcome them into the group – without overwhelming them of course.

The consolidation process now continues in the cell and the next step is to present the Pre-encounter Bible studies which lead the new believer into their first steps of discipleship and prepares them for the Encounter Weekend.

From Pre-encounter to Encounter

18

Imagine, for a moment you have just put your trust in Christ and you are a brand new, born again believer. What might you need to understand about the journey you have just begun? Looking back on your own Christian experience, what do you know now, that would have been helpful to know when you first came to Christ? Pondering questions like this will enable you to become an effective consolidator.

New Christians must receive more than Bible teaching, although it is essential for their growth. They need to experience the warmth of fellowship and the reassurance of Christian friends who care about them. Think how you might present the following spiritual truths to a new believer and re-enforce this teaching through the relationships within the cell group:

- It is important from the very beginning that you become strong in your faith and that you set your life in the right direction – the direction of Christ and his glory.

- Christ, who saves you by his grace, leads you step by step into the fullness of the Father's kingdom.

- He is always with you by his Holy Spirit and he draws other believers around you so that you can grow together as his disciples.

- The moment you believe in Jesus, trusting him and him alone for your salvation, you are perfectly qualified for heaven. In fact, you are already seated with him in heavenly places and your life is now hidden with Christ in God.

- The assurance of God's loving acceptance and divine favour encourages you to change the way you live. The Holy Spirit in you transforms you to be like Christ.

- God wants you to become fruitful. This will happen as you discover more about the Lord Jesus, his everlasting kingdom and the blessings he has showered upon you.

- The consolidation process helps make sure that new believers understand and experience all these important truths at the beginning of their Christian life.

THE THREEFOLD ENCOUNTER PROCESS

As we have seen in our overview of the Ladder of Success in Chapter 14, the Model of 12 helps lead new Christians through a threefold process of consolidation: Pre-encounter, Encounter, Post-encounter. It begins the moment they make a declaration of faith in Christ. Ideally, the ground has already been prepared by the cell members who were instrumental in bringing them to Christ.

The two part Pre-encounter Bible study helps ground new believers in basic Christian teaching and prepares them for the Encounter Weekend. During this period, the new believer is taught some basic principles of life transformation. Their relationship with other cell members deepens and they begin to anticipate the Encounter Weekend where they will have a profound experience with Christ.

The New Believers Encounter is then followed by the Post-encounter course which we call *Living Free!* This is a 10-week programme, during which a Facilitator leads the small group discussions which follow the main preaching sessions. I shall cover the Encounter and the Post-encounter steps in the following two chapters. But first, I shall examine the Pre-encounter process in detail.

THE PRE-ENCOUNTER

Relationship building is of paramount importance in the Pre-encounter stage of a new believer's life. We seek to foster a sense of belonging so that the person can begin to develop in an environment of acceptance and genuine friendship. The care extended through the cells is both practical and spiritual. The new believers can freely ask questions, share their problems and joys as well as express their fears and doubts. Practical needs are also met in the true spirit of community. As relationships develop the cells rapidly become a 'second home' for the new converts.

As we have seen, cells are not just small midweek church meetings. Cells are groups of people in committed relationship with each other and the Lord, seven days a week. Discipleship is 'caught' through example and imitation. The new believer becomes part of a group of Bible-believing practitioners of Christ's way, not those who merely study the Bible together once a week. Establishing new believers in the cell groups is one of our primary objectives during the Pre-encounter stage of their development.

New Believers' Log Book

Early on in this process, each new believer is given a booklet entitled *My Spiritual Journey* which contains some teaching on the cell vision and highlights key stages of their spiritual growth. It helps encourage them to progress in their spiritual life as they walk step by step through the cell vision, beginning with their decision to follow Christ until the moment they open their own cell group, and go on to influence their world for Christ.

The new believers record their personal journey in the log books where each stage is clearly indicated. They can easily see the next step and are encouraged to take it. This is not a pressure technique, but a useful tool for discipleship. Each major stage in the journey is marked by a 'certificate' which is signed by the cell leader when the new believer completes that step:

- First-time commitment or public affirmation of believing in Christ
- Baptism in water
- Baptism in the Spirit
- Pre-encounter studies
- Encounter Weekend
- Post-encounter (*Living Free!* Course)
- Evangelism of 3 (Prayer and witness triplets)
- Leadership Training (Terms 1 & 2)
- Re-encounter (preparing prospective leaders)
- Opening a new cell.

The first part of the Pre-encounter teaching is a four week Bible study series called *Walking with Jesus*. The second part is another four week series entitled *Preparing for Your Encounter with Jesus*. The cell leader is responsible to make sure every cell member receives this teaching. It can take place during the cell meetings, if there are a significant number of new believers present. It can also happen before, alongside or after the cell meeting, if there are only one or two new believers in the cell group.

Sometimes, we organise special Consolidation Groups consisting entirely of new believers. These groups are an ideal way of starting new cells where existing cells cannot accommodate the geographic, relational or scheduling needs of the new believers. Our *Discipleship Cell Explosion* booklet, *Consolidation Groups* gives a detailed explanation of how these groups function and how they are led.

Another approach is to hold the consolidation Bible studies at a central venue before or after the main Sunday services. A pre-service breakfast meeting is ideal, especially if the new believers are taking time to settle into a cell group. The key is to provide many ways for a new believer to be consolidated so that no one is left out of the process.

Pre-encounter Bible Studies

The preliminary teaching is called *Walking with Jesus*. We deal with four topics.

Study 1: A change of direction – repentance and faith

This study stresses the importance of building the Christian life on the firm foundations of God's grace and forgiveness. We talk about being born again and show the importance of repentance and faith in the life of a new believer. We emphasise Christian assurance, showing that salvation comes by pure grace and is received by simple faith.

We lay this foundation of grace carefully, because we know that without it the Christian life simply cannot flourish. Doing the cell vision is difficult for most people in today's spiritual climate, but it is *impossible* unless the passion of Christ is first planted in their hearts. The glory of the New Covenant is the grace and forgiveness God gives us in Christ. The cell vision operates out of the overflow of this grace at work in our hearts and it leads to a life of passionate service.

Study 2: Becoming a disciple of Jesus – water baptism

In this study, we introduce water baptism as Jesus' ordinance of Christian initiation. In other words, we show the new believer that he or she is entering into the new life of Christ as part of the Christian community. We see water baptism as the beginning of the life-long discipleship process and not the graduation ceremony at the end of a discipleship course.

The new believer begins to understand that Christian living is more than having an assurance of heaven – it means following Christ on the earth. We teach that discipleship is "the life that springs from grace." God's grace shapes our hearts so that we want live for Christ and serve him as his disciples.

Study 3: Power for living – receiving the Holy Spirit

This teaching emphasises our need for the Holy Spirit as God's enabling presence. We show that the Holy Spirit comes to reveal Christ to us, lead us in his ways and empower us for his service. We also speak of the gifts of the Holy Spirit as tools for our Christian ministry and encourage new believers to be ready to exercise these wonderful endowments as the Holy Spirit moves in their lives.

Study 4: The church: belonging to the family of God

This important study helps the new believer connect to the body of Christ, understanding that the church is divinely-conceived and is not merely a human institution. We show that the church is God's family and speak of Communion as the 'family meal'. We show that through the Communion we continue to participate in the body and blood of Christ, enjoying by faith all the benefits of his death on the cross.

We also stress *ekklesia* and *koinonia*, the Greek words for 'church' and 'fellowship', showing that these words speak of the continual relationship with have with Christ and with each other. Church is living with Christ and fellow believers 24/7, not just during Sunday services. We draw out the implications of this truth by showing that the cell vision enables us to '*be* the church' right where we are, and not just to '*go* to church' at the weekend.

We direct people away from Sunday-only Christianity towards being an effective witness right where they are. We introduce the new believer to the Great Commission of Matthew 28:18-20, and show that we are saved to serve the Master who has called us to make disciples of all nations. Each cell member understands that they are called to be ministers of Christ.

The second series of Pre-encounter studies is called *Preparing for Your Encounter with Jesus*. The Encounter Weekend is usually held at our own Encounter Centre, Annan Court. The Centre is located in a peaceful part of the English countryside – a welcome relief from the busyness of London!

Both the leaders and the delegates prepare for the Weekend ahead. The Encounters are effective only if this preparation is in place. Leadership preparation is dealt with in the next chapter, but I outline here the teaching and personal preparation each delegate receives before they go on the Encounter.

We base the Encounter Preparation on four Bible studies. However, this is only the teaching material. The real preparation happens through personal discussion and interaction. The cell members share their experiences of the Encounter and this builds expectation and motivates the new believers to take this next step in the Ladder of Success.

Study 1: Introduction to Encounters

We begin by introducing the new believer to the importance of having an encounter with Jesus. We teach people to expect God to meet them at the Encounter Weekend. The New Believers Encounter often proves to be a landmark in the lives of the delegates. Invariably, their relationship with Christ is deepened and they discover the peace, assurance and freedom available in him.

We explain that the Encounter will help the new believers receive a divine intervention that will encourage them to give up their past life, experience inner healing and deliverance and hear his call to win, nurture, train and release disciples of Christ. We outline the major themes of the Encounter which build on the Pre-encounter teaching they are receiving. As there is a cost element to the Weekend (for food, transport and accommodation), we help them prepare for the modest fees that will become due when they register for the Encounter.

Study 2: Getting to know Jesus

This study focuses on the life-long process of getting to know Jesus. It is worth remembering that towards the end of his ministry, the apostle Paul's great desire was 'to get to know Jesus'. By that time, Paul had already pioneered the Gentile mission and built two great centres of sending Christianity either side of the Aegean Sea – one in Corinth and the other in Ephesus. He was also well on the way to writing, under the inspiration of the Holy Spirit, two-thirds of the theology of the New Testament. And yet, his dream was still to get to know the Lord.

We inspire the new believers with the greatest adventure of all – developing deep intimacy with the Lord. That way, they will never fall into the dull weekly routine of 'going from church to home, from home to work, from work to home and back to church again'. Instead, we show that church is a lifestyle of living in Father-facing obedience, leaving our sin and past life far behind, and going forward, attaining to our high call in Christ.

Study 3: Real change – heart transformation
This topic begins to focus on the heart – the "wellspring of life" (Proverbs 4:23). We emphasise that God is not looking for behaviour modification. His grace leads us into something deeper and more lasting than that – heart transformation. We show that gospel obedience is about becoming who we are in Christ and not striving to be what we are not. We keep the new disciple focussed on Christ and his power.

In this way, we show what it is to be led by the Holy Spirit and how to avoid falling into legalistic forms of Christianity. We help the new disciples understand that it is only the Holy Spirit who can enable us to 'put off' the old life and 'put on' the new life which Christ has given to us. This teaching links with what they will learn on the Encounter and will be developed even further during the *Living Free!* Post-encounter sessions.

Study 4: Being set free
The final study highlights freedom in Christ through the victory he won for us at the cross. We speak of Jesus' absolute victory over Satan and all the forces of darkness. This prepares the new

believer for the deliverance they experience during the Encounter. We assume that every believer will face great spiritual battles in their life and we help equip them with the spiritual weapons they will need both in the present and in the future.

We lay the foundation for further teaching which will be given on this topic during the *Living Free!* Post-encounter sessions. We want the new believer to develop a victory mindset and a freedom mentality. We teach them how to deal with the accusations of the enemy by showing that all believers are "perfect in Christ". We show them that they are greatly blessed, highly favoured and deeply loved in him. This revelation is the greatest weapon they will have as they fight fear, doubt and temptation in their own lives and in their ministry to the lost.

The new believer is now ready for the Encounter, and the cell leader makes sure that a place is reserved for them. In the following chapter, I describe how we organise the Weekend itself.

The Encounter

Annan Court, our residential Encounter Centre, is set in 14 acres of East Sussex countryside with undulating grounds of woods, streams and gardens. Virtually every Friday in the year, different groups of people from the cells leave the pressures of London behind and enthusiastically set out for their Encounter with Jesus.

Our Encounters are charged with a palpable sense of the presence of God as the team leaders have spent weeks preparing, fasting and praying down the manifest presence of the Holy Spirit. From the first session on Friday evening through to the concluding session on Sunday at noon, there is only one way to describe what is happening – people are meeting with God. Compelling worship, relevant and practical teaching, words of knowledge and personal ministry directed by the Holy Spirit, combine to make the experience unforgettable and life changing.

The Encounter finishes with a Communion service followed by a Sunday lunch, and the delegates make their way back to London filled, blessed and transformed. They have met with God. During the following week, they share their experiences with their family, their friends and their fellow cell members. The victories won on the Encounter are underlined by the *Living Free!* teaching – the 10-week Post-encounter programme. From there, the new believers will be trained in the Leadership School, become cell leaders themselves and begin to grow in their ministry.

ENCOUNTER TESTIMONIES

The testimonies that flood in each week from the Encounters speak of every conceivable blessing and experience with Christ. In the presence of God, expectations are met and needs are filled. People are healed, set free, baptised in the Spirit and receive the gift of tongues. Other spiritual gifts are also regularly released.

People who have been on an Encounter speak of a new hunger for God, a new passion for Christ and a new intimacy in their relationship with Jesus. They testify to a receiving a love for souls, a clear sense of God's call and a determination to serve him as never before. Quite simply, they are brought closer to God and learn to trust him more as they discover the Father's unconditional love and acceptance. They leave with a new boldness, assurance and confidence in their faith.

As people are released from inner pain, hurt, bitterness and resentment, many marriages are healed and many families are reconciled. Anger and domestic violence are dealt with. In the powerful presence of God, burdens are lifted and sorrow and despair evaporate. The Holy Spirit ministers deeply into people's hearts, bringing supernatural peace and joy.

People also testify to the miraculous provision of jobs and finance, as well as remarkable answers to prayer for accommodation and other practical needs. The atmosphere is charged with prayer and faith, and it encourages the delegates to experience intimacy with God. Deliverance from demonic bondages is frequent as well as freedom from other life-controlling problems such as drug, alcohol and sexual addictions.

PREPARING NEW BELIEVERS FOR THE ENCOUNTER

In the previous chapter, we examined the first steps of the Pre-encounter process. This begins with the After Service Counselling people receive when they publicly commit their life to Christ and leads to the Bible studies we give them as they settle into the cell groups. The goal is always practical and not just to communicate knowledge. This teaching builds a solid foundation for the Encounter experience.

The new believer is assisted practically and receives counselling for any problems they are facing. There is always opportunity to ask questions and to talk about any fears and doubts he or she may be experiencing. The goal is to encourage and assure the new believers that Christ is with them and the family of believers is there to help. The Pre-encounter material builds anticipation and the expectation in the people that they will meet with Christ at the Encounter. It also reiterates the basic message of the gospel.

One of the common mistakes consolidators make as they try to ground people in the faith is to assume that new Christians understand exactly what has happened to them. Many people are moved to respond to God in a public meeting, but they are not exactly sure what is happening to them. The understanding of the gospel and what it means to believe in Christ come later.

From the beginning, we must carefully explain what it means to be born again. Jesus described the new birth as a mysterious working of the Holy Spirit (John 3:8). We do not always know the precise moment it happens, although we can recognise its effects straight away. A new believer is a "new creation" – they think differently, believe differently and begin to behave differently.

Evangelical Christianity often identifies a person's conscious decision to follow Christ as the very moment the re-birth takes place. This sometimes obscures the fact that coming to Christ is a process. The Holy Spirit has usually been working in a person's heart for some time before he or she makes a public commitment to Christ. Also, the point of decision is usually followed by a growing awareness of what it means in practice to follow Christ. That is why consolidation of new believers is so important.

Throughout the consolidation process we keep on explaining the gospel to those who have responded to the appeal to follow Christ. We repeat the gospel message in the After Service Counselling session and in the early consolidation Bible studies. Our goal is to give the Holy Spirit room to do a deep work in people's hearts. We want the new convert to be clear about the facts of the gospel and the response it calls for.

The Encounter Weekend provides an ideal setting to make sure the new believers meet with Christ personally and confirm their own decision to follow him. Some look back at the New Believers Encounter and realise they genuinely met with Christ for the *first* time during this Weekend. Others testify that the Encounter led them into a *deeper* experience of Christ. Obviously, we cannot make this happen. It is a work of the Holy Spirit. However, we can prepare our hearts, pray and make room for the Holy Spirit to work.

DIFFERENT KINDS OF ENCOUNTER WEEKENDS

In this chapter, I am focussing on the New Believers Encounter. However, we have several different kinds of Encounters in the cell vision. In addition to the New Believers Encounter, we have Annual Cell Members Encounters and Annual Leaders Encounters. There is also an Encounter for those who are about to become cell leaders. We call this the 'Re-encounter' or the 'Leaders Preparation Encounter'.

Both the New Believers Encounter and the Annual Encounter for cell members are held for each of the Nets – men, women, youth and children. The Leaders Encounters are usually mixed in gender and we encourage every leader to go on one each year. This is to help us all keep fresh in our relationship with the Lord and to re-energise us in our personal life and ministry.

I will say more about the Re-encounter and the Leaders Encounters in Chapter 21, where I show how we train our cell leaders. During these Encounters we focus on vital leadership issues and important spiritual disciplines such as prayer and spiritual warfare, as well as holiness and purity.

We prepare specific material for the Annual Encounters for cell members as well as for the Annual Encounters for cell leaders. Each Encounter is preceded by careful planning, preparation and prayer. Sometimes, we have a specific theme each year. Some recent themes for the Annual Encounters for cell members are *Joy for the Journey*, *Going for Gold* and *Prepared for Battle*.

We often begin the year with a special Leaders Encounter for the Primary 12 leaders. During this Weekend, we focus on the goals and strategy for the coming year and spend time seeking God for fruitfulness. This Encounter sets the direction for the coming year and is a time of re-consecration to Christ and his ministry.

At the New Believers Encounter, we teach the material we have developed and published as a manual entitled, *My Encounter with Jesus*. But we always leave room for flexibility. In the rest of this chapter, I will show how we prepare for and conduct the New Believers Encounter.

THE NEW BELIEVERS ENCOUNTER

Leadership preparation
The success of the Encounter Weekend is sensitivity on the part of the leaders both as they prepare themselves and as they minister throughout the Weekend. We conduct special training sessions on how to lead an Encounter and we take seriously the important role the Encounter leaders have throughout the Weekend.

As in everything, preparation is the key. We have already seen how the delegates are prepared for the Encounter, but what preparation do the leaders undergo?

The Encounters are lead by a team, specially chosen from the Primary 12 teams and the wider cell leadership. The whole team meets to pray, plan and prepare for the Encounter. The preparation usually begins around four weeks before the Weekend. The team allocates the different roles and responsibilities needed for a successful Encounter.

The *Spiritual Leader* is in overall charge of the Weekend. He or she is assisted by a *Co-ordinator* and who is responsible for all the administrative and practical arrangements, and the *Facilitators* who help lead the small group sessions during the Weekend.

Leadership roles

The Spiritual Leader

The Spiritual Leader is usually from the first generation of cell leaders – a member of the Primary 12, and must be both spiritually mature and experienced. He or she will be in charge of the teaching and the ministry times. The Spiritual Leader helps shape the Encounter, sets the teaching agenda and allocates the topics to the other teachers who may be sharing in the teaching. He or she also ministers to the Facilitators during the preparation meetings and explains the direction the Encounter will take.

While there is a set manual of teaching covering the New Believers Encounter, each Weekend is different. The manual contains teaching for 16 different topics and has extensive supplementary material in the Appendices. This is far more than is needed for any single New Believers Encounter and so there is scope for freedom and flexibility.

Through prayer and attentive listening to the leading of the Holy Spirit, the team will develop a particular emphasis for each Encounter. What is most important is that the whole team hears from the Lord concerning the particular needs of the people who will be attending the Encounter. The teaching can then be shaped to meet these needs. There may be a special emphasis on deliverance, inner healing, self-image or some other particular need the Holy Spirit highlights.

The team will spend much time in prayer and fasting in order to 'win' the spiritual battle in advance of the Encounter. Prayer prepares the way for the Holy Spirit to work in the hearts of the delegates.

The Co-ordinator

The Co-ordinator is responsible for all the organisational elements of the Encounter. He or she will be supported by a team of helpers – the Facilitators who will be present at the Encounter themselves and other cell leaders who may only be involved in the preparation period. The Co-ordinator must have both spiritual maturity and organisational skills. Co-ordinating an Encounter is an onerous task. There is the registration process which includes sending out letters explaining all the practical details delegates need to know in advance of the Encounter. Other practical matters include transport arrangements, collecting the registration fees, organising the musicians and the PA system and making sure that the bookstall is well stocked with relevant spiritual literature that will help inform and encourage the delegates to go deeper into the topics.

In every preparation meeting, the Co-ordinator helps lead the prayer times and prepare the team spiritually. He or she will also help the Spiritual Leader allocate the messages each teacher will be presenting. The Co-ordinator will be constantly in touch with the Spiritual Leader making sure that every detail is in place, that the spiritual direction is clear and that every Facilitator is adequately prepared.

The Facilitators

The Facilitators must be cell leaders. They can only pass on to others what they have first received and proved in their own lives. The Encounter is not just a spiritual retreat. It is part of the process of making, maturing and mobilising disciples through the cell vision. The Encounters must never lose their cell focus. The Facilitators will be leading groups of up to 10 people each. That way the Encounter can have up to 120 delegates who will all receive personal attention.

Ideally, the Facilitators will look after the same new believers they have personally led through the Pre-encounter teaching. The Encounters are most effective when the cell leaders prepare the delegates from their cells and bring them to the Weekend. The relationships in the cells prepare the way for the deep ministry offered at the Encounter. The Facilitators are on hand, not only to minister, but also to follow up after the Encounter and bring their cell members to the Post-encounter sessions after the Weekend is over.

ENCOUNTER TEACHING

The teaching and personal ministry on the New Believers Encounter has a specific overall purpose. It is designed to lead the delegates to encounter Christ, to experience his loving acceptance and his deep assurance, to discover his freedom and to hear his call to become a real disciple and an effective disciple-maker of others. Therefore, the teaching is never lengthy or complicated. It is targeted and practical and is always followed by prayer and personal ministry – either to everyone together, or in the small groups led by the Facilitators.

Each topic has a specific objective, main teaching and key points. This keeps the teaching focused and ensures the Encounter stays on track. As we have seen, the Spiritual Leader of the Encounter shapes the sessions using both this material and also the other messages freshly prepared for each Encounter.

The New Believers Encounter themes
The Encounter Weekend focuses on a number of key themes.

- The Father's Heart – learning to receive the Father's unconditional love and acceptance.
- Assurance of Salvation – knowing for sure that you are saved and that you have eternal life.
- Repentance – breaking the habits of the past.
- The Cross – seeing what Jesus did for you on the cross.
- Inner Healing – finding release from rejection and inner pain caused by life experiences.
- Deliverance – being set free from evil powers at work in your life.
- Breaking Strongholds – a thorough deliverance from everything that binds you to the past.
- The Favour of God – learning how to walk in the favour of God.
- The Holy Spirit – experiencing the fullness and power of the Holy Spirit.
- The Ministry – understanding and responding to Jesus' call upon your life.
- Life Transformation – setting the direction of your life, now and for the future by enrolling in the *Living Free! Life Transformation Course*.

The New Believers Encounter teaching
Each of the delegates receives a copy of the Encounter Manual entitled *My Encounter with Jesus*, containing 16 separate messages, all of which may or may not be covered during the course of the Weekend. The focus is on the grace of God and builds on this foundation, climaxing in the response of a transformed heart. Christ and his cross remain central to the whole Encounter. The key text is:

From the fullness of his grace we have all received one blessing after another. For the law was given through Moses; grace and truth came through Jesus Christ. No-one has ever seen God, but God the One and Only, who is at the Father's side, has made him known.

John 1:16-18 NIV

The following is a summary of each topic:

Part one: Assurance

You are greatly blessed, highly favoured and deeply loved in God's beloved Son

Message 1 – Face to Face with God

Objective: To lead you meet God face to face.

Main message: Like Jacob, you can meet with God.

Key points:
- Repentance comes from seeing God face to face
- Brokenness means coming to an end of yourself
- Wholeness comes from depending entirely on God.

Message 2 – The Father's Love

Objective: To lead you into genuine repentance by getting to know the love of the Father.

Main message: You find repentance in the loving arms of the Father.

Key points:
- The Father's love is unconditional
- We find repentance in the Father's arms of acceptance
- We come as we are, in all our sin and he freely forgives us through the cross
- We love and serve him because he first loved us.

Message 3 – Accepted in the Beloved
Objective: To help you come out of shame into the favour of God in Christ.

Main message: You are accepted in the Well-beloved.

Key point:
• You are greatly blessed, highly favoured, and deeply loved in Christ.

Part two: Christ's perfect work on the Cross

You have forever been made perfect by the one, perfect sacrifice of Jesus.

Message 4 – The Divine Exchange
Objective: to strengthen your faith in the blood of Jesus so that you will depend the cross for your every need.

Main message: The exchange that took place at the cross (teaching material by Derek Prince).

Key points:
• The exchange of the cross means that Jesus endured what was due to us so that we might receive what was due to him
• How to enter into the blessing of God.

Message 5 – The Sacrifice of Jesus on the Cross
Objective: to focus on the glory of the cross.

Message: You owe everything to the cross

Key points:
• The cross shows the love and grace of God
• The 'religious mind' cannot understand it
• Jesus gladly suffered the shame of cross for us
• The Holy Spirit reveals the glory of the cross.

Part three: Freedom in Christ

At the cross, Jesus paid for your complete deliverance and gave you absolute victory

Message 6 – It is for Freedom Christ has Set You Free
  Objective: To show you your absolute freedom in Christ and how to walk in grace through faith.

  Main message: You have been set free by the blood of Christ.

  Key points:
  • The death and resurrection of Jesus brings us into freedom
  • Victory is complete and it is a gift of God's grace
  • We reject the legalism of the flesh and we stand firm in our freedom in Christ.

Message 7 – Freedom from Sin
  Objective: to show you that Christ has set you free from the penalty and the power of sin.

  Main message: "Neither do I condemn you; go and sin no more."

  Key Points:
  • First, Jesus lifts condemnation from your life
  • Then, he gives you power to live a life free from sin
  • God's grace is a delivering and an enabling grace.

Message 8 – Freedom from Demonic Bondage
  Objective: To show you that on the cross Jesus totally set you free from all demonic bondage.

  Main message: You have been delivered from the powers of darkness.

  Key points:
  • The devil tries to steal your freedom through demonic attack
  • But, as you focus on our righteousness in Christ, you can overcome his every attack.

Message 9 – Freedom from the Curse of the Law
Objective: To show you how you can avoid falling back under the effects of the curse of the law.

Main message: Don't fall back into the bondage of the law.

Key points:
• You have been set free from the curse of the law
• No other curse has any hold on you
• You are blessed and not cursed
• The devil cannot curse those whom God has blessed.

Message 10 – Freedom from Negative Judgements
Objective: To show how you can be free from the bitter-root judgements you may have made against others and yourself.

Main message: Dealing with negative judgements (against yourself and others).

Key points:
• Bitter-root judgements come from your inner pain
• You make them against yourself and others
• Forgiveness is the key
• You release others and yourself by living in the grace God has given to you.

Message 11 – Breaking the Strongholds of the Mind
Objective: To show you how you can overcome Satan in the key battleground of the mind.

Main message: Defeating Satan through your position in Christ.

Key points:
• Accusation is the greatest weapon of the enemy
• He tries to bring you into bondage by convincing you that you are still under the condemnation of your sins
• And that you are not worthy of God's blessing
• But you do not have to do more to be free or to be blessed
• You simply assert your freedom in Christ over the strongholds of the mind.

Part four: Living in the favour of God
You will bear fruit and prosper because you are under the favour of God

Message 12 – Walking in the Favour of God
Objective: to show you that you are under the favour of God because you are in Christ.

Main message: By grace, God brings you under his divine favour.

Key points:
- Favour depends on God's grace shown to you in Christ
- You can walk in the favour of God by faith
- The favour of God extends to every part of your life.

Message 13 – The Blessing of the Spirit
Objective: To show you that God's blessing flows from his Holy Spirit and to lead you into the fullness of the Spirit.

Main message: Blessing flows through the gift of the Holy Spirit

Key points:
- The Father has promised you the gift of the Spirit
- Jesus is the baptiser in the Spirit
- God wants you to receive his Spirit and be released in the gift of tongues
- He wants you to stay in the flow of his Spirit.

Message 14 – The Powerful Effects of Water Baptism
Objective: to show that water baptism is a powerful means of cutting off your past.

Main message: Water baptism, marks the end of the old and the beginning of the new.

Key points:
- Water baptism is the burial service of the old life
- Water baptism speaks of dying to the old and rising in newness of life.

Message 15 – Following God's Vision for Your Life
Objective: to show that grace produces effective labourers who willingly serve the Lord.

Message: You are called to the ministry of Jesus.

Key points:
- You have been saved by God's grace that you might serve him by this same grace at work in you
- The Great Commission is your responsibility
- Jesus is with us to help you
- The cell vision is an effective way fulfilling Jesus' command to make, mature and to mobilise disciples.

Message 16 – Communion
Objective: to show that Communion is God's powerful way of confirming his covenant with you.

Main message: What happens when you have Communion.

Key Points:
- Communion is a powerful instrument of the Spirit
- God pledges to act to fulfil his covenant promises when you take Communion
- Communion helps you focus on Christ
- As you focus on Christ, you are transformed to be like him.

At the New Believers Encounter each delegate signs up for *Living Free!* – the Post-encounter phase of the consolidation process. We look at this in the next chapter.

The Post-encounter

20

The Encounter Weekends are powerful times of personal liberation as people discover their freedom in Christ. However, real change takes time to be established in a person's life. It cannot be accomplished in a weekend away from the daily circumstances of life. That is why the Encounter is followed by a 10-week Post-encounter discipleship course which we call *Living Free!*

Once new believers understand that they have been set free from the penalty and the power of sin at the cross and have been delivered from every connection and association with their past life of sin, they are ready to develop new patterns of thinking and living. This kind of change is progressive as people learn to put off the old and put on the new.

This process called 'sanctification' is life-long, but we teach the new believers during the Post-encounter training how to begin to identify some basic aspects of their life that need to change and to bring them to the Lord and his transforming power. We explain that the 'new man' has been created in Christ as a gift of his grace, however we also make it clear that we all have to learn to walk in the lifestyle of our new identity in Christ.

We must learn to put off the old ways of thinking and acting and to put on the new attitudes and behaviour consistent with our identity in Christ. The Holy Spirit enables us day by day to replace the things that belong to our former way of life with the new ways of life in Christ.

The course is usually conducted in a central venue with the help of the cell leaders. Each Primary cell leader could run his or her own *Living Free!* programme. However, the centralised approach seems to suit most people.

LIFE TRANSFORMATION

The *Living Free!* Course is demanding but rewarding. Both new believers and long-established Christians, speak about it in glowing terms. By thorough discipleship training, it enables people to get to grips with the practical outworking of their new life in Christ. The goal is life transformation.

The first objective is to help the people on the programme to develop a delightful, daily devotional life. A devotional guidebook in the form of a spiritual journal called *120 Days with Jesus* takes the delegates through a daily scripture reading, following the themes from the *Living Free!* teaching. They share what they receive from this devotional each week in the small group sessions during the course.

The second part of the course helps the new believer grasp the process of putting off the old and putting on the new, as they connect with the deeper issues of the heart. We concentrate on transforming the inner person, showing that behavioural change is the result of the renewing of the heart and the mind in the power of the Holy Spirit.

Finally, those on the course select an area of their life they feel the Holy Spirit is directing them to change. The *Living Free!* Manual presents a wide range of life issues to choose from. The objective is for each person to experience change in one important area. Once they have seen this change, they can continue to respond to the Holy Spirit's call for change in other areas, once the Post-encounter is over.

The *Living Free!* teaching takes place one evening a week alongside the Leadership School. All the students meet together for worship before going to their respective classes. We begin with the teaching for the evening which is followed by small group sessions led by trained Facilitators who help the students apply the teaching to their lives personally. We call this the *Transformation Track* and it is where the real work takes place. The Facilitators, often the cell leaders of those in the groups, involve each person in the process of sharing, asking questions and doing the practical assignments.

Everything is designed to help establish the new patterns of life and living. The new believers begin to grasp what life in Christ is all about – walking in the grace and favour of God, surrendering to his Holy Spirit and living out their call to be like Christ in life and ministry.

Normally, everyone who is on *Living Free!* has been through the New Believers Encounter before enrolling for the course. However, each person on *Living Free!* is invited to attend a special *Living Free!* Encounter Weekend during the course and receives ministry for the issues the course highlights. This Weekend re-enforces the Post-encounter teaching and gives time for the Holy Spirit to do a deep work in people's hearts.

The course climaxes with Jesus' command to make, mature and mobilise disciples, and by the final session each new believer is ready to go through the Leadership School.

LIVING FREE! TOPICS

There are 10 topics, one for each week's main teaching session:

1. Your Devotional Life
2. The Family of God
3. Your Testimony
4. Real Change
5. The Fruit of the Spirit
6. Inner Healing
7. Handling Your Emotions
8. Free Indeed
9. The Spirit-filled Life
10. Serving God.

THE TRANSFORMATION TRACK

Each week the Facilitators take their groups through the themes presented in the Transformation Track:

1. Why Change?
2. The Dynamics of Change
3. Sharing Your Testimony
4. Renewing Your Mind
5. God Meets All of Your Needs
6. Discovering Your Idolatrous Beliefs
7. Walking in Freedom
8. Choosing to Change
9. Putting-off and Putting-on
10. Making Change Stick.

LIFE ISSUES

During the last stage of the *Living Free!* Course, each person works through *one* specific area of change selected from the following Life Issues:

1. Emotional Problems
2. Sexual Problems
3. Freedom from Homosexual Sin
4. Marriage and Family Problems
5. Children and the Family
6. Returning to God's Order in the Home
7. Freedom from Occult Bondage
8. The Ministry of Deliverance
9. Developing a Healthy Self-image
10. Forgiveness and Inner Healing
11. Dealing with Drug and Alcohol Problems
12. Financial Problems.

At the end of the course, certificates of completion are presented to each person and there is a time of testimony and commissioning. By now the new believers are well established in the life and ministry of the cells, and have completed the consolidation process. This evening coincides with the end of the Leadership School (*Mastering Leadership*). Everyone meets together for celebration, awarding of certificates, testimony, and progresses to the next step in the Ladder of Success. The *Living Free!* students sign up for *Mastering Leadership*, and those who have completed the leadership training go on to plant their own cells.

Throughout this process each cell member is encouraged and supported by the cell leader and the rest of their group. The Sunday preaching continues to motivate and inspire them to live for God and witness to the world. The whole church is involved in serving God and taking up the Mandate of Christ to make disciples and to extend his kingdom. The consolidation is thorough, and the cell leaders work through the process with patience and understanding. No one is forced to go faster than they are able or willing.

We teach that everyone must follow the 'pace of grace' according to their own personal experience. No one can grow faster than the rate at which they receive revelation from the Holy Spirit and apply it to their lives. Some complete the consolidation process within six months, while others take much longer, and a few opt out for a time.

Everyone receives encouragement and acceptance whatever their progress. Those who struggle in their Christian life receive the most care and attention. We teach each cell leader to be a sensitive, caring shepherd and, like the Good Shepherd, to lead gently and compassionately. At the end of the Post-encounter teaching we have not only kept the fruit of evangelism, but we also have dedicated disciples ready to follow the Lord into his mission.

Over the last five chapters, we have been looking at every aspect of consolidation. I would like to end this section with some testimonies from people who have experienced the blessing of good consolidation. It is perhaps one of the greatest joys for us as leaders – to see the fruit of evangelism remain in the church and for new believers to go on and become solid disciples of Christ.

TRANSFORMED LIVES

As with the Encounter Weekend, the Post-encounter course brings a flood of testimonies of how people have met with the Lord and have had their lives changed. At this moment, I have on my desk stories of deliverance from debt, offence, rejection, insomnia, anxiety and rejection. Others have written to me telling of other blessings they have received during the 10-week programme including:

- Increased dependence on God
- Growth in confidence in studies and at work
- Peace
- Financial increase
- Boldness and effectiveness in witness to others
- Employment
- Family restoration
- Physical healing
- Inner healing
- Release of spiritual gifts

Here are some examples of current testimonies:

"I received deliverance from shame. I feel so completely free and relaxed. I am so happy and feel at peace!"

"God brought together things that were scattered in my life and strongholds of the mind have been broken."

"God has given me a clear focus and I feel all the baggage I have been carrying has been lifted and the work has started – God is able to continue."

"I experienced inner healing due to the feeling of being loved, special and equipped for God's service. My life has value and I can truly accept who I am. God has given me more clarity regarding my purpose and greater understanding of how to use the Bible as a manual for life."

"The Lord showed me areas of life that I needed to surrender to him. I feel empowered to be on the look-out for every chance of being used by God to minister to those around me."

"Working through the material I have found my confidence, knowledge and understanding is growing in leaps and bounds. People say the difference can be physically seen in me."

"I'm changing my thinking concerning my pursuits, aspirations and goals. I'm now pursuing holiness and spending more time and fellowship with the Father. I love every bit of it and I'm trusting God more. It certainly is a life transformation for me!"

The *Living Free! Daily Devotional* helps those on the Post-encounter Course learn how to develop their devotional life, feeding on God's Word and talking to him in prayer. One cell leader told me about the progress of one of her cell members during the course:

"She found the teaching on God's love life-changing. She now realises who she is in Christ, and also her position in him. The Daily Devotional has helped her grasp the revelation that she is 'accepted in the well-beloved'. She had a really bad childhood experience caused by her parents, but through the teaching she has forgiven them and found healing for her damaged emotions."

The final testimony shows how the course encourages people to change from the inside out:

> *"My testimony is that it seems my eyes were closed and when the facilitator was explaining about emotions I started to see things differently. I began to understand how my fulfilment comes from God and not through the things I have been depending on. I have started to believe God to meet my needs and my faith is growing. I just trust God more and focus on him. I know he is in charge of my life and I now have hope."*

The Post-encounter helps new believers through the early stages of Christian living by showing them how to fix their hearts on God and develop the lifestyle of transformation in Christ. It prepares them for the next step – leadership training.

Training Cell Leaders

21

Training is part of the culture of the cell vision. Without an effective method of raising new leaders, the cells cannot multiply and be fruitful. That is why we place a strong emphasis on training cell leaders in the Model of 12. The training really works. It is the most effective method we have ever used for the equipping and releasing of leaders into the church.

The main job of the Primary cell leader is to train, mentor and release cell leaders into a flourishing cell ministry. Therefore, the Primary 12 group is the main setting for leadership development and this training happens alongside the Leadership School which takes prospective leaders through every aspect of cell ministry. We aim to prepare them for the work of planting and growing cells as well as pastoral care and evangelism.

The dearth of leadership in churches today stems largely from the defects of the traditional church model with its approach to 'ministry by the few'. Some church leaders with this approach see the highest form of ministry for their members is serving in the church. As we have already seen, the cell vision's goal is set the church to work in the world – not just to get people involved in church work. Many churches do release their members into commendable ministries in the community. However, without adopting Christ's vision of making, maturing and mobilising disciples, church ministry can become activity-based and lack the overall focus on the Great Commission.

The Model of 12 unashamedly sees Jesus' command of Matthew 28:18-20 as the job description for every person in the church. Everything must be about this objective. Therefore, training must be focussed on showing people how they can grow in their own discipleship and on equipping them to become disciple-makers of others.

As we have seen, we stress that daily life in the community is the place of mission. The daily occupation of cell members is the location of their true vocation. Cell groups can penetrate and see kingdom transformation come about in every layer and setting in society. That's why we train our members to become cell leaders and to reach people for Christ, right where they are.

John Maxwell's definition of leadership as *influence* is helpful. Every believer is called to influence their non-Christian family, friends and colleagues by their witness as disciples of Christ. Discipleship implies leadership. My own understanding of leadership has to do with accepting *responsibility*. We are all called to accept responsibility for the Great Commission and the growth of the church. The true ministry of Christ is accomplished through his body.

We have already noted that specialised leadership functions such as those mentioned in Ephesians 4:11 are given by Christ in order to "prepare God's people for works of service". That is why we believe that every Christian is called to be a leader. We are all called to lead people to Christ and to lead our brothers and sisters deeper into the faith. This is our responsibility before God. Cell leadership is an ideal way of developing the leader inside every believer. I will say more about how the fivefold ministry operates in the cell vision in Chapter 29.

Some object to this thinking and cite extreme examples of believers with severe disabilities such as mental illness and reject the notion that *everyone* can become a leader. Of course these kinds of limitations mean there are exceptions to the rule. The strong must protect the weak, not expect them to do what they cannot manage. However, the vast majority of believers do not suffer from these seemingly insurmountable problems.

UNLOCKING PEOPLE'S POTENTIAL

The real problem is that many with clear leadership potential, as well as those who seem to lack ability and confidence, are being held back by an unbiblical view of the church and its ministry. As we saw in Chapter 8, the traditional system upholds the vested interests of the professional elite – the so-called 'ministers'. We must combat this unbiblical and crippling tradition and release the body of Christ to do its work. Training our people to "win, consolidate, disciple and send" will overcome this restriction on church growth and vitality.

On the other hand, we do not underestimate the challenges involved in cell leadership. The qualities, gifts and skills cell leaders need are considerable. The training must be effective and be supported by a caring and encouraging church body, so that every prospective leader can draw from the wisdom and expertise of others.

Cell leaders are the first line of pastoral care in the church. They must be ready to give themselves to the principles of godly shepherding. They must have a heart for people and a love for souls. They will need to develop communication, teaching and management skills. They must be servant-hearted and not authoritarian in their leadership. They must be able to gather people and be faithful in the ministry of Christ. The keys are effective training and on-going support from their leaders in the cell structure.

We have other courses besides basic cell leadership training, and these equip cell leaders, who are committed to 'life-long learning', for every aspect of spiritual ministry. Through on-the-job training and a commitment to continue to develop their leadership knowledge, attitude and skills, cell leaders can rise to the highest level of their gifts and calling in the church and the world.

We have developed a series of 12 manuals entitled *The Sword of the Spirit*. These manuals provide on-going doctrinal and practical teaching on a wide range of biblical themes. Cell leaders are resourced well into their ministry with this kind of teaching. We provide Sunday teaching sessions, midweek meetings and on-line learning tools to provide as many training outlets as possible and to make these courses accessible.

Alongside our cell leadership training known as *Mastering Leadership* we have a full-time Bible School called *The International Bible Institute of London*. Each student is first trained as a cell leader and then is equipped to fulfil their ministry as an apostle, a prophet, an evangelist, a pastor or a teacher. This full-time school is open to students from around the world who come to learn about the cell vision and to take it back to their own nation. Whereas the Bible Institute focuses on the fivefold ministry, our basic cell leadership training concentrates on raising up leadership for the cell vision in our local church.

CHARACTER DEVELOPMENT

Cell leadership training uses the discipleship model and the Primary leader is responsible to see the prospective cell leader grow in their character and Christ-likeness. The classroom work in our *Mastering Leadership* programme would be totally ineffective if the Primary cell leader did not accept his or her responsibility to disciple their members into leadership.

We look at a person's character and not just their ability, spiritual gifts, or personality. It is interesting to notice that of all the many qualities the apostle Paul considered necessary for spiritual leadership (in particular, elders and deacons) in 1 Timothy 3:1-13, only one has to do with desire and only one to do with ability. The rest are about Christian character. I breakdown these leadership qualities in the following way:

1. A desire for service (v1)
2. Without blame (v2)
3. Faithful husband (v2)
4. Temperate (v2)
5. Able to teach (v2)
6. Not a drunkard (v3)
7. Not violent (v3)
8. Gentle (v3)
9. Not quarrelsome (v3)
10. Not a lover of money (v3)
11. A good leader of his family (v4)
12. Has the respect of his children (v4)
13. Not a new convert (v6)
14. A good reputation with the non-Christians (v7)
15. Worthy of respect (v8)
16. Sincere (v8)
17. Honest (v8)
18. Genuine in faith (v9)
19. Proved to be faithful (v10)
20. Not an evil talker (v11).

This list shows us what our training should focus on. But we must be patient. It takes time to make and mature a good leader. Cell churches are often accused of putting people into leadership too soon. However, we take seriously the need to prove every leader to be faithful and mature before we appoint them. Every potential leader must first be proved to be a faithful servant in the cell and always has a mentor or coach to help them develop.

On the other hand, we recognise that spiritual maturity is not always related to age or the length of time people have been Christians. It is about having the qualities that Paul sets forth as the standard for leaders. We must also remember that not everyone carries the same level of leadership calling and some will grow into positions of stronger responsibility and authority than others. The beauty of the cell vision is that there is a place for everyone to develop the ministry God gives them.

'RAW MATERIAL'

The leadership cells are an ideal context for developing the character of Christ from the 'raw material' of people's lives. Before Michelangelo sculpted his masterpiece 'David', he 'saw' the potential in the stone. God does the same with each one of us. As the apostle Paul declared "We are God's workmanship (God's 'work of art') 're-created' in Christ Jesus to do good works which God prepared in advance for us to do" (Ephesians 2:10). Primary cell leaders depend on the Holy Spirit for the ability to see what God sees and the skill to shape people for their destiny.

Prospective cell leaders will be diamonds in the rough, needing to be formed and shaped. Formation is the principal work of the Group of 12. Jesus' disciples were at first unproven and unlikely candidates for apostleship. I doubt they would have been chosen for great positions in today's church. But Jesus worked with them for three years or more and gradually shaped their character, disciplined their behaviour and trained them for ministry. Then he released his power upon them sending them to be his witnesses to the ends of the earth.

The key here is potential. The man who mentored me, Wynne Lewis, was the former senior pastor of Kensington Temple, and he often said, "Any fool can see the obvious, but it takes discernment to identify the potential that someone has." We find it easy to see people's faults but often fail to recognise their potential as leaders. When developing a leader, we must learn to look beneath the surface and see the hidden treasures within them. Once you understand this, you can then help bring this potential out and develop them as leaders.

Some time ago, I invited a particular man to be part of my Primary 12, but he was not quickly accepted by the others who could see no reason for his inclusion. I pointed out to some of them that many at first had not seen their potential as leaders either. Now this member of the team has seen much fruit and proved his leadership many times over. I am glad that I listened to what the Holy Spirit was telling me about him.

KNOWLEDGE AND SKILL

In addition to character development, any training programme seeking to equip people for a specific role will involve imparting the knowledge and practical skill required to do the job. The Leadership School pays attention to these two key elements.

The students must develop a good understanding of the cell vision and what is required of them as cell leaders. They will also a good knowledge of the Bible and basic Christian theology. They will need to understand the principles of leadership and become aware of the most effective leadership styles and how to develop these.

They must have a good understanding of how to motivate people, respect their individuality and build strong relationships. They also need a thorough grasp of the small group dynamic and how to teach, encourage and involve every person in the group. They need to know how to handle 'difficult' people – those who talk too much, participate too little, dominate or disrupt the group, and so on.

As we can see the skill set a cell leader needs is diverse. They must develop good people skills, study skills and planning skills. They need to be able to organise their time, be self-disciplined and be able to delegate well. A successful cell leader will have good pastoral and counselling skills. He or she will be able to work with and develop a team. Cell leaders must be skilled in both evangelism and follow-up. They must be humble, teachable and always available.

This long list of requirements for cell leaders makes the task of leadership training seem like 'Mission Impossible'! However, we have found that we can develop leaders quite rapidly if we apply some basic principles of cell church training:

1. On-the-job training – we best learn by doing

2. Discipling, mentoring and coaching by people who are active in the cell vision – nobody is left to go it alone

3. Focussing on oral teaching – we avoid complicated written material

4. Using a wide range of accessible, easy to understand training resources – we do not get too technical

5. Working in teams – people learn in a group and benefit from peer input

6. Practical training – people begin to put into practice what they learn from the very beginning

7. On-going development of cell leaders – we do not expect the cell leader to be fully-developed before they open their first cell. We offer on-going training after the Leadership School.

BASIC CELL LEADERSHIP TRAINING

We call our basic cell leaders training programme, *Mastering Leadership*. There are two terms each lasting 10 weeks, and they are held on the same evening of the week as the Post-encounter *Living Free!* Course. We regard *Living Free!* as an introduction to leadership as well as a new believer's discipleship course. We find this foundation to be solid and cell members who complete the course are ready to go onto the Leadership School.

The teaching given at the Leadership School is simple, yet effective. We focus on the cell vision itself, helping the students develop the knowledge, awareness and skills they need to become cell leaders. This training is supplemented by a course on doctrine so that they gain biblical understanding on the major doctrines of the faith.

However, the emphasis is on practical training that equips the student to become a good cell leader. Each evening begins with the lecture and is followed by a practical session in small groups during which the students learn how to apply the lecture in their own lives.

We have a training manual for the Leadership School which contains all the material we use. Therefore, I will limit myself here to an overview of the course to show the topics we cover and the kind of training we offer our prospective cell leaders. The following topics are covered in the basic cell leaders training programme. Our additional training expands on these as well as adding other topics so that the cell leaders can continue to develop after they have graduated from the School and started their cells.

Mastering Leadership Topics

Vision

The Vision of our Church
We want our students to understand that the Kensington Temple Mission Statement drives all that we do as a church. It is 'London and the World for Christ'. We explain the recent history of our church and what brought us into the cell vision. The students begin to understand where they fit into this vision.

The Principle of 12 – The Heart of our Vision
We seek to establish why the principle of 12 is at the heart of our cell vision. We explain our vision for growth by multiplication according to the principle of 12. We also seek to instil desire and faith in the students to have a vision for their own Group of 12.

The Benefits of Cell Church

The purpose of this teaching is to ensure that the students understand the importance and value of cell ministry. As leaders, they will need a thorough knowledge of this and be able to explain to others the benefits of the cell vision.

Spirituality in the Cell Vision

Grace

Knowing that an experience of grace is essential for spiritual passion, we ensure that every cell member's Christian faith is thoroughly rooted in God's grace. This section shows that service flows out of a deep experience of Christ's love and that enabling grace is the only sure motivation for cell leadership.

The Anointing of the Holy Spirit

Total dependence on the Holy Spirit's power is essential in every aspect of service. We teach the cell leaders how to be continually filled with the Spirit and how to release his gifts into their ministry.

Prayer

We explain that the cell vision will not work as a model apart from a deep spirituality. We want the students to understand that nothing in the cell vision can be accomplished if it is not founded on prayer. We teach the basic principles of effective prayer.

Faith

The objective is to show the students the importance of growing in faith as a leader. We establish the fact that the vision will only be effective as we exercise our faith. We explain the principles of dynamic faith that lead to effective action.

Leadership

Responsibility and Servanthood

We explain that mature discipleship involves taking leadership responsibility for other people's lives. We look at the call of Moses to show it is important for the students to know they are called to lead. We stress that our model of leadership is servant leadership. We also motivate the students to be disciplers of others.

Accountability

This teaching emphasises the importance of example in the cell leader's life. We show the students that they must model the Christian life and cell vision to their members. We also emphasise the crucial aspect of integrity in leadership. We also stress that accountability leads to success and blessing. We explain that the cell leaders are accountable to God and to their leaders and that they are not to be 'lone rangers'.

Leadership Styles

This topic helps the cell leader examine his or her leadership style and to be aware of the advantages and disadvantages of various leadership approaches.

Daring to Dream

This theme has to do with setting vision, goals and strategy in the cell. It begins with learning to dream God's dreams and ends with the disciplines of goal-setting and reporting.

Introduction to Pastoral Counselling

The goal is to give the students a basic understanding of what counselling is and how to counsel a cell member.

The Cell Church Strategy

The Model of 12
We give the students an introduction to the Model of 12 and help them see the basic components of cell ministry and why they are important.

Win – Personal Evangelism
We aim to stimulate a passion for soul winning and to demonstrate the necessity of praying for the lost. We also explain the steps to effective personal evangelism in a cell context, emphasising the Evangelism of 3 strategy.

Introduction to Consolidation
The objective is to help the students understand the importance of taking care of new believers. We explain the principles and the process of consolidation. We also encourage the students to enrol in the next School of Consolidation.

Train – Turning Disciples into Leaders
We show the students that discipleship always results in leadership. We explain that the way Jesus worked with his 12 disciples is the primary model for all our leadership aspirations and our training in the Model of 12. We speak about the basic principles of leadership and character development.

Send – Starting an Open Cell
Well before the end of the course, we encourage the students to take practical steps to prepare and plan to start an open cell. We teach what it means to be a leader of an open cell and focus on two things: personal discipleship and evangelism.

Starting a Cell Group

Open Cells and Leadership Cells

We make sure the students know the purpose of the two kinds of cells in the Model of 12 and how to lead each of them successfully. We explain that it is vital for cell leaders to understand the difference between the open cell and the leadership cell. One of the most common mistakes in the cell vision is a misunderstanding of the distinction between the two types of cells and how to operate them.

How to Kick-start Your Open Cell

Towards the end of the training we ascertain the progress of the students on the Ladder of Success. We also assess their progress in preparing to open a cell and help them devise a plan to follow in order to reach that goal in the coming weeks. The students attend this session with their cell leaders.

Principles of a Well-run Open Cell

We instruct the students on the principles of a well-run open cell. Most of this teaching is presented in question and answer form, returning to the things that have already been taught.

This also helps the students think about how they will prioritise their efforts as cell leaders. We ask them to consider how they will practically balance all the different duties – home, family, personal, work, study. We ask them how they would delegate responsibilities. We find out how they plan to maintain their own spiritual, mental and physical health in the light of the pressures cell leadership brings.

Cell Group Dynamics

This theme examines how a cell leader should lead a cell meeting and make the most of the dynamics of a small group setting. It covers how to lead a conversational Bible Study and how to involve the whole group in discussion and sharing. It shows the leader how to handle the different personalities that are often present in a cell meeting – from the quiet to the talkative.

The Friendship Factor

We help the students understand how the 'friendship factor' makes a cell successful. They look at how they can incorporate this into the life of their cell. Friendships are a rewarding part of our existence and should be the basis of a healthy cell group.

Open Cell Start-up Workshop

The aim is to review the students' progress in opening their cell. The session takes the form of a workshop in which the students' cell leaders are present and share testimonies about how they started their own cells and especially how they overcame the challenges. This helps the cell leaders to be more involved with their cell members on the course.

The Leadership Cell: Growing Your 12

The objective is to ensure the students understand the principles of the leadership cell. Once they grow an open cell, their next major focus will be to build their 12.

COMMISSIONING CELL LEADERS

During the final session of the Leadership School the students offer their evaluation of the course and share their experiences – how it has changed them and what their next steps will be in starting their own cell. This is followed by a commissioning service which is linked to the final week of the Post-encounter course. The *Mastering Leadership* students encourage the *Living Free!* students to sign up to the Leadership School.

ONGOING TRAINING

The Leadership School is not the end of their training. It is only the beginning. They will continue to grow as leaders through discipleship in the leadership cell to which they belong. We supplement this through regular training sessions on an evening in the week and during our quarterly training weekends. These present on-going opportunities for leaders to develop and to extend their skills.

Once the cell leaders have graduated out of the Leadership School and start to lead their own cells, we expect them to continue their training through other specialised Training Schools. Many of these are one day courses and are held periodically in the central church building. The main schools include the following:

- Consolidation
- Evangelism
- Missions
- School of Teachers
- School of Encounters
- Counselling
- Ministry in the Spirit.

From all this, we can see that training is central to the cell vision and that it becomes part of the culture of the church. Many churches who are interested in the cell model are sometimes reticent to adopt it, because they don't know how to grow their own leaders. The Model of 12 is effective precisely because it is successful in producing leaders.

The central training programmes are effective, but the real focus is on the cells, where people are discipled into leadership and receive on-going mentoring and coaching. As cell members discover they have a calling and begin to express it in the cells, they have the opportunity to grow through on-the-job training.

People rise to the standard you set for them and the cell vision provides the context for both the swift recognition of spiritual gifts and for these gifts to be developed. The myth of "I could never do that!" is exploded. People can grow rapidly if the conditions are right and the willingness to learn is there. But, once again, I emphasise that no one is forced into leadership and each person is able to set their own pace.

Leadership is the ability to gather and grow a group of followers. We identify those who are successfully making disciples and encourage these people to take bold steps in leadership. We present everyone with the opportunity to develop as a leader, but we know that it will be a longer process for some than for others. The heart of Jesus is to send out effective workers into the harvest field, and we never lose sight of that.

LEADERS' ENCOUNTERS

In Chapter 19, we dealt with the basic New Believers Encounter. I explained that we encourage every new believer to go on an Encounter early on in their Christian life. We also ensure that every cell member attends an Annual Encounter. It is good practice to keep our experience of Christ fresh. These Annual Encounters follow a similar format to the New Believers Encounter, but the material is usually specifically prepared each time.

I also explained that we have Encounters specially designed for leaders. The first one is timed for those just about to graduate from the Leadership School and is seen as a 'Re-encounter'. That is, it follows on from the New Believers Encounter material, going over some of the same ground and introducing some new topics. The purpose of the Re-encounter is to prepare the prospective cell leader for the ministry he or she will soon be taking up.

The Re-encounter helps prospective leaders prepare their hearts for leadership by developing their personal discipline, growing in prayer and intercession and being trained in spiritual warfare. Also, we encourage those on the Re-encounter to experience deeper levels of the fullness of the Holy Spirit and to understand that without the anointing, we simply cannot be effective leaders.

Existing leaders are also expected to attend an Annual Leaders Encounter. These Leaders Encounters are varied in content and focus. Each one is unique, emphasising aspects of spirituality and leadership according to the needs of the moment and the particular themes currently being ministered in the wider church body. For example, the focus may be on holiness, spiritual renewal, ministry in the Holy Spirit, grace, evangelism, intercession or spiritual warfare.

Leadership issues are also included on each Leaders Encounter. However, the emphasis is more on the heart than on leadership techniques. It is an important time for the leaders to receive spiritual refreshment and renewal. At these Encounters, the leaders rededicate their lives to Christ and his mission, keeping the cell vision burning within them.

Having looked at the way we train leaders and help them maintain their own levels of spirituality, we now can look at the process of planting new cells. This is the focus of the next chapter.

Planting a New Cell

22

The final stage in the Ladder of Success is '*Send*', and this is about planting new cells. The new believer has been grounded in their Christian life through the Pre-encounter Teaching, the Encounter Weekend and the *Living Free!* Post-encounter Course. He or she has also been through basic cell training on the Leadership School and is now ready to plant their own cell. Clearly, this is a big step for which there must be thorough preparation.

The prospective cell planter has been continually surrounded by the prayerful support of their Primary Cell leader and the Primary 12 group to which they belong. The Net Leaders (those who head up the Men's, Women's, Youth and Children's Nets) also meet with their Primary 12 group of leaders each week. That means every existing and prospective cell leader is accountable to the 'top level' leadership of the church. This is an important factor in maintaining unity and purity in the cell vision.

The cell planters have been increasingly involved in leadership within their own cell and have already begun to win and consolidate new believers themselves. They attend weekly leadership meetings held by their immediate team leader and will be encouraged and supported at every stage of the cell planting process.

I am often asked how long after someone has come to Christ do we expect them to open their own cell. The answer is that it depends on many factors. If the cell member progresses through the Ladder of Success in the minimum possible time and has developed the necessary spiritual maturity, then they will be ready to graduate from the School of Leaders within one year. The *Mastering Leadership* course prepares the prospective cell planter in the last stages of the second term to begin their cell as soon as they have finished the training. But this only applies to those who are already winning people to Christ and have proven that they are capable of taking these new believers forward.

Rapid and effective leadership development

It is by no means rare to see relatively new believers start their own cells. We have many cells being led by people who were saved within the last 18 months. The Model of 12 is the most effective way of training and releasing leaders I have seen anywhere in the world. Spiritual maturity is not about age, or how long you have been a Christian, it has to do with how much you have allowed the Holy Spirit to shape your life. Some new believers devour the teaching the cell system provides for them and make rapid progress in faith, doctrine and Christian character.

We must resist the traditional thinking that does not believe leadership can develop rapidly. The apostle Paul appointed Elders in churches during his first missionary journey, having founded these churches perhaps as little as six months earlier (Acts 14:23). The cell church model allows people to begin to serve the Lord and develop their leadership potential right from the very beginning and it is structured to nurture and support that process.

The general culture of the cell vision fosters an environment in which leaders develop rapidly. But no one is forced into leadership, or indeed allowed to take it up until they are adequately prepared for the task. Again, let me remind those who are sceptical about this that each leader meets once a week with their leader where they receive on-going support and mentoring. The main point is that everyone is allowed to develop *at their own pace*. No one is pushed into leadership before they are ready for it.

How to plant an open cell

We saw in Chapter 18 that some cells are planted through Consolidation Groups formed for the nurture of new believers. But, what other ways do we start new cells?

The seeds of cell planting are sown into every cell member. Multiplication is part of the DNA of each cell. The group grows through evangelism as each cell member identifies people they can reach with the gospel. We encourage people to think about whom they could most naturally reach with the message of Christ. They are taught to identify and pray for this target group which is usually those they work with, share common interests with and with whom they have the closest affinity. Long before they start their own cell, the cell member will have been evangelising their target group. Our eyes are always on the harvest fields.

Before the launch of a new cell, the cell leader will have been helping the prospective cell planter gather some cell members who will form the nucleus of the new cell. These will probably be those he or she has won for the Lord and already begun to disciple. Unless someone can reach out and win souls, they will never be a successful cell leader. Prospective cell leaders are taught to agonise over souls. Like every other aspect of evangelism and mission, cell planting is birthed through prayer, fasting and spiritual warfare. It is like being pregnant, with intercession being the labour pains.

Group, Gather, Grow

The cell is launched when the new cell leader has several people who will form the core of the new cell. Those in the core group of the new cell bond together tightly in a covenant-type commitment to serve the Lord together and to develop the cell. They meet daily to pray and to plan for growth. They evangelise together seeking to win people in their target groups to Christ and to draw the new converts to the cell.

Those in this initial group begin to gather 2 or 3 other people each into the cell. They focus on the vision God has given them to be totally committed to Christ and to grow the cell. This process takes time and much effort, but those who are determined to succeed keep the passion burning. Then the whole extended group makes it their priority to grow the cell. A group of 3 or 4 becomes 9 or 12, and they continue to grow by adding new believers through evangelism and outreach. The pool of new converts is increased by referrals from the church's consolidation teams as well as through the team's own efforts.

Once the cell group begins to grow, the emphasis shifts to discipleship, and each new convert is taken on the Encounter and then progresses to the *Living Free!* Course. The new cell leader seeks to inspire every new member with the vision of Christ for the church, stressing that he has entrusted his Great Commission to each one of them. The sense of fellowship is developed through sharing life experiences, social events and by developing deep friendships. At the same time, they continue to reach out to others. This 'group, gather, grow' strategy is illustrated by Figure 2 on page 243.

DIFFERENT WAYS OF PLANTING CELLS

The 'group, gather, grow' strategy can be applied in many different ways. There is no one way to plant a cell that suits every situation. If a church is transitioning into the cell model, new cells can be formed from existing church members and then begin to grow and multiply by implementing the Ladder of Success. The cell leader will begin with a group of 2 or 3, who will each immediately gather 2 or 3 others and then begin to grow by reaching those outside the church. However, if there is no 'pool' of existing believers to draw on, a leader will have to gather others and grow the cell entirely from new converts through the Evangelism of 3.

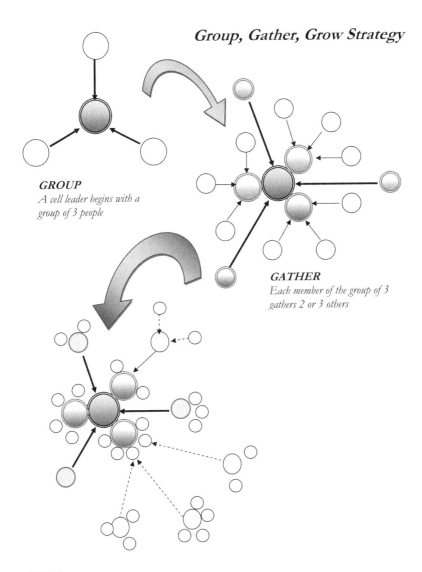

Group, Gather, Grow Strategy

GROUP
A cell leader begins with a group of 3 people

GATHER
Each member of the group of 3 gathers 2 or 3 others

GROW
The Cell grows as each member reaches out to others

Figure 2

When the cell vision is established in the church, there are many other ways in which the cells can multiply. The traditional cell model emphasises growth through division. A cell with a leader and an assistant leader grows to around 15 members and then divides into 2 cells. This process is repeated producing many new cells in the future.

In our model, many cells are planted from a single cell. We aim to see the original cell plant up to 12 cells, before it transitions into a Leadership Cell, or Primary 12 group. As the first cell grows through evangelism and discipleship, the leader encourages groups of 3 to develop within the cell. These groups of 3 can become the nucleus of new cells. When a sufficient number of people have been won for the Lord, the new cell members can become part of the new cells as they are launched.

This system of multiple cell planting works well when the original cell has a number of promising potential leaders. They grow and develop within the larger group, like babies developing in the womb. As we saw in Chapter 12, a leader who is looking after several other leaders with cells will often draw all the leaders and their members together into macro cell gatherings. One reason for doing this is to prepare for planting new cells. When cell planting is the main agenda, these macro cells are either called 'launching groups' (in the men's ministry) or 'birthing groups' (in the women's ministry).

One cell leader, who is currently using this method, meets with all the cell leaders and members in his generation of cells once a week and has grown this launching group to around 50 people. Within this macro cell there are already 4 leaders who have their cells and 5 potential leaders who are currently going through the Leadership School. When they graduate, each one will have their own cell with 5 to 6 members. The original open cell will have multiplied itself 9 times over. This macro cell multiplication is illustrated in Figure 3 on page 245.

Macro Cell Multiplication

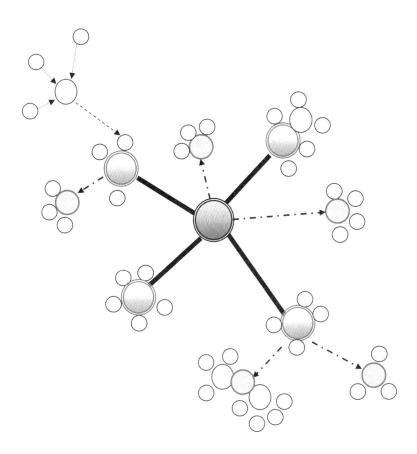

MULTIPLICATION

In this macro cell, 4 leaders have their own cells with strong bonds of friendship developed in their groups. 5 Potential leaders are gathering their groups of 3 through the macro cell contacts, preparing their own cells for launch.

Figure 3

TRANSMITTING DNA

As in the case of biological cells, each new cell carries the genetic material transmitted to it by the parent cell. This principle is vital in planting new cells. The potential new cell leaders and members must carry the vision and values of the church body. That is why the discipleship method is so successful. The parent cell carries the DNA of the body to which it belongs and reproduces this DNA in the new cell leaders and members.

In this way, the character and integrity of the body is upheld and the spirit of independence is checked. As we began to see in Chapter 9, cells in the human body are not independent, autonomous organisms. Each cell carries the unique genetic blueprint of the body to which it belongs. They work together to form organs, tissue and biological systems which function interdependently for the good of the whole body. However, each single cell is a functioning unit it its own right, regardless of its place in the body. In Chapter 29, I will suggest some other helpful parallels between a cell church and how cells operate in the human body.

GROWING THE NEW CELL

As the cell group grows, the cell leader introduces basic cell structures assigning responsibilities, introducing evangelistic strategies and helping people to develop the groups of 3 within the cell. He or she begins to delegate significant responsibility to the most promising cell members helping them train and expand their own leadership skills. The primary objectives of the leader are to foster heart relationships, solidarity and unity of purpose in the cell. He or she shows the cell members their duty to stand together, to support one another and to pray constantly for their fellow cell members. The leader makes sure that every cell member gets to know the Model of 12 thoroughly and that they understand the part they play in reaching out to others and to build the cell.

Developing a leaders' cell

When the open cell grows to a significant number, it is time to think about multiplication. The cell leader will have been preparing cell members for leadership, delegating more and more responsibility to them and ensuring they attend the Leadership School. One by one, these cell members prepare to plant their own cells. The cell leader gives concentrated time to these prospective cell planters, meeting with them separately before or after the regular cell meetings. When a sufficient number of cell members have their own cell, the open cell transforms into a leadership cell and the cell members from the original cell who are not yet leaders become part of a cell belonging to new cell leaders.

The leader of the original open cell now has a Primary cell, made up of leaders. The agenda changes from evangelism and nurture of new believers to leadership development. The leader is on the way to have his or her own 12. This team of disciples models its agenda on Jesus and his 12. This group stays together indefinitely and it is the real strength of the Model of 12 cell structure. The commitment levels are high, friendships are deep and the team grows in effectiveness. I will say more about developing and leading a Group of 12 in the next chapter.

The groups of 12 which are at the heart of the Model of 12 continue to multiply their cells aiming for the 144 level. This is when a leader's 12 have their own 12 leading cells in their 'generation' of cells (see Figure 1 on page 111). Multiplication according to the factor of 12 can bring rapid and lasting growth as every cell leader is both being discipled and discipling others.

Here we can see the importance of working the Ladder of Success. The whole process depends on every person learning how to win, consolidate, disciple and send. It is like a revolving escalator – a continuing cycle. The passion to serve Christ effectively drives the process forward. We assume nothing and 'inspect what we expect'. We monitor our progress at every stage making sure that we are not neglecting one thing in favour of another. We follow through on every convert's journey through all the stages knowing that "he who began a good work in us will bring it to completion (Philippians 1:6). This is effective disciple making.

Building your 12

23

As we have seen, there are two kinds of cells in the Model of 12. The *open cells* are evangelistic and also take care of new believers. The *leadership cells*, also called the Primary 12 groups, develop and grow cell leaders. Usually, a cell leader begins a leadership group when the members of the open cell start to form their own cells. Growing your open cell is therefore the first step towards building your Group of 12.

BEGINNING TO BUILD YOUR TEAM

As you begin to disciple your cell members, you will soon identify those who show leadership potential. The Holy Spirit will help you build a strong spiritual connection with these members. Gradually, they will start their own cells and could eventually form your leadership team.

One-to-one contact

The first step is to meet individually with these promising cell members. Do this outside the regular cell meetings so that you can get to know them better and encourage them to take bold steps for the Lord. Teach them the cell vision and begin to delegate some responsibility to them as they are able to carry it. For example, they can assist you in organisational matters, by helping collect reports, by communicating to cell members, and so on. As they grow spiritually, you can train them to assist you to teach, to consolidate new believers and to disciple members in the cell.

Prayer

Because calling your 12 is a spiritual process, the most important factors are prayer and sensitivity to the Holy Spirit. Jesus spent the whole night in prayer before he chose his 12. He did this for 3 reasons. He wanted to be sensitive to the Father's will. He wanted those the Father had given him to be ready to respond to his call. He also wanted those in close discipleship with him to prosper and flourish.

Not only did Jesus call his 12 through prayer, but his prayers also kept them in the place of effective participation in his mission. Jesus' prayer in John chapter 17 shows this. He prayed for them to be kept resolute and faithful to the kingdom of God.

Informal gatherings

When you have a several cell members who are beginning to develop as leaders, start meeting with them informally. This group could form the core of your future Primary 12 group, but it is important to keep things low key at this stage. Your main concern is to help these cell members grow and develop their leadership potential without carrying any commitment that neither you nor they are ready for.

Fruitfulness

Leadership is a function not just a title, and fruitfulness plays an important part. In fact, fruitfulness is at the heart of the Model of 12 and we hold that leaders without fruit are a contradiction. In churches today, there are many people who are leaders in name and position only. They never (or rarely) lead a soul to Christ and have few if any who are following them. Others may be leading services, running committees and even preaching sermons, but they are not making disciples themselves.

The cell model corrects these tendencies by insisting that people are only recognised as leaders if they are bearing fruit by making disciples and growing them in the cell. Once your

Group of 12 is complete, each member will have become a leader with their own cells. However, it is a mistake to wait until potential leaders have a cell before you begin to mentor them and disciple them into leadership. Jesus called his 12 before they bore fruit in order to form them into fruitful leaders.

Spiritual growth

Take time to help your leaders in every area of the Christian life. Bring them to the Leaders Encounter Weekends so that they can meet with Christ, be healed and set free from bondages to sin and emotional problems. The experience of Christian freedom is necessary so that your team members can step out in ministry without barriers or hindrances.

Uppermost in your mind at this stage of development, is to help bring each member of your potential 12 to be truly consecrated to Christ. Once people are truly passionate for Christ, the cell vision is a delight to them. If they are half-hearted in the things of the kingdom, they will never truly flourish as leaders.

Knowing your own total inability to serve God without the anointing, you will want your disciples to know how to depend on the Holy Spirit. This will happen as you become transparent and open yourself up to those you are leading. Let them see your weaknesses and help them recognise that fruit comes from the Lord and not your own ability. As you minister to your disciples they will discover the principles of ministry anointed by the Spirit.

As you evangelise the lost, pray for the sick, deliver people from demons, receive words of knowledge and wisdom for others, let your disciples see the dynamic process that is taking place through the Spirit. Explain to them what is happening and how you are experiencing his power at every stage of the process. This way you will model ministry in the Spirit, and will give your team of potential leaders a life-long hunger for his anointing in their lives.

Planting new cells

Finally, the goal at this point is to help these potential leaders open their own cell. Encourage them to go to the Leadership School. The teaching is given by the especially gifted teachers in the School, but as the Primary 12 leader, you remain the main trainer and discipler. Make sure you follow the progress of each cell member in the school, helping them and encouraging them throughout the course.

As well as supporting them through the Leadership School, you need to work with the potential leaders, helping them win and consolidate new believers. Without new converts, there can be no new cells, no growth and no fruit. Ideally, when the months of leadership training are over, the work that has been happening alongside the teaching in the Leadership School will have borne fruit, and the person can begin their new cell as they graduate from the school.

LAUNCHING YOUR LEADERSHIP CELL

You launch your Primary 12 group when you have several leaders who have started their own cells. At this point, there must be a stepping up of value and commitment on the part of those who are now included in your 12. This is a significant and joyous occasion as one of the greatest privileges we can have in the ministry is to have our own Primary 12 group or to be part of someone else's leadership team.

You can begin with 3 or 4 members in your 12 who have their own cells. But you can also incorporate others who do not yet have their cell, providing they are actively working towards that goal. Keep working with the whole group until all 12 have their own cell, and then you will have formed your Group of 12.

But that doesn't mean your work has finished. Having chosen your 12 and brought them to the place of fruitfulness, your task now is to develop your team into greater levels of leadership effectiveness. They will need on-going care and encouragement, correction and motivation, as well as further training. Help them develop their ministry and reach for the greater goals that lie ahead. Much of this happens in the weekly leadership meeting.

THE PRIMARY 12 WEEKLY MEETING

Your main purpose for the Primary group meetings is to develop relationships and to build your team. The weekly meeting of the 12 should be an exciting and uplifting experience, a real highlight of the week. This will not happen without careful planning and preparation. You have a full agenda to follow which will demand much prayer and serious thought. The important thing is to keep the meetings lively, relevant and interesting. Avoid doing exactly the same things week after week. Ensure variety and freshness by making a list of what you want to accomplish and then find creative ways to cover each of these things, focussing on different components each week.

I have listed below 20 things that I seek to do regularly in my own Primary 12 meetings. I include some of these elements every week and make sure I cover the rest over a period of time.

1. Worship

Corporate worship is one of the main joys of gathering as believers. Jesus manifests his presence and our hearts are melted in love and unity. That's why we should learn to be passionate worshipers and value highly such worship in the Primary 12 meetings. Sometimes this can be simple and unaided by music or other outward expressions. We simply meditate quietly on the Lord and his goodness. But we also usually want to take the opportunity to worship God with music and singing.

2. Preach the Word

The ministry of the Word is essential every time you meet with your 12. Seek God for a relevant word for them that will meet their need at that moment in their lives. The message could be a word of encouragement, doctrine, challenge, prophetic insight, correction, revelation or instruction. You should make it a matter of priority regularly to preach your way through every aspect of the cell vision.

3. Ministry in the Spirit

Minister to your 12 as often as you can through personal prayer, laying on of hands and the exercise of spiritual gifts, such as prophecy. Remember your 12 are always giving out, and can easily become spiritually drained. Therefore, they need to be continually filled and refreshed. During your own times of private prayer and intercession for your 12, ask the Lord to give you revelation about their spiritual needs. This will help you always to be sensitive to those you lead. The Holy Spirit knows just what they need to hear and exactly when they need to hear it.

4. Relationship

Each Primary 12 meeting should be about promoting relationship by encouraging honest interaction, sharing of needs and other forms of relationship building through personal interaction. Without relationship the vision cannot function. I often give time for my Primary 12 members to share together in groups of 2 or 3 and in order to pray for and minister to one another.

5. Encouragement

Always make a conscious effort to ensure your meetings are encouraging. When things are not going so well and difficulties surface, that's the time to be most encouraging. Avoid the temptation to remonstrate with your 12, especially if you think they have been remiss or are not rising to the mark. As you verbally acknowledge the things that are being done well, you can also raise the areas that need strengthening by saying such encouraging words such as, "Let's look together at how we can make this better", or by asking, "How can we be more effective in this area?" That way, you bring correction where it is needed and you also help maintain high levels of encouragement.

6. Vision building

At some point each meeting, you will need to help the group maintain the focus on the cell vision. You must constantly hold the vision up before their eyes. It is easy to take for granted the things you have previously established, only to discover they have been let slip, sidelined or dropped altogether. But this is not just a matter of maintenance. We all need to grow in our understanding of the vision which is always developing.

International co-operation between ministries across the world means that we often share new insights concerning the cell ministry in various conferences, on the internet and through other forums. As we develop our understanding of the cell model and discover new ways of making it effective in our churches, we can immediately work these insights into the life of the church through the Groups of 12.

7. Leadership issues and problem solving

Leadership development is an ongoing matter. Issues arise all the time as leaders confront situations in the course of their ministry. Address these issues and minister to the felt needs of the group, making sure your teaching is practical and relevant. Use the wisdom of the whole group to help answer questions and solve the problems others are facing in their leadership. It is also good to anticipate leadership training needs through a programme of leadership development and teaching. Read widely and make sure that you are always growing in your understanding of leadership.

8. Reporting

This is an important part of the cell ministry. Good reporting will provide the information you need to manage your cells. The more data you have to enable you to track the progress of each cell and each cell member through the Ladder of Success, the more effective you will become in helping each person through the various stages of the cell vision.

We use a *Leader's Log Book* in which each person logs the progress of their cells. This is an important tool for leaders as it helps them personally keep track of their cells. It also gives them the data they need to prepare their regular reports. The Primary 12 meeting is an ideal place to discuss this data and formulate strategies to reach your goals.

9. Strategise for growth

The Primary meetings are like 'summit meetings' where strategic and tactical thinking is explored and where plans are drawn up for their effective implementation. This comes out of the prior commitment made by every member of the 12 to take up the responsibility for the growth of the church. Utterly committed to healthy expansion, the 12 will want to work tirelessly, looking for ways of being more effective in reaching out and discipling others. If something appears not to be working, we come together as a Group of 12, and ask why. Leadership becomes effective only when correct strategies are devised and implemented. We are solution seekers and problem solvers, not people who are negative or defeatist. We are conquerors, not quitters!

10. Helping each other

Being part of a team means that no one person is ultimately above any other person, in terms of significance or importance. We all need each other. It is said that in League Football, individuals win goals, but teams win tournaments. The same is true for Primary 12 teams. There can be no competition between us, except spurring one another on to achieve greater things for God. That means we are always willing to help each other, share the things that we have found to be effective and to pass on the secrets of our success. It also means helping bear one another's burdens and be willing to help, counsel, support and correct each other. Just as in the book by Stephen Ambrose made famous by the Steven Spielberg TV series, *Band of Brothers*, we too, are fellow soldiers at war and we need each other to help us make it through and achieve our important mission objectives.

11. Strategic prayer and intercession

Prayer is the power plant generating spiritual energy in every aspect of ministry. The Primary 12 meetings should be powerful times of effective intercession. Prayer is the greatest testimony we have of our belief in the power of a supernatural God and of our own inability to do what he calls us to do. Targeted, informed and anointed intercession will bring more results and solve more problems than hours of mere discussion, soul searching, arguing or debating. Keep prayer alive and powerfully working at every level in your ministry and with your 12.

12. Soaking in the Spirit

Do all that you can to make sure that your experience of the Spirit and that of your team remains fresh. Every team member should know what it means to be filled with the Spirit and to continue to be saturated on a daily basis. The weekly meetings are ideal times to 'top up' your levels of Holy Spirit fullness. You should encourage regular 'soaking' times with your 12, allowing the Holy Spirit to minister just as he pleases – in healing, empowerment, acceptance and revelation. Give God time to work in the meeting as you and your team wait expectantly in his presence.

13. Sharing testimonies

This can be one of our most effective tools of encouragement. When we share with each other a victory, an effective strategy or any other way that God has blessed us in the cell vision, we can all rejoice together as well as learn from what has been shared. Try to give regular time for testimony. You will be encouraged yourself, and also learn a great deal about what is actually going on in your generation of cells.

14. Feedback

Always make time for feedback. Communication is a two way process, so don't fall into the error of the meeting becoming mere 'top down' communication. Invite questions, give opportunity for the team members to let you know what they are thinking and feeling and make time for their suggestions to be heard.

15. Doing the vision

Help the team practically with any area of the Ladder of Success they are struggling with. It is good to take frequent audits of the vision to check out how things really are on the ground. Help brush up the leaders' skill in such areas as consolidation, planning, networking and training.

16. Fun

Keep the 'fun elements' alive in the meeting. It is easy to begin to take ourselves too seriously. We are dealing with important issues in the cell vision, but that is all the more reason to 'lighten up' from time to time. People are more motivated when they are having fun. Humour is a sanity preserver. Learn to laugh at yourself. Keep people's morale high. Make time in your agenda for recreational activities. It may mean sometimes cancelling the meeting and all going out for the day or for a couple of hours, doing something everyone enjoys. Be creative. Be interesting.

17. Gift Development

An important part of leadership is developing the gifts in others. That means you need to identify the abilities in your team and help them grow in this area. When you know the strengths of each team member, you can then help them develop their gifts and release them within the team. That way, someone strong on evangelism, for example, can help those who are not so gifted in this area. In the same way, those who need help with teaching skills or pastoral ministry issues can call on those who are strong in these things.

18. Mentoring

Mentorship is a proven method of someone more experienced developing others who are less experienced. I strongly recommend you implement a mentoring and coaching strategy in your cells, beginning with your Primary 12.

19. Evangelism

As has already been mentioned, this should never be off the agenda of the 12. As well as planning various evangelistic events for the cells, the team should always be actively engaged in evangelism themselves. This can be a lot of fun and richly rewarding. It maintains an outward focus and prevents the group from becoming too introspective or self-serving.

20. Motivation

Almost everything that you do in a Primary 12 meeting is about motivation. Make sure that the whole experience is inspiring and encouraging. Learn to rejoice at what God is doing and maintain high levels of expectancy. Our ultimate joy comes from knowing that we are about the Father's business and are seeking to be authentic followers of Christ by placing the Great Commission at the centre of our lives.

PASTORING YOUR 12

One of the main advantages of the Model of 12, above some other cell models, is that it is essentially a model based on relationship. The relationship between the Primary 12 leader and his or her team is not that of a supervisor or manager, but a fellow-player and coach. The leader is responsible for the pastoral care and development of the team. Primary leaders should master the principles of pastoral care and actively pastor the group.

As you minister to the needs of your team, they will grow and become strong in the Lord and will show the same care to those they lead. Pastoral leadership is about feeding the flock, teaching them, counselling them and guiding them in their life and relationship with the Lord. Only then will the team respond to the high levels of commitment you ask of them in the cell ministry.

LEADING BY EXAMPLE

Leading by example is the only way to be effective, because people will follow what you do more easily than what you say. In fact, *they* will only do what you say if *you* do what you say. As you continue to develop your 12, this principle becomes ever more important to remember.

When a Primary 12 leader successfully raises his or her 12 from the open cell, the original cell becomes a leadership cell and the members who are not yet cell leaders are distributed among the cells of the 12. That means the open cell is no longer available to the Primary leader as a means of modelling such activities as evangelism and consolidation. This can be a real problem because if the leader stops evangelising or doing the other things associated with ordinary day-to-day ministry, the whole generation of cells seems to lose their enthusiasm for these things as well.

The only way to make sure that your 12 continue to win, consolidate, disciple and send, is to keep on modelling these things yourself. That means being involved with them by opening another cell yourself or by helping your 12 work with their cells.

MAINTAIN WHAT YOU ATTAIN

Primary leaders are in place because they have successfully mastered many principles of leadership. Make sure you maintain these and take them even further as you focus your energy, time and your passion on your 12. Continue to pray and intercede daily for your 12. Know their life, their family and their intimate needs. Listen to God on their behalf and sustain them through your life of intercession.

Keep teaching, training and equipping your 12. As you grow in your leadership, pass your knowledge and expertise on to them. Make sure you follow their progress as leaders, and regularly input them as a coach, highlighting areas of play and working on the skills of the players.

Work hard to maintain personal contact and develop your relationship with your 12 outside the cell meetings. Doing things socially together, spending time with each other and generally keeping in personal contact can be difficult in our busy lives, especially in big cities or remote rural areas where transport is difficult, and so it pays to be creative and optimise every opportunity to be together with your 12. You can read more about developing your team of 12 in the booklet, *Growing Your 12*.

An important part of Primary 12 leadership is strategic planning, and a crucial part of that process is goal-setting. In the cell vision, we emphasise the need to set clear, identifiable and manageable goals in every aspect of the strategy. Goal-setting is the topic of the next chapter.

Working with Goals

Any serious venture will involve setting and fulfilling clear-cut goals. The cell vision is a journey. Like any other journey we need to know what the destination is, why we should go there, how long it will take and what we may need on the way. That is why goal-setting is necessary.

GOALS AND FAITH

Goals are faith statements. They declare the specific things we believe God wants us to have achieved at a certain point in the future. This means our goals must be inspired by God. They are grounded on faith, not human logic. Goals set by human reasoning alone do not take into account the supernatural power of God. If they do not stretch our faith they lead to underachievement. A goal inspired by the Holy Spirit may not seem possible to us, but if we have truly heard from God, it can be done. On the other hand, over-ambitious goals rooted in unreality or pride are presumptuous. Unrealistic goal-setting is de-motivating and leads to discouragement when they are not fulfilled.

In the 1990s, one pastor told me that he had a 'goal' of growing his church from 20 to 2,000 people in a just a few years. It was not an impossible goal, but he had no strategy in place to achieve it. It was just a good idea – inspired by the Millennium. His catch phrase was "2,000 by the year 2000". He never achieved his goal because he was not seriously working to do so, and it was doubtful that God had given him this goal in the first place.

Spiritual goal-setting is about having God's vision of the future and determining to bring it about. As disciples of Christ, we must have a healthy future focus. God has given us a future and a hope and we must be able to see it clearly in order to bring it about. He has a prepared purpose for our lives that we can delight in fulfilling.

Living in the past is boring. Getting stuck in the present is short-sighted and causes you to drift without aim or focus. The best days are always ahead. Living with a future-looking perspective engenders hope, enthusiasm and excitement, because God is always developing us, always giving us new challenges and always leading us forward.

Goals help us lay hold of God's plans and purposes and anchor them in the world of space and time. This does not mean that every Spirit-inspired goal will be achieved. We must act in purposeful obedience, doing what he tells us to do. The keys to partnering with God are always keen listening and active obeying. Faith without actions is fruitless.

TAKING THE LIMITS OFF GOD

Be prepared to be challenged when you agree to work with God. One of the greatest faith-motivators I ever met was my mentor Wynne Lewis. We worked together in Kensington Temple as I assisted him when he was the Senior Pastor. When I succeeded him in 1991, he told me to expect great things from God. He believed that the church would grow from strength to strength under my leadership. He challenged me to press into God's greatness for my life. He passed away in 2009 and, on the day he went to be with the Lord, we shared some precious moments together.

Despite the limitations of his own body now reaching the end of its earthly usefulness, Wynne spent most of the time talking about the great things God was going to do in the future. His final sermon was to a small group of pastors in

France and he focussed on the theme "Taking the limits off God". Using as his text, Psalm 78:41 which reads, "…they limited the Holy One of Israel", Wynne told us to dream big, think big and act big! This is not arrogance, but dependence on God as you partner with him.

God wants you also to dream big dreams. God is able to do exceedingly above and beyond all we can think or imagine. Without this kind of faith it is impossible to please God. Audacious faith delights him. Nothing is impossible – if only we believe God. Real faith is rooted in revelation. It is not about telling God what we want, but hearing what he wants and then going out and doing it. God wants to challenge our human smallness with his divine greatness and this should be reflected in our goals.

As we spend time in God's presence listening to his voice, he will reveal the things he wants us to achieve and the great possibilities that are in his heart for us. The devil will tell you that it cannot be done. But God says "Do not be afraid. I am with you!"

Some are nervous about goal-setting because they do not want the pressure of the commitment and accountability that comes with it. They don't set goals because they don't want the embarrassment of not achieving them. But all this means is that nothing gets done! They just go on doing church as usual, never standing up and admitting that they are achieving very little.

There can be no more urgent need for the church than to get before God and receive his vision concerning what he wants us to achieve in this generation. Where there is vision, there will be passion, and where there is passion there will be goals.

As we have seen, the cell vision aims for a fully-mobilised church, equipped and empowered for the worldwide work of making, maturing and mobilising disciples. It is a vision to penetrate every part of society with small groups of Christian disciples being good news and showing God's love through the gospel. It is about having a determination to see the church grow into a strong and influential disciple-making community, shining as a lighthouse in a dark and dangerous world.

We have also seen that the strategy for fulfilling this vision is to organise the church into cell groups, the basic functioning unit of *ekklesia*. Structures are put in place for every member of the church to be active in fulfilling the Great Commission – to win, consolidate, train and send disciples into the world to continue the Master's work.

However, implementing and maintaining the vision will take more than a good model. It requires continual sacrificial service and total dependence on God. Faith, prayer and practical action are all part of the sustained spirituality the cell strategy demands. Inherent in all this is the need to set goals. Deciding to work with the cell model shows that we are serious about fulfilling our intentions to serve God. Goal-setting is the first step we take in turning our intentions into action. Vision, faith and intention all lead to strategic goal-setting.

CORPORATE GOAL-SETTING

Goal-setting is part of strategic planning. We set goals for every part of the cell vision because we seriously intend to implement it. We make sure that every step in the process is clearly-defined by specific, time-related goals. We set goals for our evangelism, consolidation, training and cell planting.

Without goals, our strategy will remain just a set of good ideas. Goals state what we are going to do and by when. They are milestones on the road that mark the steps we need to fulfil in order to arrive at a certain place at a certain time.

God himself is the great goal setter. First, he determines the end he wants to see come to pass. Then, he plans his work. Finally, he works out his plan in perfect harmony with his will until his purposes are perfectly fulfilled. Partnering with God involves corporate ownership of goals and working together to see them fulfilled.

Good goals are clear-cut, manageable and inspiring. They help release the energy of God's people as everyone works together to fulfil them. They express what we want to achieve together for God and are made plain for everyone to see and follow. Our goals should be bigger than anything we can do on our own, and show that every member of the church needs every other member to get the job done. They demonstrate the value of working together and reveal the part individuals have to play in the overall plan.

HIGHLIGHTING RESOURCES

Goal-setting highlights the resources we need in order to achieve our objectives. For example, if we want to start 100 new cells within a given time frame, we know we will need at least 100 leaders, probably with another hundred assistant leaders working alongside them.

That means we will need to have an effective training programme ready to produce leaders for these cells. We will need to know what proportion of students on the Leadership School will be ready to plant a cell at the end of their training. Depending on their experience, maturity, ability and availability, it could be approximately 7 out of 10 students. That means we will need to have up to 150 leaders in training in order to plant 100 new cells.

But it does not end there. Who will be in these cells? 100 cells, each with at least 5 or 6 people, means that we need to think in terms of having 500–600 people ready to go into cells. Where will these people come from? If they are not yet in the church, it means we have to win them to Christ and consolidate them into the cells. So we think of the number of people we have to win to Christ to ensure a sufficient number can be consolidated to furnish each cell with at least 5 members.

From this simple exercise, we can see that a seemingly straightforward goal of planting a specific number of cells will provoke an intensive process of strategic thinking and serious planning. It will also cause us to spend a lot of time in prayer! After all, we are talking about spiritual things. Only God can compel life and grant growth. At this point people tend to pull back and resort to what I called in an earlier part of this book, 'Evangelical notionalism'. We affirm our belief and at best hold seminars about what we believe, without actually doing anything!

BASIC GOALS FOR THE CELL VISION

Usually, the first goal for most churches is to transition into cells. This takes time, particularly if the church has a traditional approach to cells or to small groups. The initial process of transitioning to a cell church according to the Model of 12 takes up to 5 years in most cases. We cannot underestimate the importance of laying the right foundations and values in the cell vision before we start to implement the Model of 12. I say more about transitioning in Chapter 26 of this book.

The next goal is to see the first Primary 12 team established and for these leaders to generate the second generation of leaders. This is when the Primary groups have established 12 other leaders each with cells. The process of growing from 12 cells to 144 cells in each of the Nets (men, women and youth) can take another three or more years.

In setting further goals for growth, it is vitally important to be realistic without, of course, excluding faith in the power of God. A goal must be born out of faith under the direction of the Holy Spirit. But it is realistic to expect steady growth for the first years of the vision and beyond that to expect a greater rate of growth.

ANNUAL GOAL-SETTING

Once the cell vision has been established in the church, you need to set annual goals for the Ladder of Success. Expect to have a working year of 10 months, not 12. This fits into the pattern of most people's lives and takes account of holidays and other 'low' periods in the church's yearly calendar of activities. It is good to focus on Evangelism for the first part of the year, and then take the new believers through the rest of the steps on the Ladder of Success for the remainder of the year. However, as we saw in Chapter 14, we think of the Ladder as an escalator with each step constantly revolving. You need to be continually winning, consolidating, discipling and sending. Last year's converts will be fully consolidated this year and this year's students on the Leadership School will probably start their cells next year.

When you set your annual goals you take account where every cell member is positioned on the Ladder of Success, as well as also their realistic anticipated progress in the year ahead. For example, suppose a cell leader has 16 members who have all been on the Encounter and are progressing through the Ladder of Success. 8 members are ready to enter the Post-encounter, 5 are ready for the Leadership School and 3 have completed the Leadership School and are ready to open a cell.

This leader might set the following annual goals for their *existing* members:

Annual Goals (existing members)
6 (out of 8) people to complete the Post-encounter
3 (out of 5) people to complete the Leadership School
2 (out of 3) people to start a new cell.

These are reasonable goals. Those who don't complete the Ladder of Success this year will be included in next year's goals.

Next, the leader sets goals for *new* members. Following the Evangelism of 3 strategy, 15 cell members will be praying for and witnessing to 3 friends each. This means there will be a pool of 45 people who they can invite to visit the cell meeting or an evangelistic event this year. The cell leader sets goals based on the realistic proportions of these people coming to the cell and progressing through the Ladder of Success.

The cell leader knows that not all those who get saved will complete the Ladder of Success this year, and takes this into account. The goals for *new* cell members may look like this:

Annual Goals (new members)

	Total	This year	Next year
Evangelism of 3	45	45	-
Visitors to the cell	34	34	-
Salvations	22	22	-
Encounter	16	8	8
Post-encounter	11	4	7
Leadership School	5	1	4
New cells	4	0	4

Finally, the cell leader adds all these goals together, and arrives at following totals:

Total Annual Goals

	Total	This year	Next year
Evangelism of 3	45	45	-
Visitors to the cell	34	34	-
Salvations	22	22	-
Encounter	16	8	8
Post-encounter	17	10	7
Leadership School	8	4	4
New cells	6	2	4

To keep this example simple, these goals assume that the existing cell members will only move forward one step on the Ladder of Success next year. In reality, many people do far more than that. Therefore, personal knowledge of each individual is necessary before the final goals are set.

Some people are ready to plant their cell within a year, others take much longer and some don't ever do it! Those who do not complete the process this year will probably do so next year, so long as the cell leaders keep on ministering to them, encouraging them and training them. It is important for us to reflect these realities in our goal-setting.

The goals increase each year as new people are won to the Lord. The cell leader in our example above is likely to begin next year with double the number of cell members, if this year's goals are met. Setting simple goals and consistently achieving them, pays off.

Once we understand how the Ladder of Success works in practice we can set realistic annual goals. We base our annual goals on the expected percentages and rate at which people will progress through the Ladder of Success in the year ahead. In our experience, 70% of people on each step, progress steadily to the next one and we begin our goal-setting with this in mind.

These calculations are only a guide to the kinds of goals we should be setting. The cell leader begins with this information but, as we have said, sets final goals based on specific personal knowledge of each cell member. Sometimes our assumptions concerning the rate people will progress on the Ladder of Success are too ambitious, and at other times they underestimate what is likely to happen. It all depends on the individual cell members and how ready they are to advance on the Ladder of Success.

In all this, we continue our 'conversation' with the Holy Spirit asking him for his wisdom and guidance. We do not want to miss what he is saying to us about the goals we should be setting!

The final goals of each cell leader are collated into the overall goals for each of the Nets and then into the goals for the whole church. I guide each group of cells during this process, inspire them and encourage them – but I do not impose goals from the 'top down'. It is better to build goals from the grass roots upwards.

ACHIEVING YOUR GOALS

The saying goes, 'If you fail to plan, then you plan to fail'. If you don't aim at a target, how can expect to hit it? But neither of these sayings guarantees that all our goals will be achieved!

An objection some people have against setting goals in the cell vision is that it puts pressure on people and makes the process of serving God stressful. I don't think this is necessarily true, provided that the goals are realistic and that they are made with sensitivity to the leading of the Holy Spirit. I also think that if you are really serious about serving God and being fruitful for him, you will set goals, plan well and focus all your attention and resources on achieving what you believe God has called you to.

Our annual goals are rooted in the practical outworking of the cell vision. If we are thoughtful in setting our goals, we will already have some idea of what it will take to meet them. For example, if we set a goal to present the gospel each year to all those on our Evangelism of 3 lists, we will make sure that we have a strategy in place to do it.

First, we make sure the Evangelism of 3 lists are up to date. The lists contain the names of people whom the Holy Spirit has laid on our heart, with whom we are in regular contact and who can be invited to the cell meeting or some event arranged especially for them. If we are to see them attend an evangelistic event, we will probably first need to spend time with them outside a formal 'church' activity. We will be fervently praying for them and we will arrange a suitable context in which we can share Christ with them – a meal, a party or a Christian concert.

We examine all the specific goals we have for the year and check to see what we need to do to fulfil them. It will mean organising intensive prayer mixed with aggressive faith, believing God to do what only he can do. The goals will determine strategy throughout the year. We break annual goals down into monthly targets and devise a detailed plan of action.

There will be times of reflection, review and adapting the plan as the year unfolds, so that we stay on track. The goals and the strategies that go with them will always be before our eyes making sure we do not let them slip. We will keep the cell members motivated and make sure they are adequately resourced with everything they need to fulfil the goals.

If the goals are not fulfilled as we had hoped, we never make people feel guilty or like failures. It all takes time, effort, focus and an ongoing desire to keep the vision alive in our hearts. This can only happen if each cell group knows the goals and is committed to them. That's why we involve every cell member when we develop our goals for the next year. That way, each person takes responsibility for their part in achieving the goals beginning with their own, personal ones.

The key is to determine at the beginning of the year what steps each cell member needs to take in order to progress along the Ladder of Success throughout that year.

SUMMARY

I conclude this chapter by summarising some important points about goal-setting.

- Goals are faith statements – they declare what we believe about the future.
- Goals must be visual – you must be able to picture them. Otherwise they are not specific enough. You will never see with your natural eyes what you cannot first see with your spiritual eyes.
- Goals must be achievable but ambitious.
- Goals must be clear, measurable and time specific.
- Goals must be written down bringing clarity and accountability.
- Goals must be supported by specific action, broken down into specific steps.

- Goals must call for real change – what to stop doing, what to start doing, and what to keep doing.
- Goals must be kept in a visible place so that you will constantly keep them in view and under review.

Now, we turn to another subject, closely-related to goal-setting. Reporting and data gathering are essential if we are to follow our progress throughout the year and check to see if we are on course to fulfil our goals.

Reporting – A Spiritual Discipline

In the previous chapter, we saw that developing and implementing a strategic plan helps turn intention into action. A strategy is a series of practical, time-related and purpose-driven steps. The function of goal-setting is to define these steps clearly. Every cell leader knows what he or she is expected to achieve each year and follows the plan they have formulated with the help of their Primary leader. The weekly Primary leadership meetings include a time of feedback on the progress being made by the cell leaders. They share their experiences and discuss any difficulties they may be facing. The Primary leader offers advice and help, making sure the cells remain on track.

KEEPING ON TRACK

The main way we follow our progress throughout the year is through our system of reporting. Cell leaders understand that without timely, accurate and precise reporting there is no way we can keep on top of our task. We need to know where we are at any particular moment in relation to our goals. I cannot overemphasise the importance of good reporting. It is more than just looking at numbers. The cell reports provide valuable information on the issues the cells are facing. Personally, without the reports I simply could not direct the work. Imagine a General in the midst of the battle not knowing where the troops are, what is their condition and what needs they have. The regular reports each cell leader is expected to make are one vitally important element in our communication system.

Once we understand the strategic significance of reporting, this spiritual discipline becomes a delight. As testimonies roll in, we celebrate our successes. When the reports highlight problems, we pray about them. As patterns emerge revealing weaknesses in our performance, we look for ways of overcoming them.

I pay close attention to the written reports I receive, as well as the verbal feedback I get from the leaders in my Primary 12 weekly meeting. I discern trends early – both positive and negative. I can then input the all the Nets through prayer, teaching and spiritual direction.

REPORTING, A SPIRITUAL DISCIPLINE

Despite these facts that confirm reporting as crucial to the cell vision, some people are a little suspicious of the whole process. Perhaps they feel they are being scrutinised or that reports will be used as a means of highlighting poor performance. Some regard reporting as unnecessary bureaucracy. Others actually consider it to be unspiritual. They recall that King David was punished for taking a census of his troops (1 Chronicles 21:1-4). But the God of the book of Numbers is certainly not against numbering. It was David's motives that were questionable.

The issues God confronted in this instance had to do with David's pride and the temptation to put his trust in the number of his troops and not in God's ability to deliver the nation. The size of Israel's army was never the decisive factor in the victories God gave her against her enemies. We must be aware of the dangers of pride, sinful ambition and competitiveness when considering numerical goals and growth. Exaggeration, never glorifying to God, is another matter of concern. God does not want us to massage either our numbers or our egos!

MORE THAN STATISTICS

When reporting, we must never treat people as if they are mere statistics, or make leaders feel that their status is only as elevated as the number of members they have in their cells. This kind of 'numbers game' is offensive to God and we must have nothing to do with it. However, the true significance of numbering is that each person counts before God. Counting people shows that they are important.

Jesus was numbered among the transgressors (Isaiah 53:12) which means his death counted on our behalf. The 12 tribes of Israel were numbered, showing that the whole nation counted as the people of God (Numbers 1:19). In John's Gospel chapter 21 every single fish that was miraculously caught was counted. John records the number: 153. Jesus' earlier statement, "Come follow me, and I will make you to become fishers of men" shows that in this miracle Jesus was directing the disciples back to their original commission. It was ultimately about people, not fish.

God holds statistics about every detail of our lives because he cares for us. He gave us the book of Numbers, showing his keen interest in his people and their history. The book of Acts is full of numbers – 3,000 on the Day of Pentecost and the 5,000 added to the church. Matthias was numbered among the 12. More personally, our days are numbered by the Lord as are the very hairs on our head. This last point came in handy one day when one of my leaders said that he did not fill in his report form because he had nothing to report. I reminded him that God numbers the hairs on our head even when we are bald – zero is a number!

REPORTING ENCOURAGES ACCOUNTABILITY

Numbering is an indispensible part of strategic planning. Before you act, you must quantify the task – whether it has to do with building a tower or going to war (Luke 14:28-32). The 12 emissaries of Moses who went out to 'spy out the land' gave a report which proved crucial to the people of God.

Unfortunately, the information gained by 10 of the spies was negatively interpreted and applied, due to their fear and unbelief. The people ignored the report Caleb and Joshua gave which was positive and designed to stimulate faith in God. The key message in all of this is that correct reporting is necessary. Reporting should record both what God has done and stimulate faith in what he is able to do. We praise him for what he has done and call out to him in dependent faith when the task seems impossible.

Reporting makes us accountable for the task assigned to us. It shows us that our work is a vital part of the whole. As each person carries his or her own share of the load, the whole vision moves forward. Keeping track of our own performance helps us strengthen the elements that we have personally let slip and maintain our focus. Without reporting we will never be able to celebrate our successes or correct our mistakes.

WHAT WE REPORT

We keep weekly accounts of what is happening in the cells and these are collected into monthly reports. We record:

- Up to date details of cell members – name, address, contact details
- Cell attendance details
- Salvations
- Testimonies
- Pastoral needs
- What is being taught in the cells
- Pastoral visits to homes
- Where cell members are on the ladder of success
- Where cell leaders are in relation to their goals – annual, quarterly, monthly.

HOW WE REPORT

We have two basic systems of reporting – paper and online. Sample reporting forms are found in Appendix V. We have different reporting forms for open cells and leadership cells which focus on the specific functions of these two types of cell meetings. Each month, the report forms are either emailed to the central office or dropped into the designated post box situated in our central church building. A copy is also passed to the Primary leader who can use it to strategise for their particular generation of cells groups.

We also use cell database software developed by Bethany World Prayer Center, the church led by Larry Stockstill in Louisiana. This programme called *Excellerate* is designed for the Model of 12, and each leader can input their cell data enabling us to generate instant and accurate reports on every aspect of the Ladder of Success. We prefer the cell leaders to use this system of reporting, but we know that some people are not used to handling computers. Our staff members make sure that the data gathered from the report forms is entered into *Excellerate* and the information is kept up to date.

Each cell leader has a *Leader's Log Book* which he or she uses to keep track of all the cell leaders in their generation of cells. Along with pages for tracking each cell member's growth through the Ladder of Success, the *Leader's Log Book* also is used to plan cell meetings, record the progress of new believers, strategise for events and chart progress towards the cell goals.

ACTING ON INFORMATION

The information that comes to us through the reports enables us to track the progress of the vision and to trace where we are in relation to our goals at any given point in time. This helps us see what we must emphasise, correct or change about the way we are doing things. It gives us cues to follow as we discern certain trends – what is working and what is not. For example, if I see that we are lagging behind in some aspect of consolidation, I can correct that trend by giving more public focus on this topic or by suggesting that the Primary Leaders address it in the regular leadership meetings. If we see that a cell leader is struggling in some area, or a certain issue seems to be recurring, we can get alongside that leader and help.

The reports give us the information we need as we devise our annual goals. We can see where every cell member is on the Ladder of Success and then create strategies to help them move forward in the coming year. The reports also enable us to track the progress of the vision at every point throughout the year. They highlight specific needs for prayer, encouragement and practical action. Without this, we would be working in the dark. Reporting is our navigation system to keep us on track. It is one of the most crucial elements that lead to success.

Part 4
Pursuing the Cell Vision

Transitioning into the Model of 12

So far in this book, I have built a foundation for the spirituality the cell vision requires, I have given some basic principles of cell church and I have begun to show how the Model of 12 works. From this point, I want to deal with the issue of implementation – how we can begin to work with the cell model.

Many church leaders reading this book may be wondering how to adopt the cell model in their church. Transitioning into the Model of 12 is a challenging process and takes considerable leadership skill. We must never underestimate the enormity of the task. Moving from traditional church to cell church involves mastering many new concepts and adopting many new values. In Chapter 8, we saw that cell church challenges cherished traditions entrenched in the way we have learned to do church in the past.

Traditional church perpetuates a weakened understanding of *ekklesia* and *diakonia* which is built into its structure and practice. For most churches, *ekklesia* is basically understood as church meetings and *diakonia* is ultimately seen as the responsibility of paid professional clergy. Even when these words are correctly expounded from the pulpit, our church structures favour the traditional approach so that what we *say* and what we end up *doing*, are entirely different.

In some cases, there seems to be reluctance to abandon old models of church. Some shy away from God's order, preferring made-made structures. Some Christians are all too willing to pay the pastors and leaders to do the job for them, and the 'professionals' are happy to accept that role. It gives them status. We must end this conspiracy of ineffectiveness.

Be prepared to wage war in the Spirit over these issues. The enemy has a vested interest in maintaining the *status quo*. Despite the crying need for a new way of doing church in the 21st Century, the lessons are hard to learn. The tendency to uphold the 'one man ministry' and to promote 'superstars' in the pulpit, means that the call for a new reformation in church order will not always be welcome. But we must persist and break free from the straight jacket of tradition.

People may be wondering that if cell church is supposed to be the glorious new way of the Holy Spirit for our day, why is it not it working better, especially in the West. We touch on the issue of culture below, but first, there are some important points to be made.

Cell church is working, all over the world. Most of the world's largest churches are cell churches. In North America and Europe there are glowing examples of cell churches using either the 5 by 5 Model or Principle of 12. Also, we must understand that many examples of failed attempts to implement cell church are the result of bad transition and not the fault of the model. I know church leaders who were full of enthusiasm following a cell conference in Bogota or Seoul. They returned home and hurriedly tried to put it all into practice. When they failed, they concluded that cell church doesn't work in their situation.

We spent about two years looking into the Model of 12, before we began to adopt it in London. We made sure we thoroughly understood what we were getting into before we did anything. Our transition was only beginning to take effect three years later, and the cell vision was probably not fully established until several years after that.

We grasped from the very beginning that the success of cell church does not lie in the structure, but in the values that underpin it and the spirituality that sustains it. Cell church does not work without the Spirit-inspired passion and dedicated surrender of every member. We spent much of our transition time preparing the church for the changes that were to come.

Transitioning into a cell church is an exciting adventure and we learned many valuable lessons during the process. In this chapter, I will offer some basic suggestions and simple guidelines for successful transition. For a fuller presentation of this subject, I refer you to my book *Transitioning into the Model of 12*, in which I look in greater detail at the issue of culture, the management of change and how to implement the Model of 12. I will stick to broad principles here.

THE PROCESS OF CHANGE

Change is a process which must be managed carefully and with precision. Generally speaking, people are insecure at the thought of change. It invades their comfort zone and challenges their vested interests. Usually, people will not be willing to change until they believe that the consequences of not changing are more severe than the pain of the change they must make. Showing them the benefits of change will enable them to overcome these barriers.

Why change?

The reasons for changing the way we do church have been expressed repeatedly in this book and I will not go over them in detail now. However, it seems to me that we must not fail to grasp that church as we know it and are doing it, is simply not working.

Church must become everything Jesus intends it to be. In effect, Jesus said, "I will build my church – *you* make disciples". This is the heart of the cell model. Transitioning into a cell church involves adopting a model that enables every member to be cared for so that they can grow as a disciple and find their full potential in Christ.

Change from what to what?

When going on any journey, it is always good to know where we are starting from and where we want to end up. The transition into cell church can only begin when we know what exactly are we seeking to change, how we intend to go about it and why are we doing it in the first place. When we have settled the decision to become a cell church and have decided on the model we have chosen to follow (in our case, the Model of 12), we need to have a clear understanding of our starting point. What are we changing from?

Some will be transitioning from a traditional church structure such as I described in Chapter 8. For others, the starting point will be a church which has already a cell or small group programme. Both will have to understand the difference between what they have now and a fully-fledged cell church. Some will be building from scratch and planting a new church. I will be dealing with that topic in the next chapter, but much of what I say here will also be helpful for church planters.

You cannot assume that when you start a new church you are beginning with a blank sheet of paper. You need to make sure that those who are working with you as well as those you will win to Christ, do not unwittingly superimpose their traditional ideas of church onto the cell church you are intending to plant.

The steps that take you there

Transition demands a clear strategy and a concrete plan for the desired change. This must be carefully worked out in measurable steps which include precise timings. There must be close management of the process of change which will include sensitive people management and ruthless revision of the plan as the need arises.

The issue of culture

It has been a long-standing view among many Western church leaders that the cell vision is only for developing nations. They have seen it work in South Korea and Colombia but tell me it doesn't work in their own nations. When I explain to them how it is working in London, they reluctantly add London to the list of places where it does work, but still do not accept that it is possible for their situation. As I have already mentioned, many negative Western attitudes concerning cell church results from the experience of those who have not appreciated the importance of managing the transition well.

Changing the culture of church as we know it and are doing it in the West is not easy. But is it true to think of cell church as essentially a non-Western model? There are some specific advantages in working with the cell vision in a non-Western context. However, the issue of national or ethnic culture is not the determining factor in its success.

In non-Western nations there is less individualism than in the West. Individualism is destroying the church in many nations and the cell vision confronts this tendency. I have found that the isolation of the individual in many Western churches is precisely why the cell vision is needed and is also one of its greatest attractions.

Jesus did not leave behind one *ekklesia* for collective societies and another one for individualist societies. God is Trinity and therefore carries community in his own nature. The church is modelled on this characteristic of God. This is as true for the tribes of Togo as it is for the 'loners' of London. We all need to understand Christ's 'body language' of collectivism expressed in our corporate *koinonia* in the church.

Concepts of time vary from culture to culture. Westerners see time as a commodity to be portioned, whereas non-Westerners tend to see time as a continuum. Try to convince someone in the West that the cell vision is good for them, and the response often is, 'How can I find time for all that in my busy schedule?' Tell the same thing to the 'average' non-Westerner and they bring the vision into their whole life – which is a far more biblical response. I often tell my people that the cell vision is not time consuming, it's a lifestyle.

Westerners with their 'Greek' education tend to see the cell vision as a set of ideas or notions. Non-Westerners respond more practically. We carry concepts in our minds and teach about them in seminars, they see truth as concrete action and get on and do it. This too is more biblical. In Bible understanding, to believe something is to do it.

All this means that we may have a harder job on our hands when it comes to mobilising Western believers into the cell vision, but it does not mean that cell church is only for non-Westerners. We simply must not underestimate the depth of the shift in thinking that the cell vision requires if we are to be successful in transitioning our churches in the West into the culture of cell church.

Resources

There are many resources available to help you transition into cell church. One of the greatest of these is the experience of those who are already working with the Model. Seeing cell church in action provides a wealth of practical examples to follow. Don't try to go it alone, or re-invent the wheel! It is good to have a personal mentor who has been through the process and can be on hand for advice and help. There is also a range of printed materials, seminar teaching and other resources available from churches around the world who are using the Model of 12. The *Discipleship Cell Explosion* website (see page 347) gives you online access to many of these.

BEFORE THE TRANSITION

Get to grips with the model

You must not begin the transition process until you have a thorough understanding of the model. You need to know what it actually looks like in practice and the reasoning behind every element it includes. Otherwise you will be tempted to take short cuts or to compromise on aspects of the model you do not understand or you think are irrelevant.

The issue of whether to 'adopt or adapt' is a real one. However, I would counsel caution on this point. It takes a lot of experience of working with cells before you can discern what is essential and what is peripheral. Always discuss your questions with someone who has more experience than you do. Their advice will be invaluable. When you are learning about the Model of 12, always look for the 'heart' of it. Ask what New Testament value lies behind the structure being proposed and what biblical principles are being put into practice at any given point.

How does the model work in practice?

The difference between theory and practice is vast. Models only approximate to reality. In spiritual matters, definitions, bullet points, flow charts and diagrams are at best weak attempts of defining the indefinable. I say this, not to negate the value of theory, but to point out that, in practice, things do not always work as neatly as we would like.

We must learn to be patient with the model and infinitely patient with people. Above all, learn to be flexible and avoid ideological dogmatism. We are dealing with principles not precepts when we are working with a model. Success lies in learning how to implement the vision with sensitivity and wisdom, particularly during the transition.

What Spirituality does the model presuppose?

No model works by itself. It has to be put into practice by the people implementing it. As we have seen, the vision presupposes a prior passion for Christ, a strong commitment to prayer and intercession, faith and an intense love for souls. Surrender to the Holy Spirit's power and grace is absolutely necessary if want to avoid burning ourselves out through self-effort. Only the Holy Spirit can convict of sin, lead people into the righteousness of the kingdom and fill people with the desire and ability to work for God. The church of the New Testament experienced all these things and that is why it was so successful. Before you implement the Model of 12, build this spirituality into the hearts of the people. They cannot hope to run with the vision until they are ready for it.

Hear from God

I would categorically state that you should not implement the model until you have heard from God and are convinced that he is calling you to do it. This is a matter for the whole leadership of the church. According to Psalm 133, we can only count on God's anointing and blessing if we are in unity. The vision will demand the very best from every existing leader calling for unimaginable commitment to change.

Unity is impossible without humility and this vision will humble you. There are times when some leaders must step aside and make room for others. Some longstanding and highly cherished programmes will be replaced with new cell-based initiatives, and this calls for high levels of grace and understanding. That is why you need to know that God is in what you are seeking to do, just as the scripture says,

> *Unless the Lord builds the house, they labour in vain who build it.*
>
> Psalm 127:1

Teach the values of the vision

As I have frequently stated, the cell vision rests on certain New Testament values. Without these, the vision becomes meaningless and cannot function. That is why it is important to lay the right foundations before you start to build with the Model of 12.

These values permeate this book and I guess you have been noting them chapter by chapter. In summary, I would say that the principal values are commitment to the Great Commission, every member involvement in the work of Christ and the priority of discipleship training.

Make your own list of all the values expressed in the cell vision and begin to preach these, avoiding the temptation just to speak about cells. People will grasp the need for cells and be excited about them when they see that the cells give them the opportunity to fulfil the values they hold dear. But they must embrace the values first.

THE TRANSITION PERIOD

The right moment

Choosing the right moment to begin the transition is crucial. Just as a ship sets sail when the tide is right, so you will want to launch the cell vision in the church at the optimum moment. As the leaders plan and prepare themselves, the church imbibes the values and teaching of the cell vision. Then, the right time for change presents itself.

You will want to wait until the consensus of the church is with you. Do not wait for the 'stragglers' but, equally, do not be pressed into a premature launch by the 'enthusiasts'. When the moment arrives, begin to implement the transition strategy you planned during the preparation period.

How to begin

There is no one, single, or correct way of beginning the transition. Some start by training cell leaders, others take the whole church through the Encounter Weekend, and others begin by taking new believers and new members through the consolidation process and gradually introduce the cell model that way. It is important to start a training programme from the beginning. As soon as you have enough cell leaders trained in the Model of 12, you can begin to encourage the church members to join the cells and the leaders can actively recruit members.

Another good way of starting is to have a pilot programme. Begin with a handful of good, effective leaders and start modestly with a few cells. Let the church know that this a pilot programme and keep them informed. When testimonies of the blessings in the cells begin to emerge, others will be ready to take up the vision.

Some find the youth to be the most open group and introducing the cell vision through them can be an effective strategy. The success of the Model in one area of the church can then encourage the whole church to get involved. However the danger in this is that the rest of the church can begin to think of the cells as merely a young people's vision.

I advise the leader to set the example by opening the first leadership cell. Take the existing leadership team on an Encounter Weekend, explaining that they must first do it before they lead others through it. The same applies to the Leadership School. You can begin with experienced leaders and do an intensive course making sure that you include all the material, even if it appears basic.

I always tell leaders and mature Christians who are learning the vision that much of the teaching is basic and they will know it already. However, I ask them to keep two questions in mind: are they actually putting the teaching in practice in their own lives? And, do they know how to communicate it to others?

That way, even the most basic teaching is a challenge to the mature and experienced.

Transition in stages

Throughout the transition period, keep focussed on the main steps you have planned in your process. Do not be pedantic with the details. Gradual implementation is wise in transition. Various programmes and activities can either be integrated into the ministry of the cells over a period of time, or gradually phased out altogether if they do not facilitate the vision.

Where there is a reluctance to let go of long-cherished programmes or practices, be gentle but firm. The church must unite in its desire to be effective in the Great Commission. We are good at proliferating programmes but not very good as assessing their value and dissolving them if they are not fit for purpose. If something we do is not producing the fruit or contributing positively to the goal of discipleship, why should we continue doing it?

Streamline the central programmes

The church's centralised programmes should be thoroughly reviewed. It is not possible to take up the cell vision while maintaining all the central activities that may have existed in the past. Nothing should be allowed to compete with the cells. The major shift in thinking comes when the whole church accepts the cells as the fundamental unit through which the ministry of the church takes place.

If some central activity such as the weekly church prayer meeting or evangelistic outreach affirms and feeds the cells, then it is good. However, if people see these as alternatives to the cells, then they will prove to be counter-productive in the long run. Centralised ministries such as consolidation, Sunday ministry teams and the midweek prayer meeting can involve the cells by working out a rota system in which various groups of cells take turns to support these activities.

Exercise pastoral wisdom

Be patient with people at all times. Understand that some good people, who have been faithful to the church's vision down through the years, may struggle with the new structure. If you have prepared the church well, by preaching the values of the cell vision, consulting and communicating with the church members and explaining the cell model carefully, people will be more willing to run with it.

Remember that people grow at different paces. Don't force anyone. Work with those who are willing. Try to include everybody. Ownership is the key. Great pastoral care and wisdom is needed to keep people onboard. Above all, don't exclude or isolate. Take as much time as it needs to do the transition well.

CONCLUDING THE TRANSITION

If you have ever been an airline passenger, you will know how frustrating it is to be kept endlessly waiting in the transit lounge. Your mind is on your destination. Transit is not the final goal, only a necessary step to get you where you want to be. While it is wrong to hurry the transition, it is also wrong to prolong the process unnecessarily.

During transition, you may retain some elements from the old way of doing things, but this is because you cannot change everything overnight. Transition means you are in the process of changing everything that must be changed in order to become what you have set out to be – a fully-functioning cell church.

You will be ready to declare an end to transition when all the basic elements of the Model of 12 are established and working. The Ladder of Success will be operating well, the majority of church members will be in cells, new leaders will be emerging, cells will be multiplying and the church will be growing. A church that has transitioned well will be a church in which the culture has changed, and not just when the cell structure is theoretically in place.

You know you have achieved this when the 'average' church member understands the cell vision, loves it and is actively involved in it. Fruit takes time to appear, so do not judge the success of your transition by numerical statistics alone. Discipleship will lead to multiplication, but exponential growth factors take time to kick in.

You know you have transitioned when the church members are engaged in the ministry and have shouldered the responsibility for the life and growth of the church. When they are winning their friends and neighbours to Christ, discipling them in the faith and are carrying the full Mandate of Christ.

The transition is a demanding time for everyone – but it is also exciting. People will have a sense that the church is getting 'back to basics' and this will restore a sense of authenticity to the Christian community. New life will begin to spring up and you will be surprised by those who take to the cell vision as the proverbial duck to water. You may also be disappointed by those who struggle to embrace it. However, the most significant blessing outweighs all the challenges – Christ and his mission will once again be at the heart of everything we do.

Planting a Cell Church

Taking into account the challenges that come with transitioning a traditional church into a cell church, some leaders approach the idea of planting new churches with enthusiasm. The opportunity to start with a blank sheet of paper is appealing. After all, you do not have to transition a church which may be reluctant to learn new ideas and you can begin building with completely 'unchurched' people who don't come with too much ecclesiastical baggage.

There is a large degree of truth in this. However, you cannot assume that traditional thinking will not be carried over into the new venture. Perhaps the founding members will unconsciously bring traditional ideas with them and automatically reproduce them in the new church. New converts will also probably have some preconceived ideas about church and some of these notions will be far-removed from New Testament concepts. Church planters will have to be aware of these tendencies and overcome them by being sure about cell church themselves and hold firmly to the vision.

In Chapter 8, we covered extensively the reasons why cell church is a good model to follow, but there are some additional advantages for church planters. The cell model is an effective way of planting simple and reproducible churches whereas the traditional model is rather cumbersome. It is usually associated with elaborate buildings, extensive programmes and established leaders who have been formally-trained through a long and costly process of education.

People working with the conventional model may start small but their goal is to move towards all the elements of traditional church. Because traditional church is based on 'come and see' rather than 'go and tell', it tends to attract spectators rather than active participators. It an 'attractional' model and not a 'missional' model. Growth is achieved through attractive programmes, rather than by reaching out through a trained and active membership.

WHY SHOULD WE PLANT CHURCHES?

It is important to be aware of the role church planting has in the Holy Spirit's agenda for today. Church planting is much more than a good idea someone once happened to have. It is the on-going plan of God for reaching the nations. Peter Wagner, the missiologist and church growth expert says, "Church planting is the best method of evangelism under heaven."

Donald McGravrin, the founder of the modern church growth movement saw the need in global evangelism for an extensive church planting strategy and said that the only way we will get the job of the Great Commission done was to plant a church in every community in the world. Church planting is needed not only to evangelise unevangelised nations but to re-evangelise nations where the church is in decline.

Established churches often carry an outmoded culture and often do not express Christ in a way that is relevant to the unchurched. New churches can more easily adapt their style and approach to the needs of our contemporary generation. Church planting brings the gospel within the reach of thousands of people who would simply not be drawn to the more traditional expressions of church. We need a new and effective church planting movement that uses a simple and reproducible model. Cell church may well prove to be it.

Kensington Temple was instrumental in planting around 150 churches in London from 1985 to 2000. We did not have the benefit at the time of the cell model we are using today.

Some of our church planters first formed a nucleus of members, then looked for a building and finally opened their church. Others lacked the vision for making, maturing and mobilising disciples and simply set about trying to attract new members to their church. They soon found themselves with a group of people who were expecting a fully-established programme in place without accepting their responsibility to become producers of growth themselves. This is the typical 'consumer Christianity' of today.

Some started as cell groups and then grew into churches without retaining the vision for cells. The initial cell members grew too numerous to meet in a home, so they began to gather in a hall. When this became too small they dreamed of having their own church building. The focus was on growing the congregation bigger and bigger. In other words, they simply reproduced the traditional church model – a pastor with a congregation and a building.

We do not do that now. We have adopted the cell church model of planting churches. We start a new church by reproducing cells, grouping them into one or more congregations, which remain part of the vision of London City Church – the name we give to our city-wide strategy of planting cells, congregations and ministries. We see ourselves as a network of all these elements working together as one church. In other words, we have a Meta church structure.

MEGA CHURCH OR META CHURCH?

The rise of the Western Mega church phenomenon in the 1980s was championed by church growth proponents who seemed to believe that the objective was to grow a single church into a huge congregation of many thousands. The primary purpose was to attract and keep as many people as possible under one roof. The preaching had to be popular and the programme polished. 'Big' became the new spirituality and 'better' the new philosphy of ministry. The small group programme was simply a way of 'closing the back door' of the church. Where all these elements successfully came together, usually under the leadership of a talented and anointed leader, the multitudes came. Some were new converts but most were drawn from other churches within a 100 mile radius.

This couldn't be further away from what David Yonggi Cho, for example, was doing in South Korea. He also had a church of many thousands and excellence was highly-valued. However, discipleship was at the centre of the strategy. People were not passive spectators in Sunday services but active members who did the work of Christ through the cells and brought their 'fruit' to the massive celebrations in the church building at the weekend. This is not Mega church, but Meta church.

Meta church is about reaching multi thousands, but it is also about building church through Jesus' method of discipleship. What is the point of attracting thousands of believers into a massive building once a week, if there is no real, intentional discipleship? Meta church seeks to train and deploy every member for the harvest, and not just to attract them into one central venue. It is about releasing people into the ministry through a network of cells, congregations and celebration gatherings resulting in a multiplicity of interrelated expressions of Christ throughout a city or region.

The term 'Meta church' comes from an important use of the Greek word *meta*. This word means 'change' or 'after' as in *metanoia*, the Greek word for 'repentance', which means 'a change of mind' or 'thinking again'. But *meta* can also mean 'beyond' or 'between'. It refers to things that stand in relation to each other. An example of this use of *meta* is 'metaphor' which refers to a figure of speech that makes a link between one thing and something else it can be compared to. Another example is 'metatarsus', which refers to the part of the foot between the *tarus* (ankle) and the toes. 'Metagalaxy' is an example of a word that incorporates the use of *meta* as 'beyond'. It refers to a complete system of galaxies, beyond the Milky Way to include all the surrounding galaxies.

Meta church, therefore, expresses the concept of church as being more than a single, isolated and independent unit, no matter how small or big. It indicates the link beyond a single, self-contained expression of church and shows the relationship between it and other similar expressions. It emphasises interdependence and interconnectedness. Mega church focuses on one, big centralised entity while Meta church is concerned with expressing church at many different levels. Everything has its place – from the small to the big, the microscopic to the gigantic.

The advantage of this idea of church is that it can release every member to grow into the fullest expression of individual ministry while remaining a functioning part of the whole. It can penetrate every part of society with expressions of church through cells and groups of cells, forming congregational communities and large celebration gatherings that can impact and transform whole cities and regions.

WHAT SHOULD WE BE PLANTING?

We have seen that cell church moves away from traditional church models, including the mega expressions of them. It seeks to express the full New Testament meaning of *ekklesia* and *diakonia* resulting in cells, congregations and celebrations linked in Meta church fellowship.

We have also begun to see the importance of the networking principle. After all, no expression of the church should be isolated in its fellowship, narrow its vision or inward in its focus. You cannot have an independent church any more than you can have an independent hand or foot. We are joined to Christ and to each other.

These are the kinds of churches we should be thinking of planting. This is the prophetic and apostolic vision of the hour.

God is progressively bringing his church to the fullness set out in Ephesians chapter 4:

> *And he himself gave some to be apostles, some prophets, some evangelists, and some pastors and teachers, for the equipping of the saints for the work of ministry, for the edifying of the body of Christ, till we all come to the unity of the faith and of the knowledge of the Son of God, to a perfect man, to the measure of the stature of the fullness of Christ.*
>
> Ephesians 4:11-13

Pragmatism and flexibility have their place, but not at the expense of God's ultimate plan. Success must be measured in biblical terms. We are Christ's representatives on earth and we must fulfil our apostolic commission to make the kind of disciples that Jesus is able to use to build his church.

HOW TO BEGIN

Simplicity, multiplication and networking are the basic principles that we keep in mind when planting a cell church. We aim to keep our structures *simple* by focussing on the most important elements of evangelism, discipleship and training. We build reproduction and *multiplication* into the DNA of the church from the very beginning. Every member becomes a worker – that's the deal. If people are not prepared to work for Jesus, they are poor candidates for church planting. Right from the start, the church planters connect with others *networking* with the wider body of Christ. They work in relationship with their parent body and in partnership with other expressions of the body of Christ around them.

In Chapter 22, we looked at the 'group, gather, grow' strategy of planting cells, and this strategy also applies to planting a cell church. We begin by planting a cell and growing that cell so that it can multiply. The cell members must understand what they are signing up to when they join the cell. They must carry the vision of the church plant and be committed to it. Unity of purpose, covenant commitment and heart relationship are the foundational values. The vision of the church plant must be established from the very beginning.

The cell is the fundament unit of functioning church and this is strengthened by the principle of 3. Companionship groups form the nuclei of the cells. They foster the Holy Spirit bonds in the group and sustain its life through mutual encouragement and relationship. Growth is established through evangelism and by attracting other like-minded people God is calling to the work. These must be released to the church plant by their leaders and not just by their own desires.

New members must be drawn into the commitment of growing in Christ together, according to cell principles. Otherwise, there will be tension when the new church begins to develop. The spiritual environment that fosters traditional church will take over and destroy the original vision. Death to selfish ambition and egotistical pride is essential or the tiny church will be hijacked by the fleshly intentions of those looking for a platform for their own ministry.

Cells, congregations and celebrations

As the cells multiply, the Primary Groups of 12 will be established. Evangelism will still be the major focus. The new church plant will be all about reaching people with the gospel and discipling them in the faith. When there are a sufficient number of cells gathering a substantial number of people, it is time to gather the cells in regular congregational meetings. The cells should continue to meet during the week. The congregation meeting could be held on Sundays and should follow the pattern the apostle Paul establishes in 1 Corinthians 14:26.

> *How is it then, brethren? Whenever you come together, each of you has a psalm, has a teaching, has a tongue, has a revelation, has an interpretation. Let all things be done for edification.*
>
> 1 Corinthians 14:26-27

The congregational setting is an opportunity for the cell groups to join together to worship God and to edify one another. It is not the same as the celebration services which are led from the platform by a few principal leaders. Congregational worship is about each person coming ready to contribute in the service as the Holy Spirit leads. It is an ideal opportunity for people to develop their ministry but only in so far as it edifies the whole congregation. It is not for spiritual grandstanding or showy performance. Instead, the family of God shares together in worship, fellowship, Communion and the exercise of spiritual gifts.

When the congregation is established the temptation is to switch the focus away from cells and adopt the traditional model that demands independence, a pastor, a building, and so on. But this should not happen. The cells produce growth through evangelism and discipleship and when these are compromised, the growth will decline, training will diminish and the members of the church will take a back seat and call for the 'professionals' to take over. The cells carry the dynamic for multiplication, and as they grow, the congregational gatherings increase in size and influence.

Congregations have a significant responsibility toward the community. Cells can influence individuals, but congregations can reach their community. Serving the wider community is part of the cell vision. Community service not only fulfils God's call to servanthood, but it can also build valuable links for gospel witness and transformational influence in society.

This is an important milestone in the new church's development, but it does not stop there. By now, the church plant will begin to feel like a church. But this has more to do with the commonly accepted understanding of what a church looks like. Leadership will have been established. Organisation becomes a little more elaborate and the congregation's visibility is noticed by others, but the church has not arrived at its destination. It must continue to multiply cells and grow.

The congregational dynamic, capable of fulfilling 1 Corinthians 14:26, breaks down when the group grows too big. When the number of people grows to significantly over 100, it becomes difficult for everyone to contribute to the worship service meaningfully. The danger is that 'the many' become passive and 'the few' begin to dominate the ministry. That is not the purpose of congregational worship. At this point, it is time to think about the next step.

The choice now is between forming multiple congregations which can preserve the integrity of congregational worship or transitioning the congregational meeting into a celebration-style service. Celebration services are appropriate for gatherings larger than 150 people. In these meetings, the ministry is mainly 'from the front' and not 'body-based'. The dynamic of the large group takes over and the focus is on celebration. Teaching and preaching is in the hands of the more gifted leaders. The service is directed by key people who lead the whole gathering as the Holy Spirit leads. These meetings are valuable and an important part of church. The Jerusalem church of Acts met in celebration style gatherings in the Temple courts as well as in the small groups gathered in the homes.

The standard cell model emphasises the cells and celebrations as being the 'two wings' of the church. However in my view, the congregational level should have an on-going place in cell church, even when numbers increase significantly.

The choice us up to the individual churches, but there is a way of expressing all three levels: *cell, congregation* and *celebration*. As the cells continue to multiply, they can be gathered into several congregations for weekly meetings on Sundays (or another day if necessary). Celebrations can be held monthly in which all the congregations gather together in a larger venue. This presents an exciting prospect – church functioning at every level found in the New Testament. We aim for the best of everything. Each different level of church fulfils its own purpose and function while working in relationship with every other level.

- *The cells* remain the basic building block of the church – where the crucial work of the church takes place. New believers are won and consolidated in the faith. Leaders begin to be trained.

- *The congregations* serve to express the community dimension of our faith, raising up strong ministries from within and reaching the community without.

- *The celebrations* provide the occasion for the Ephesians 4:11 ministries to flourish and for the people of God to express their identity as part of a large and vibrant group.

The first generation of Primary 12 cells will produce the second generation making 144 groups, and then the third generation multiplies to 1,728. Finally, a vibrant Meta church emerges, with each part a living and active component of the whole. A church functioning like this can have a strong influence on its society and can be a solid base for missional activity further away from home. We look at the place of world mission in the cell vision in the next chapter.

Cells for Mission

The Great Commission is expansive, embracing all nations. Christ died for all and the gospel belongs to the whole world. From the first missions of the apostle Paul to the present day initiatives to take the gospel to all peoples, God has been directing his church to disciple the nations. The cell vision instils this vision through its emphasis on Matthew 28:18-20. We actively encourage all the cells to engage passionately in world missions through prayer, giving and going. The cell vision is a part of God's global move to reach the nations of the world through evangelism, discipleship and church planting. Mission is always on the agenda.

Kensington Temple has 119 different nations represented in its membership, and so we find it easy to focus on international ministry. We send missionaries to the harvest fields of the world and organise short term missions through the cells. Each Primary 12 leader 'adopts' a mission field and begins to promote missions through his or her generation of cells. Strategic plans emerge through research and networking with existing initiatives on the ground. We support local churches overseas through equipping, enabling and encouraging. Where appropriate, we initiate new strategies to extend the influence of the gospel in any particular nation.

The cells pray for the mission fields the Holy Spirit lays on their heart and give to the work of God taking place in that nation. These funds support on-going initiatives of church planting, training and evangelism. We plant Bible Schools, children's homes, community projects and other aid initiatives. Every cell member is a part of this ministry and we encourage every person to go overseas for at least one short term mission. We find that this brings life to the cells and broadens their vision. Jesus said, "Lift up your eyes and look at the fields, for they are white for harvest!" (John 4:35). Every new believer joins a cell which is immersed in the vision of Christ for the nations.

This aspect of cell ministry means we are marshalling our people power for the worldwide work of making, maturing and mobilising disciples. The more we grow, the more we can achieve. Our resources are not being depleted but rather are increasing. A devolved, rather than a centralised approach to missions in the church, makes sure that the vision for mission does not run out of steam. The cell vision ensures that the more we grow, the more we can do.

We believe that global vision is as important as worship and Communion. Historically, every major move of God in the church has provoked intensive prayer and extensive missions. We are inspired by the example of the Moravian church of the 18ᵗʰ Century.

ZINZENDORF AND THE MORAVIANS

200 years after the Protestant Reformation began in Germany through the work of Martin Luther, the nation witnessed a new move of God that would have a far reaching effect on missions. Many began to turn away from the cold formalism that had become associated with Lutheranism. Led by men like Philip Spener and August Herman Franck, this new move centred in the Danish University of Halle, and was called Pietism. Franck was a professor at Halle and he turned the university into a centre for evangelism and mission.

Soon missionaries were sent out into India and met with success. Back in Germany, however, these men were severely ridiculed and criticised. They were called "priests of Baal" and "false prophets". Sermons were preached against the new movement even in Wittenberg, the birth place of the Reformation. One such sermon closed with the ditty:

'Go into all the world' the Lord did say;
but now, 'Where God has placed thee,
there he would have thee stay.'

This shows how far the church had fallen from her original purpose. Despite the Protestant Reformation, world mission was resisted as a concept. The standard approach to church was still predominantly that of the 'state church', in which every citizen was 'christened' at birth. The national church's responsibility was to its own nation. However, the concept of the 'gathered church' introduced by the Anabaptists of the 16th Century was slowly gaining ground. The Anabaptists emphasised the importance of vital, personal Christianity and opened the way for the concept of growing the church worldwide through prayer and world missions. Evangelising the nations and not Christianising them was recovered as Christ's way of building his church. Mission became the spiritual call to surrender to God's kingdom, his dynamic rule, and not to extend the borders of Christendom.

One young man who came under the influence of Franck's Halle University was Count Nicholas Ludwig von Zinzendorf. Zinzendorf soon began to burn with intense missionary vision. In 1719, he dedicated his life to the Christian ministry. In 1724 he founded a Christian community on his estate for those who fled to Germany escaping religious persecution.

In 1727, revival broke out in the community, and birthed the two passions that were to shake the earth and result in massive Christian expansion: a passion for missions and a passion for prayer. A round-the-clock prayer vigil was started that was to last for over 100 years. In the next 20 years the Moravians (as they were called) sent out more missionaries than the whole of Protestantism in the previous two centuries. Missions were started in the Virgin Islands (1732), Greenland (1733), North America (1734), Lapland and south America (1735), South Africa (1736), and Labrador (1771).

We saw in Chapter 9, that the Moravians emphasised the place of small groups in the Christian community. These were the means of stirring spiritual passion and keeping the fires of revival alive. The missionary movement of the 18th Century could never have been sustained without this fellowship of believers in small groups where they met for mutual encouragement and edification.

CELLS, THE WORKFORCE FOR MISSION

Today, the world is a 'global village' and most of us have access to news, information or global travel. Every church can be a 'world church' and every cell can be involved in world missions. In Kensington Temple, specially devised mission offering envelopes are used in cell meetings. Giving is linked to praying in the cells. We publish a monthly missions article in our church magazine, *Revival Times*, with prayer points the cell groups use during that month. We hold regular missions revival prayer meetings. In this way, we motivate people to pray for and give to missions in the cells.

We provide notes for use in the cell meetings to promote mission and regularly supply teaching outlines to enable the cells to keep the missions focus. Each cell has a Missions Pack giving general information concerning world missions, our denominational guidelines for Short Term Missions and information on Kensington Temple's international vision. We update the cells with current news from our mission fields and invite prayer for any new developments that are in view. We also provide missions training through our Missions Course. In this way we keep the fire of missions burning.

Many of our members come to London from abroad for business or study and return home as 'missionaries' to their own people. The cells are like mini factories engaging in missional activity and releasing workers into the harvest fields of the world. This is the body of Christ in action.

The Marvellous Body of Christ

Imagine a world without the church. Where would society be without the light of the gospel shining from countless communities of Christian believers all over the world, both large and small? Think of the many benefits churches bring to the world. Hospitals, schools, drug rehabilitation, marriage counselling, care for the dying, feeding the hungry and clothing the naked – these and a myriad other works of compassion express the love of Christ in a broken and hurting world.

Think also of the Christian values embedded in the foundations of many societies, especially in the West. Despite the efforts of liberalism, atheism and false religion, Christian influence still permeates many institutions. The church is the biggest blessing the world has seen since the actual physical presence of Jesus of Nazareth, the Word made flesh.

All this comes through the gospel of Jesus, the message of hope for a dying world. The beacon of light, ignited by Christ himself more than 2,000 years ago, continues to shine through his church, which he called, "the light of the world". The grace and truth of God that is Jesus, was first manifested in the incarnation, and is now being expressed to the world through the church and the message he has given us to proclaim.

Jesus said, "A city set on a hill cannot be hidden", and then he went on to say,

> *Let your light so shine before men, that they may see your good works and glorify your Father in heaven.*
>
> Matthew 5:16

Through actions, words and miraculous demonstrations of his power, the church makes visible the invisible kingdom of God. Truly, the body of Christ is marvellous.

COMPARING THE CHURCH TO THE HUMAN BODY

In Chapter 9, I introduced some similarities between biological cells and cell groups in the church. In subsequent chapters, we examined the Model of 12 in detail. Now, we can identify more parallels between human cells and how the cells operate in the body of Christ.

The analogy between the human body and the church was first made by the apostle Paul. He described the church as the "body of Christ".

> *Now you are the body of Christ, and members individually.*
>
> 1 Corinthians 12:27

Paul develops this analogy speaking of headship, unity, diversity, functionality and interdependence. Recent discoveries of modern biological science help us apply Paul's analogy to the cell church model. The development of the electronic microscope has added to our understanding of the human body as a multi-cellular organism. This technology shows us that cells are amazingly complex and finely tuned functional entities.

All living matter is composed of cells, and the human body is no exception. It is made up of up 75 trillion cells (7.5×10^{13}). This is sheds new light onto the truth of the scripture which says,

> *I will praise you, for I am fearfully and wonderfully made. Marvellous are your works.*
>
> Psalm 139:14

If the human body is so marvellous, can we expect anything less of the body of Christ? We should certainly not build doctrine on biology, but modern science helps us understand Paul's analogy in a deeper way.

The correspondence between how the cells of the human body function and the workings of the body of Christ are remarkable. I will list some of these now, restating those I have already touched on in this book, and adding a few more to the list.

1. The human body is structured into cells. Cell church follows this principle by encouraging every member to be an active part of a cell group.

2. The cells of the human body are the basic functioning unit of the life of the body. Cell groups are also the basic unit of life in the cell church.

3. Cells in the body have a nucleus which acts as the control centre of the cell. Cell groups also have a system of leadership which regulates the group according to the vision of the church.

4. Human cells carry the DNA of the body they belong to. The characteristics of *ekklesia* are present in microcosmic form in the cells groups. They also carry and reproduce the spiritual DNA of their church.

5. Cells in the human body reproduce and multiply. Cells in the church also reproduce through evangelism and discipleship.

6. Human cells do not have a totally independent life of their own. Cell groups also are not independent. They have an interdependent relationship with each other and the body of Christ.

7. Individual human cells work together for the good of the whole body, each having a special place and function. Cells in the church also work together for the common good. Every individual cell is needed for the growth and development of the whole body.

8. The cells in the human body have systems of communication and reporting. The cell groups also communicate and report to the church.

9. Human cells generate power and energy. Cells in the church are also centres of power and energy for the good of the body of Christ.

10. Human cells are comprised of mini organs (organelles) which function at a sub-cellular level making sure the cell stays healthy and fulfils its function. Cell groups are also organised into sub-groups, such as the groups of 3. Cell members have specially-assigned responsibilities enabling them to function efficiently and effectively.

11. Human cells have specialised functions. Cells groups can also develop areas of expertise and can have specialised ministries reaching different members of the community. These can be ethnic groups, professional groups or those with special interests such as the arts or science.

12. Some cells (stem cells) in the human body have the capacity to transform or differentiate into cells of a different type in order for the body to develop every necessary capacity. This is also seen in cell groups where an open cell transforms into a leadership cell.

FULLY MOBILISED

This short excursion into the world of human biology highlights the benefits of the cell vision. Healthy cells mean a healthy body. The cell model enables Christ's body on earth to function effectively. The body of Christ is his 'agent' in the world. Just as our bodies enable us to be present in any specific place and do what we want it to do, so Christ acts in the world through his body. Whatever he wants to do on the earth, he must use his body do it. As the apostle Paul says, "The Head cannot say to the body, 'I have no need of you'" (1 Corinthians 12:21).

That's why his body must be mobilised, not paralysed. We would never wish the tragedy of physical paralysis on anyone. We should be equally concerned to see the body of Christ fully active and mobile. However, for the most part, we expect Jesus to work through a severely restricted body.

Estimates vary, but active members are definitely in the minority in most churches. Usually, only 5 to 10% of church members are involved in evangelism, nurturing new believers or any other kind of effective Christian ministry. However, 80 to 95% of the members in most cell churches are actively involved in the work of Christ.

Imagine the effects on our nations and the world at large of a fully-mobilised body of Christ, where every believer is a disciple and every disciple is a minister. This must be our goal. The only way the church will rise up and accomplish the task set by the Master, is for every member of his body to be fully responsive to the direction of the Head. This is in line with the New Testament's view of the church. The whole is only brought to fullness as each part does its share of the work:

> *…the whole body, joined and knit together by what every joint supplies, according to the effective working by which every part does its share, causes growth of the body for the edifying of itself in love.*
>
> Ephesians 4:16

In order for the church to be healthy and grow to maturity, all the ministry gifts of Christ must be active in the body. Only then will every member be equipped to do the work of Christ. Cell churches take account of this and make sure all the five ministries of Ephesians 4:11 are active in the church: apostles, prophets, evangelists, pastors, and teachers.

Jesus exercised all these ministries while he was on the earth. Now, he operates them through specially-selected and suitably-anointed people. These gifts are distributed to the church and make up the full complement of the ministry of Christ in his body.

The fivefold ministry gifts are a permanent part of the church's ministry on earth. They are valid and necessary in every generation, and will continue to operate:

> *...until we all reach unity in the faith and in the knowledge of the Son of God and become mature, attaining to the whole measure of the fullness of Christ.*
> Ephesians 4:13

All these gifts are needed until the whole church grows into the full maturity of Christ. Only then will the church be fully equipped to complete the Mandate of Christ. These gifts are given to men and women who have a 'life calling' in one or more of them. However, their purpose is to prepare God's people for the ministry of Christ. The cell strategy recognises how the fivefold ministry operates both in the wider body of the church as well as in the cells.

Understanding the fivefold ministry

Apostles provide the foundational framework for church life. They are gifted in initiating key functions, thereby moving the church forward into God's vision. They have the ability to bring structure and growth into the body of Christ.

Prophets exercise more than the regular gift of prophecy in the church. They are prophets to the church, and sometimes to the wider world. They are the eyes, ears and mouthpiece of the body. They bring revelation and give direction in a wide range of situations.

Evangelists are the 'promoters' of the Christian faith. They are gifted in leading people to Christ and proclaiming the good news. Their ministry is to draw people to the point of making a decision to follow Christ.

Pastors are the shepherds of the flock. They gather the sheep, care for them, feed them and guard them from dangers. Pastors are like anchors in the church, keeping it steady in turbulent times. Like glue, they hold the church together in unity and strength. Their focus is the regular, day-to-day ministry of the church.

Teachers are gifted in understanding the scriptures and have the ability to communicate the truths of God to others in a practical and understandable way. The teaching ministry is closely associated with discipleship. Teachers form disciples through their instruction and practical example.

Equipping the saints

As I have just pointed out, the scriptural purpose of the fivefold ministry is "to prepare God's people for works of service, so that the body of Christ may be built up". Leadership exists to equip every member of the church for the ministry, that is, to do the work of Christ.

Cell churches are ideally structured to exercise the fivefold ministry according to its true purpose. The cells are where these spiritual gifts begin to be indentified and developed, because the cells are the breeding ground of ministry. They are also at the cutting edge of mission – the cells are where people are won to Christ, consolidated in their faith, discipled into leadership and sent out into the world.

We can easily see how each of the five ministries of Christ finds its expression in the growth, expansion and multiplication of new disciples. This presents us with a bold and radical vision of a modern day, 'New Testament' church.

The fivefold ministry and the cells

At every point in the cell vision, one or more of the five main ministries must be functioning. As the cell leaders and cell members come under the influence of the fivefold ministry, every person is equipped to participate in every stage of the cell vision. That way we are all able to 'Win, Consolidate, Disciple and Send'.

I say more about this in my book *The Fivefold Ministry*, in which I explain in detail the nature of all the five ministries and how they operate in a cell church. I will give a short summary here of how I see the fivefold ministry working with the cells by equipping every believer to do the work of Christ.

- The apostolic ministry grounds the cells in the principles of grace. It spurs the cells on towards growth and multiplication. New cells spring up as new initiatives are taken under apostolically influenced cell leaders.
- The prophetic ministry brings breakthrough revelation in the lives of cell members. It helps the cells remain in touch with the heart and mind of the Spirit.
- The evangelistic ministry motivates and equips the cells for evangelism and for producing new life.
- The pastoral ministry helps nurture the cell members and consolidate the new believers.
- The teaching ministry builds up the cell members and helps disciple the believers, showing them also how to become disciple makers of others.

In my Group of 12, all the fivefold ministries of Christ are in evidence. These leaders are growing other leaders who reflect the same ministry strengths. Over time, everyone receives ministry from all the five major gifts of Christ, especially in our celebration services. I know whom to send to help cell leaders struggling in one area of ministry or another. No one person has all the gifts, but we can all grow in every area because the fivefold ministry is functioning.

When all the ministries are working together in harmony and equipping the body to do the work of Christ, we become a formidable entity. We are able to take the presence of Christ into our daily lives, evangelise the lost and bring transformation to our society. In Kensington Temple, we have a name for this aspect of our vision. We call it 'taking the giants'.

TAKING THE GIANTS
Jesus told his church to be salt and light in the world. That is, to penetrate society with the healthy influence of our salt-like

presence, and to illuminate society's thinking with the light of gospel values. We cannot withdraw from the world as if we were not living in it, and neither can we allow the world to remain in us, neutralising our saltiness and dimming our capacity to shine. The cell vision is not just about growing our numbers, but making disciples who influence the world.

The cell groups are part of the 'go and show' thrust of the church. Traditional church has a 'come and hear' emphasis and largely holds its activities within the sanctity of its buildings. Cells have the capacity to penetrate every part of society and to exercise influence for Christ in the heart of the *agora*, or market place of today. That is where the church is needed most. Christianity is a lifestyle and we are called to be good news right where we are – in our homes, our places of work, our centres of education and in every other part of society. I have quoted several times in this book our dictum to our members who spend most of their life in the market place of our society: *your occupation is the location for your true vocation.*

When Christ sent the first generation of his disciples into the world to preach, to heal, to deliver and to demonstrate his love through the gospel, he did not intend that we simply get involved by working in the church. His purpose was to put the church to work in the world. The cell ministry seeks to fulfil the Great Commission, not just in the church building, but through the cells *at the point of their greatest influence.* Cells reach people where they are.

We equip our members to 'take the giants' for God. The giants of our society are the great institutions and professions which exercise the most influence over our lives. We hold regular giants forums in which cell members from each of the major professional or occupational groupings can get together to encourage one another, and find ways of influencing their environment. That way we are facilitating cells in every major profession and section in society. We group the giants in the following way:

The giants of influence:

1. Business and Finance
2. Ecology and Environment
3. Education and Training
4. Law and Order
5. Marriage and Family
6. Media and Arts
7. Medicine and Health
8. Politics and Government
9. Religion and Belief
10. Science and Technology
11. Sport and Leisure
12. Thought and Philosophy.

As believers become active witnesses to the kingdom of God in these areas, people are won to Christ, discipled, and begin to exercise a godly influence over these giants. It is not just about having Christians working in these sectors, but disciples influencing their environment for Christ. We are aiming for the total transformation of our society. That is exactly what the body of Christ is called to do.

CHURCH WITHOUT WALLS

Cell church is church without walls. People are reached right where they are. Christian witness happens in the market place and not just in the meeting place. Beginning with the obstacle of building-bound church, barriers between us and the lost are broken down and removed. The cells build bridges for the community to see Christ in action. Cultures are penetrated through the informality and accessibility of cell ministry. Discipleship happens through relationships formed from within the heart of the non-Christian community and not merely through church programmes which appear to be mere religious institutions to those outside.

This is the church as it is meant to be – not a closed book, but "living letters, known and read by the world". This is the vision of Christ, the very heart of God expressed in the living, breathing body of Christ on the earth. The plan has not changed. God is still working out his purposes on the earth through his church. Every believer in Christ is a part of it, and cell church enables the vision to become a reality.

The Multitudes are Coming!

God's vision for the church will be fulfilled. He is totally committed to it. He sent his Son to bring the church into being through his death, resurrection and ascension to heaven. From there, Christ sent his Spirit to bring life, power and holiness to his people on the earth. He promises to be with us until the end of the age when his glorious purpose for the church will have been accomplished.

The apostle Paul gives us a glimpse of the finished product in Ephesians chapter 4,

> *...till we all come to the unity of the faith and of the knowledge of the Son of God, to a perfect man, to the measure of the stature of the fullness of Christ; that we should no longer be children, tossed to and fro and carried about with every wind of doctrine, by the trickery of men, in the cunning craftiness of deceitful plotting, but, speaking the truth in love, may grow up in all things into him who is the head – Christ...*
>
> Ephesians 4:13-15

A VISION OF FULLNESS
These verses reveal God's vision for the church. He wants us to work for this goal by growing together to be like Christ, so that he can fully manifest himself through us to our lost and dying world. Our goal is to build up the body of Christ until it becomes strong and healthy, and that will only happen when all God's people truly begin to serve in the ministry of Christ. There can be no fullness in isolation, but only as we draw

together and corporately rise to Christ's purpose. According to the apostle Paul, it will only come to fulfilment when the church enters into the following four things.

1.   The unity of the faith (Ephesians 4:13)

God's vision is for a church which is mature in understanding. Disunity is always present where there is immaturity and lack of spiritual knowledge. But the time is coming when the body of Christ will grow in wisdom and knowledge to the point when petty divisions will be laid on one side and we will embrace the unity of the faith.

The unity of the faith is more than right belief. The goal of doctrine is to mould character and to guide behaviour. God is looking for love that flows from a pure of heart. This love causes us to look beyond our personal doctrinal preferences and to hold onto the important things that unite us as Christians. God wants us to grow in this kind of love so that we can be free from jealous factions and selfish ambitions.

True unity is never merely cosmetic. It replaces competition between groups with genuine co-operation. This level of co-ordination can only flow from a complete acceptance of each other and of our common role to make Christ known in the world.

2.   The full knowledge of the Son of God (Ephesians 4:13)

When the Church reaches fullness we will have attained to the full knowledge of Christ. Christ will be fully revealed in the church. There will be a maturity of corporate knowledge and experience of Christ.

Down through the ages there have been many great men and women who have entered into this deep knowledge. But the Church of fullness will bring that same experience to every believer! It hardly seems possible, but God's Word makes clear that before the return of Jesus Christ, the Church on earth will attain to the full knowledge of the Son of God. This will not be the perfection of heaven, but the full practical outworking of all that God has shown us about Christ now.

3. Maturity (Ephesians 4:13)

The New Testament church was an infant church, but the endtime church will be a mature church that is strong and fully developed. When the church comes of age it will be able to stand against all the antagonism and deceitfulness of the enemy. The endtime church will rise to greater power and effectiveness than at the beginning. We see in the book of Acts and the rest of the New Testament what the infant church was capable of. Just imagine the glory of the church in maturity! It will be an effective instrument of world harvest. The Church will rise up and get the job done.

4. The whole measure of the fullness of Christ (Ephesians 4:13)

This is God's ultimate goal for the church on earth – Christ filling his body to capacity. The one who fills everything in every way, already fills the church (Ephesians 1:22-23). But this fullness, which we know by faith now, will one day be fully experienced by the church. Christ wants to manifest the fullness of his power, his wisdom and his authority in the church. He wants us to demonstrate to the world the fullness of his love and his grace. He wants us to attain to the fullness of holiness and joy so that he would have a credible body of witnesses on the earth through whom he can manifest his salvation to the world.

It must be the goal of the church in any age to move towards this manifest fullness, and there are some encouraging signs in our generation. All over the world, the body of Christ is rising up and laying hold of the person and presence of Christ. The

Holy Spirit is falling on whole nations. The gospel is sweeping over 100,000 people into the kingdom every day worldwide. The growth of the Christian faith, particularly in the so-called developing world, is phenomenal. And in the West, too, there is some progress. We must not falter now. We are on the verge of the church's finest hour. In our day, we could well see the fullness of Christ manifest in the church!

God's vision for the church will only be fulfilled when the church truly acts as his representatives on the earth doing the great work he gave us – reaching the world with the gospel. It is something worth dreaming about. It is something worth being a part of. Paul clearly saw the time when it would happen. It must become our goal as individuals and our goal corporately. That is what cell church offers.

THE MULTITUDES ARE COMING!

God has only ever had one plan – to have a very large family! Beginning with the call of Abram (who became Abraham), right through the Bible, ending with the prophecies of the book of Revelation, God's purpose is clearly seen – to bring together in one body people from every nation, tribe and language. This company of people will share the eternal splendour of Christ in the kingdom of God, shining in glorious testimony to his grace and power.

It began with what God said to Abram,

> *"Get out of your country, from your family and from your father's house, to a land that I will show you. I will make you a great nation; I will bless you and make your name great; and you shall be a blessing. I will bless those who bless you, and I will curse him who curses you; and in you all the families of the earth shall be blessed."*
>
> Genesis 12:1-3

Salvation is God's blessing promised to all humanity – to all nations, peoples and families. The promise came through the seed of Abraham, which is Christ (Galatians 3:16). In Christ, the church inherits this blessing of Abraham (Galatians 3:13-14). We are going to see multitudes from all nations come into the church of God. Our calling is a mirror image of the call of Abraham.

Movement – "Get out… of your country"

Abram had to be willing to change his position. For some, this will be a literal, physical relocation, for others it will be a change in attitude, a willingness to leave the comfort zone – and for some, it will mean transitioning into the cell vision – but in one way or another, we must all move forward.

Separation – "Leave… your kindred and your father's house"

God wanted to do something new. He didn't want the past to hold Abram back. He wanted a separation from the world he knew. This speaks of a willingness to break from all our fleshly ties to the past – both personally and in the way we do church.

Faith – "A land I will show you…"

Humanly speaking, we often want to see something with our physical eyes before we believe it and act on it. But God's way is by faith – believing and obeying his Word as we look forward to the outcome God promised. Lack of this kind of faith would have kept Abram in Ur of the Chaldees, and the same lack of faith will leave us where we are. However, bold and daring faith will give us the courage to move forward, towards the future where his promise awaits.

Destiny – "I will make you into a great nation… and make your name great."

God specified to Abraham what his destiny was, to be "the father of many nations." God has placed the seeds of greatness in our hearts. He wants us to discover our destiny through the

Mandate of Christ. God never does anything small. Even his apparent smallness is true greatness. No two snowflakes are the same and even our fingerprints are unique. The beauty of God's greatness is seen in the details. Cell groups appear to be tiny and insignificant compared to the vast national populations that make up the billions of people living on planet earth. But, as these cells multiply, the multitudes are won to Christ.

Blessing – "I will bless you… and you will be a blessing!"

As we take up the promise of Abraham, we move from curse to blessing, from futility to favour. Active in the vision, launched by God in Abraham's day which was accomplished in Christ and is being outworked in the church, we live under God's New Covenant blessing. The blessing is in the seed (Christ) and, therefore, we have been called to minister Christ – to show and offer him to the nations so that they can be blessed.

Multitudes – "I will make you exceedingly fruitful"

The ultimate blessing of Abraham is influence through fruitfulness, as the promise in Genesis chapter 17 shows.

> *I will make you exceedingly fruitful; and I will make nations of you, and kings shall come from you.*
>
> Genesis 17:6

Blessing always leads to multiplication, but the order is important. First God blesses, and then we become fruitful and multiply. Genesis 1:26-27 shows this principle was embedded in the original Creation Mandate and it is certainly evident in the New Creation Mandate of Matthew 28:18-20. The blessing of Abraham is given to us through God's promise of his Spirit (Galatians 3:14). The crowds that followed Jesus were the firstfruits of the multitudes that would ultimately come into the church.

Jesus taught the multitudes (Mark 6:34) he provided for them (Mark 8:2-3), he healed them (Matthew 14:14) and he gathered them (Matthew 9:36-10:1). He set in motion his principle of 12 – reaching the multitudes through training and releasing a small group of leaders and commissioning them to do the same.

The multitudes began to come on the Day of Pentecost. The Spirit was outpoured, the gospel was proclaimed with signs and wonders and 3,000 were added to the church. In Acts chapter 5, another 5,000 were brought in. Then the Word of God spread and the multiplication of believers kicked in (Acts 6:7). After that, the churches began to multiply (Acts 9:31). In the end, thousands and thousands in Jerusalem from every section of society had come to Christ and the whole city was evangelised.

A GREAT MULTITUDE NO ONE CAN NUMBER

The book of Revelation gives us a glimpse of the multitudes that are coming. It will be a number no one can count and it will be made up of people from every conceivable corner of the earth, every culture and every society of the world. Read these exciting verses:

> *And they sang a new song, saying: "You are worthy to take the scroll, and to open its seals; for you were slain, and have redeemed us to God by your blood out of every tribe and tongue and people and nation.*
>
> Revelation 5:9

> *After these things I looked, and behold, a great multitude which no one could number, of all nations, tribes, peoples, and tongues, standing before the throne and before the Lamb, clothed with white robes, with palm branches in their hands.*
>
> Revelation 7:9

Through the cell vision everyone can be a part of God's big plan. Every one of us can win, consolidate, disciple and send. We can all live under the blessing of fruitfulness and multiplication.

The multitudes are coming! Not just through big meetings and evangelistic crusades, but through the cells meeting in the homes, the streets, the cafes, the offices, the theatres, the farms, the fields and the factories that make up the *agora* of today. God has a plan for you. He has included you in his purpose for the nations. He has promised you fruitfulness. He has called you to reach the multitudes.

As we work out the Model of 12 in our lives and churches, it is always important to keep the main purpose in view – to make, mature and mobilise disciples. It is vital to maintain the three essential elements of daring faith, bold prayer and total dependence on the anointing of the Holy Spirit. These will ignite and sustain our passion for Christ and make sure that we build his vision in the world.

Crossing the Abyss

A young man by the name of Bill Phillips, who is a highly successful health and fitness expert, has made a fortune in the fitness industry with his book *Body for Life*, together with his magazine and food supplement products. Bill was surprised by how many people spoke to him after attending his seminars and said how much they loved his book and his magazine. And yet, one look at many of these dear folk would show him that they had not even begun to implement his principles of diet, fitness and body building!

Bill wondered how they could find his products so helpful and yet make no change in the way they ate, exercised or took care of their bodies. He called what they were facing "the infinite chasm between knowing and doing". He said they needed to know how to cross this "abyss". Bill then issued a challenge, "Get fit, build your body using my method and send in a before and after photo." He offered prizes of up to $1,000,000 for outstandingly successful candidates of his method. Soon afterwards 100,000 people accepted that challenge and began to change!

Jesus' salutary words to his disciples during the last supper also show that it is one thing to know what you *should* do, but to go on and *actually* do it is quite a different matter!

> *I have given you an example, that you should do as I have done to you. Most assuredly, I say to you, a servant is not greater than his master; nor is he who is sent greater than he who sent him. If you know these things, blessed are you if you do them.*
>
> John 13:15-17

The abyss exists in whatever sphere of life we care to discuss – that of a student, a parent, a teacher. We all have to cross this chasm as we seek to put God's Word into practice in our ministry, our professional occupation, and in our home and family.

PASSIVE PARTICIPATORS

All too often, knowing something, agreeing with it or giving mental assent to it passes for actually doing it! We live in a highly passive culture where there are many spectators but few participators. Take sports, for example. There are relatively few actual participators in the Olympic Games, and yet millions regularly view this event on television. Television makes us 'passive participators' in the world's affaires. We watch, get emotionally or intellectually involved, but it ends there. We are in the end, mere spectators.

We are told that in every sphere of life, 80% of the results are achieved by 20% of the people. In the church also, the spectators outnumber the participators. But God wants us to move from being passive spectators to become active participators.

EXPERTS IN KNOWING WITHOUT DOING

All too often, we are experts in knowing what Jesus wants us to do, but we never actually do it. We say "Jesus is Lord" but we don't follow him as Lord. We hear about taking up our cross and following Christ, but in practice, we live for self and not for Christ. We are told to love God with all our heart, soul, mind and strength and to love our neighbour as ourselves. We know it, but we don't do it as we should.

As I have stated throughout this book, perhaps the most neglected area of all, is the Mandate of Jesus which should be adopted as our manifesto for life (Matthew 28:18-20). The Great Commission is Christ's command for us to make, to mature and to mobilise disciples of Jesus. God doesn't want us merely to affirm it, sing it, shout it, hear it, read it, preach it, pray it, agree with it, watch it or applaud it. He wants us to do it. The Bible clearly identifies the difference between knowing and doing.

Hearing and doing

According to James, we have a tendency to be hearers of the Word, and not doers of the Word.

> *But be doers of the word, and not hearers only, deceiving yourselves.*
>
> James 1:22

Faith and works

James warns that faith without corresponding works is barren and unfruitful.

> *Thus also faith by itself, if it does not have works, is dead.*
>
> James 2:17

You who say… do you…?

Paul spoke of the scandal of religious people saying one thing and doing another. This was dishonouring to God in New Testament days and is equally dishonouring to him today.

> *You, therefore, who teach another, do you not teach yourself? You who preach that a man should not steal, do you steal? You who say, "Do not commit adultery," do you commit adultery? You who abhor idols, do you rob temples? You who make your boast in the law, do you dishonour God through breaking the law? For "The name of God is blasphemed among the Gentiles because of you," as it is written.*
>
> Romans 2:21-24

You honour me with your lips but…

Jesus quoted from Isaiah the prophet in order to describe the religious pretence apparent in his day. What we do, not just what we say, is what we really believe in our heart.

> *These people draw near to me with their mouth, and honour me with their lips, but their heart is far from me.*
> Matthew 15:8

Paul – I don't want to be disqualified

Paul wanted to avoid at all costs the error of preaching one thing and doing another.

> *Therefore I run thus: not with uncertainty. Thus I fight: not as one who beats the air. But I discipline my body and bring it into subjection, lest, when I have preached to others, I myself should become disqualified.*
> 1 Corinthians 9:26-27

Moving from knowing to doing

As we have seen, the abyss represents the gap between what we know and what we actually put into practice concerning the will of God. For the church in general, it has to do with the failure to build church around the Great Commission. We pay lip service to it, but lack the boldness to place it at the heart of church life and to organise ourselves in such a way as every believer is equipped to fulfil it.

For us as individuals, the abyss may represent our reluctance to serve God, to honour his call or to surrender some area of our lives to him. How can we take the first step onto the bridge of obedience and cross the abyss?

Begin by making a decision to change

There has to be an act of your will – you really need to make a decision that you will make a significant change in your life. You need to be specific about it, and be able to complete this sentence: "I am going to change from… to…" For many that sentence will read, "I am going to change from *being a passive spectator in the body of Christ* to *being an active participator in the Great Commission.*"

Know why you are going to change

This has to do with your motivation. If you do not understand why you need to change something in your life or your church, you probably will not see it through. There are a number of good motivations for making godly changes in your life:

- You want to honour God
- You also want to bless others
- You want to be blessed yourself.

Set goals in line with your God-given dreams

The saying goes, "Happy are those who dream dreams and pay the price to make them come true!" Cesar Castellanos says, "Dream and you will win the world." We must learn the power of a godly dream. Castellanos also says, "Dreams and visions are the language of the Holy Spirit." This is because our imagination is the God-given capacity by which he can impress upon our lives his dreams for us. As we focus on the vision God gives to us, we can begin to establish the goals and strategies needed to make that vision a reality.

Take the step – cross the abyss

The well-known Chinese proverb states, "The journey of a thousand miles begins with a single step." The cell vision is just such a journey, both for the whole church and for every individual member. We might think the journey is too difficult, especially when we realise how far we are from our destination. However, we will get there if we simply take the first step and keep on going. That is the only way we move from knowing to doing, from saying to acting and from dreaming to accomplishing our dreams.

THREE ESSENTIAL ELEMENTS OF DOING GOD'S WILL

I believe there are three main elements in effective Christian ministry. Each one is indispensible for a successful outworking of the cell vision. I have referred to these at many points in this book, and I will end by restating them briefly but emphatically.

Faith

The vital connection between knowing and doing is faith. Faith begins by hearing God and seeing as he sees. God uses the creative imaging capacity of our hearts and plants in us the vision he wants fulfilled. We will never see with our human eyes the realisation of God's will for us until we have seen it with the eyes of faith. We must see the invisible if we are to do the impossible. We must see the vision for cell church, and believe that it is possible by the power of God. Otherwise, we will be defeated from the start.

Faith as spiritual vision is one of the fundamental ways in which God works. This kind of faith activates God's promises and takes us into the realm of divine possibilities. The childless Abraham saw in advance his innumerable children when God showed him the stars in the night sky – and he believed. This vision grew in him and became fully formed in his spirit long before it was fulfilled in practice. He was able to live in the promise as though it had already been realised – that's faith. Paul says,

> *Abraham… believed God, who gives life to the dead and calls those things which do not exist as though they did.*
> Romans 4:17

Paul continues,

> *He did not waver at the promise of God through unbelief, but was strengthened in faith, giving glory to God, and being fully convinced that what he had promised he was also able to perform.*
> Romans 4:20-21

Abraham's faith activated him and gave him the ability to fulfil the will of God. In the same way, we must continually carry God's vision before our eyes and allow supernatural faith to activate us to do his will.

This means our goal-setting must not just be a human exercise in strategic planning. We must receive a revelation of God's will, see that will as having already been accomplished in the purpose of God and work it out in practice. Faith-filled vision will shape every aspect of our lives into the likeness of what God has revealed. The cell ministry necessitates these high levels of vision, faith and action.

Prayer

Believing prayer is essential in order to fulfil the cell vision. Every element must be birthed in prayer, and saturated by it during every stage of its development. One of the hallmarks of cell churches in South Korea and South America is the breadth, depth and quality of their praying. One cannot imagine any other single most important ingredient in the cell vision.

Prayer is the effective operation of God's power. James teaches this when he speaks of the power of effective, fervent and earnest prayer in James 5:16. Prayer is crucial in getting things done because it releases the operative power of God. This is what we need to fulfil the cell vision. It is a supernatural work. We cannot do it in our own ability. It has to be God, or nothing. That's why we teach our people to pray continually and to soak every aspect of the cell ministry in prayer and intercession.

This kind of praying can remove obstacles, clear the spiritual atmosphere, draw souls to the kingdom of God, overcome our weaknesses and create a climate in which God can work. We have learned to add to our prayers fasting, praise, sacrificial service and practical actions. These are all winning combinations. Prayer demonstrates that we believe only God can enable us to do what he has called us to do.

The anointing

The anointing of the Holy Spirit is the exact opposite of human effort. It makes the decisive difference. Every aspect of service in the Old Testament Tabernacle and Temple worship had to be anointed with the sacred anointing oil. The same applies to our service today. The anointing of the Holy Spirit upon our lives speaks of separation from sin and dedication to the service of God.

In a sense, the cell vision is itself anointed because it has arisen out of spiritual desire and follows biblical principles. The Holy Spirit has been invoked at every stage of its development and this process is on-going. However, the vision itself cannot work unless we carry the anointing, both personally and corporately.

The anointing reminds us that without him we are nothing and can do nothing, but when we carry his supernatural presence and power, we can do all things. That's why we focus on maintaining our spiritual anointing and seek ever higher levels of fullness in the Holy Spirit. We depend on his gifts and his grace. We seek to be saturated by the Spirit, soaking in his presence and listening for his promptings. This kind of sensitivity to the Spirit opens the way to the miraculous manifestation of the power of God. We value both the fruit and the gifts that come with the anointing of God.

In Kensington Temple, we have found that, by applying these principles to the cell vision God has given us, we can begin to be what he calls us to be, and do what he calls us to do – to make, mature and to mobilise disciples of Christ.

Bibliography

Astin, H. (2002) *Body and Cell*, London, Monarch.

Beckham, W.A. (1997) *The Second Reformation*, Houston, Touch.

Coleman, R.E. (1994) *The Master Plan of Evangelism*, USA, Sprire.

Comiskey, J. (1999) *Groups of 12*, Houston, Touch.

Fajardo, C. (2004) *Consolidation*, London, Dovewell.

Finnell, D. (1995) *Life in His Body*, Houston, Touch.

Gustitus, P. (2000) *Destination Cell Church*, Ephrata House to House Publications.

Lewis, C.S. (2001) *The Weight of Glory*, New York, HarperCollins

Neighbour Jr, R.W. (2000) *Where Do We Go From Here* (Revised edition), Houston, Touch.

Phillips, B. (1999) *Body for Life*, New York, HarperCollins

Stockstill, L. (1998) *The Cell Church*, Ventura, Regal.

Yonggi Cho, D (1994) *Successful Home Cell Groups*, Monmouth, Bridge Publishing.

Further Reading

To find out more about different aspects of the Cell Vision the following booklets are available in the *Discipleship Cell Explosion* (*www.cellexplosion.com*) series:

Introducing the Cell Vision
A clear and concise introduction to the cell model according to the Model of 12.

Consolidation Groups: Leaders Manual
A guide for leaders detailing the process of consolidation, and includes the eight Pre-encounter Bible studies.

Why Cells
A detailed explanation of why a cell strategy is the best method for making, maturing and mobilising disciples today.

The Friendship Factor
An examination of friendship and its role in the kingdom of God, and how it is expressed through the Groups of 3 operating in the cells.

Ministering to Youth
An insight into the youth of today and how they can be reached with the gospel and discipled through the cells.

Kids in the Vision
How the cell ministry can be effective in ministering to children and raising them into leadership.

Growing Your 12
A guide to raising disciples and growing them into an effective team of leaders.

Dance: Shaping Lives through Creative Movement
A detailed description covering the spiritual and practical aspects of building a dance ministry.

A Willing Heart
The principles of motivation that will help you raise people to their full potential ready to work for Christ and rise to the challenge of the cell vision.

Introducing the Church
Understanding and applying the principles of New Testament church to the body of Christ today.

Transitioning into the Model of 12.
A practical, step-by-step strategy of transition into the Model of 12 examining the issues of cultural setting, change management and sensitivity to the Holy Spirit.

Evangelism through the Cells
A guide to involving every member of the cell in sharing the gospel and reaching the lost.

All the teaching material covered by the Pre-encounter, Encounter Weekend, Post-encounter and Leadership Training has been drawn together in a series of four manuals.

My Encounter with Jesus
Includes the 8 Pre-encounter Bible studies and 16 sessions for the Encounter Weekend.

Living Free!
The complete 10-week Post-encounter course. Includes teaching material, the Transformation Track and Life Issues sections.

Living Free! Daily Devotional
120 Daily devotional Bible readings that complement the Living Free! Post-encounter Teaching.

Mastering Leadership
The complete 20-week leadership training programme.

The *Sword of the Spirit* is a complete training course in 12 manuals, each with its own student handbook, covering key topics: that build into a sound biblical foundation.

> *Effective Prayer*
> *Knowing the Spirit*
> *The Rule of God*
> *Living Faith*
> *Glory in the Church*
> *Ministry in the Spirit*
> *Knowing the Father*
> *Reaching the Lost*
> *Listening to God*
> *Knowing the Son*
> *Salvation by Grace*
> *Worship in Spirit and Truth*

See *www.swordofthespirit.co.uk* for more details.

The *Equipping the Saints* series is designed for cell members and leaders to equip them in their ministry to make, mature and mobilise disciples. Titles include:

> *The Fullness of Christ: Fulfilling your ministry*
> *Anointed to Serve: How to minister in the Spirit*
> *The Fivefold Ministry: Building the church today*

There are a number of other books by Colin Dye which help to address different aspects of the Christian life, including:

> *Mastering Your Emotions*
> *Staying Pure in a sex-charged world*
> *Prayer That Gets Answers*

All these titles are available through www.ktshop.com.

People with a Passion

Model of 12 Website

The *Discipleship Cell Explosion* website *www.cellexplosion.com* is a Model of 12 platform for those in the cell vision.

- It contains teaching material on the cell vision, including an introduction to the Model in different languages.
- The Media Centre has downloadable audio and video recordings for use in your church.
- The Forum is for discussion and interaction between church leaders working with the vision.
- The website is linked to an online bookshop service giving access to various publications on the cell vision and related topics.

Part 5
Appendices

People with a Passion

Overview of the Cell Vision

Ladder of Success

PUBLIC DECLARATION
Making the decision to DEDICATE or REDEDICATE your life to Jesus

PRE-ENCOUNTER
4 Bible Studies for New Believers

A CHANGE OF DIRECTION: Repentance and faith
BECOMING A DISCIPLE OF JESUS: Water Baptism
POWER FOR LIVING: Receiving the Holy Spirit
THE CHURCH: Belonging to the family of God

JOIN A CELL
Fulfil Christ's command to love one another and build up each other in fellowship and become motivated to fulfil Christ's call upon every believer: win the lost and "make disciples" (Matthew 28:19).

ENCOUNTER PREPARATION
4 Bible Studies to prepare for your Encounter Weekend

INTRODUCTION TO ENCOUNTERS
FINDING JESUS
REAL CHANGE
BEING SET FREE

ENCOUNTER WEEKEND
Confronts you and your past and uproot its negative influences totally from your life. You will be able to reflect on your daily life and in faith plan for a better future.

POST-ENCOUNTER
Living Free! Life Transformation Course
One session each week for 10 weeks and a *Living Free!* Encounter will help you learn to live out your life in freedom and victory in Christ.

LEADERSHIP SCHOOL
Mastering Leadership
Two terms of 10 weeks each to prepare you to be a cell leader with the ability to win lives for Christ and to disciple them until they become successful leaders.

RE-ENCOUNTER WEEKEND
Further training and more in depth ministry that will prepare you to minister through the cells.

OPEN YOUR OWN CELL

Cell Leader's Job Description

II

The success of the cell ministry, in a large part, is due to leaders creating team spirit. Cell leaders will relate 'inwards' to their Primary 12 groups and 'outwards' to their open cells.

It is your responsibility as the Cell Leader to:

See the Harvest of the Lord reaped, assimilated and discipled through the Ladder of Success:

- Win
- Consolidate
- Disciple
- Send.

Win – enthusiastically win the lost to Christ, actively seeking to:

Consolidate – systematically disciple new believers through:

- Pre encounter Studies
- Encounter Weekends
- Post-encounter Studies

Leading them to fulfil Christ's Great Commission to:

Disciple – Attend the Leadership School where they will be trained and equipped to start a cell of their own and:

Send – release them to start a cell of their own and reproduce in others what they have received from God.

1. Model discipleship (as a leader) by your own personal involvement in the 'Consolidation process' and 'Leadership Training School' and encourage each cell member to play a full part in the same.

2. Maintain the focus of the four components of a cell in a healthy balance:
   - Worship
   - Nurture
   - Fellowship
   - Outreach.

   i To facilitate Christ-centred worship in creative ways, being sensitive to the needs of new believers.

   ii To oversee the nurture of members from the Word of God preached at the Sunday services.

   iii To promote healthy fellowship and prayer, developing team-spirit and providing strong pastoral care among all members of your cell.

   iv To prioritise winning the lost at every meeting, keeping track of your members' outreach to the unsaved (thus, not allowing yourselves to be a 'fellowship-only' group).

3. Maintain the 'Five Components' by acknowledging the five-fold structure ('Cell Agenda') of cell meetings:
   - Worship
   - Word
   - Witness
   - Welfare
   - Warfare.

4. See every member as a potential leader and seek to multiply cells by developing their leadership potential.

5. Work with the homogeneous principle within the Nets.

6. Be a link between the church's leadership and your cell group, attending your Primary 12 and Net Meetings, promoting the Sunday services and any appropriate annual meetings.

7. Identify and employ members' giftings in the administration of group meetings.

8. Follow up referrals of new members.

9. Participate in verifying/counselling respondents at Sunday Services

   i   Phone call where necessary within 48 hours (delegate to other members when you are prevented)

   ii Personal visit within 7 days and invite them to your cell

   iii Forward response to the Consolidation Department on 8th day

   iv After the second week, report on the referral's cell attendance and readiness for Pre-encounter and Encounter.

10. Spend adequate time in the week before the meeting in preparation.

11. Follow up absenteeism with personal calls and arrange meeting where necessary.

12. Arrange a prayer-chain among members.

13. Devote yourself and your members to prayer and fasting for new members prior to them attending a Freedom Weekend.

14. Read your Bible consistently and apply it daily as a personal discipline and a role-model to your members

15. Pray daily for:

    i   The Senior Minister, his wife and family by name

    ii Your Primary Leader and their family by name

    iii Your Cell leader and members

    iv Your own ministry goals

    v   Your own family.

16. Sign the 'Discipleship Cell Explosion – Model of 12 Code of Conduct'.

Cell Leader's Code of Conduct III

In order to facilitate the working of cells the following principles apply:

1. Each cell is under the direction of the cell leader who is responsible to the Primary 12 groups led by the Senior Leaders of the Nets.

2. Each cell will follow the teaching as laid out by the Senior Minister.

3. The group will not be used for the promotion of any kind of business or outside ministry.

4. Any promotion of events will need to be approved by the Primary 12 leader.

5. No offering to be taken in the cell group, other than that directed by the Net Leaders.

6. Any additional activities requiring finance to be cleared by the Primary 12 Leader.

7. Effective weekly records to be kept and monthly reports sent by the first Monday in each month.

8. Each cell leader will support the vision and ministry of [your church].

9. If at any time the leader of the cell decides to leave the church then the group will be handed to Primary 12 Leader who will facilitate the process of transition of leadership.

10. Each cell leader will acknowledge that they are a part of [your church] and will conduct himself/herself in an appropriate manner. This is a voluntary role.

11. Spiritual Gifts are to be used in a way to build and encourage people and for confirmation. Prophecy needs to be regulated so as not to include subjects such a person's future partner or key financial decisions. Spiritual Gifts are to be exercised by the standard and disciplines set by the Scriptures. All prophecies must go through the process of testing involving both the cell leader and the primary leader. Words of basic affirmation or encouragement are to be submitted to the cell leader. Words of personal direction of any type to any person on any matter *must* be submitted to the primary leader before they are to be in any way considered as appropriate.

12. Before any counselling is undertaken the cell leader must be consulted. The cell leader is responsible for seeking the guidance of the primary leader on all such matters.

I agree to abide by all the stipulations of this charter and accept them as binding in all matters in regard to my cell group ministry in [your church].

This is signed by both the new cell leader and their Primary 12 leader.

New Cell Registration Form

NEW CELL REGISTRATION FORM

Cell Leaders Details

Name of New Cell Leader:	
Address:	
Postcode:	Tel (Home):
Mobile:	Tel (Work):
	E-Mail:
Your Primary Leader:	Your Cell Leader:

Your Training Profile

Encounter Weekend ☐   School of Consolidation ☐

Post-encounter ☐

Leadership School ☐

Have you Read and signed the Cell Leader's Code of Conduct: Yes / No

Your Cell Profile

Men ☐   Women ☐   Youth ☐   Children ☐

Your Cell Profile (Descriptive)

(e.g. Scandinavian Men / Young single mums) etc.:

Your Cell Details

Cell Venue:	
Postcode:	
Day of Meeting:	Time of Meeting:

Your Cell Members

First Name	Surname	Contact Number	Email Address

Sample Cell Reports

NAME:

MONTH:

Primary 12 Leader's LADDER OF SUCCESS Progress Report (Down Line Cells)

Cell Member's Name	Number of Cells	Cell Goals	No. of people Incl. Cell leader	Consolidate				Leaders	Leadership Training School
				Pre-Enc	Enc	Post-Enc	Re-Enc	Enc.	
Cell Leader's Details:									
Total:									

OPEN CELL: LEADERS MONTHLY REPORT

My Open Cell

| Cell Leader Name: | | Primary Leader Name: | |

| Net: | | Month Reported: | | Date of Report: | |

How many open cell meetings have you had this month?

Where is your cell held? | | When is your cell held?

How many people (distinct) attended in the month?

What is the average attendance of your cell each week?

How many members did not attend one meeting this month?

How many home visits have you done this month?

Statistics & Goals

	Actual (mnth)	YTD	Goal (Year)		Actual (m)	YTD	Goal (year)
Visitors				Win (Decisions)			
Consolidate (Encounter)				Disciple (L Free)			
				Disciple (ML1)			
				Disciple (ML2)			
				Disciple (Revival)			

Testimonies

Questions/Feedback

LEADERS CELL: MONTHLY REPORT

My Leaders Cell

Cell Leader Name: | Primary Leader Name:

Net: | Month Reported: | Date of Report:

How many leaders cell meetings have you had this month?

How many of your 12 do you have?

Where is your cell held? | When is your cell held?

How many (distinct) people attended in the month?

What is the average attendance of your cell each week?

How many members did not attend one meeting this month?

How many trained leaders are in your leaders cell?

How many of these leaders lead their own cells?

Goals

No of cells to be planted next month: | So far YTD | Year Target:

Names of new cell leaders:

Names of developing leaders:

Themes Covered This Month

Plans and Goals for Next Month

PRIMARY 12 LEADERS MONTHLY REPORT

Primary Leaders Cells

Primary Leader Name:

Net: | Month Reported: | Date of Report:

How many leaders cell meetings have you had this month?

How many of your 12 do you have?

How many of your 144 do you have?

How many cells do you have?

How many (distinct) people attended in the month?

How many members did not attend one meeting this month?

How many trained leaders are in your downline?

How many of these leaders lead their own cells?

What is the average size of the cells in your downline?

How many cells have you planted this month? | How many closed?

Statistics & Goals

	Actual (mnth)	YTD	Goal (Year)		Actual (m)	YTD	Goal (year)
Visitors				Win (Decisions)			
Consolidate (Encounter)				Disciple (L Free)			
				Disciple (ML1)			
				Disciple (ML2)			
				Disciple (Revival)			

No of cells to be planted next month: | Year Target?

Names of new cell leaders:

Names of developing leaders:

Multiplication Strategy:

How many leaders-in-training do you have? (ML1, ML2)

How many consolidators are operating in your cells?

How many of your leaders are in Premium Cell Program?

Vision/Word for this Month

Index

The basic elements of the Model of 12 are found under the relevant Chapter headings found in the Table of Contents. For additional ease of reference, this INDEX lists a number of topics that are covered in various places in the book.